The

LOST
PRIME
MINISTERS

The
LOST
PRIME
MINISTERS

Macdonald's Successors Abbott, Thompson, Bowell, and Tupper

Michael Hill

DUNDURN
PRESS

Publisher: Scott Fraser | Acquiring editor: Kathryn Lane | Editor: Dominic Farrell
Cover designer: Karen Alexiou
Cover images: John Abbott: Library and Archives Canada C-000697, Box 3426 ID# 3191858; John Thompson: Library and Archives Canada, Box 4423 ID#3623484; Mackenzie Bowell: Library and Archives Canada Item # 60368 ID# 5033893; Charles Tupper: Library and Archives Canada ID#3000516; paper textures: Ivan Gromov and SJ Objio on Unsplash

Library and Archives Canada Cataloguing in Publication

Title: The lost prime ministers : Macdonald's successors Abbott, Thompson, Bowell, and Tupper / Michael Hill.
Names: Hill, Michael (Michael Gerald), 1952- author.
Description: Includes bibliographical references and index.
Identifiers: Canadiana (print) 20210361565 | Canadiana (ebook) 20210361573 | ISBN 9781459749320 (softcover) | ISBN 9781459749337 (PDF) | ISBN 9781459749344 (EPUB)
Subjects: LCSH: Prime ministers—Canada—Biography. | CSH: Canada—Politics and government—1878-1896. |
  LCSH: Prime ministers—Canada—History—19th century.
Classification: LCC FC626.P7 H55 2022 | DDC 971.05/50922—dc23

We acknowledge the support of the Canada Council for the Arts and the Ontario Arts Council for our publishing program. We also acknowledge the financial support of the Government of Ontario, through the Ontario Book Publishing Tax Credit and Ontario Creates, and the Government of Canada.

Dundurn Press
1382 Queen Street East
Toronto, Ontario, Canada M4L 1C9
dundurn.com, @dundurnpress 𝕏 f ◎

To my parents: Alma Honor Joslin and Albert Percy Hill,
who encouraged and enabled my love of history.

CONTENTS

———— ◈ ————

CONTENTS

AUTHOR'S NOTE

———— ◇ ————

The *Conservative* Party, also known as the *Tories*, included members who ran under what was actually the official name of the party until 1873, the *Liberal-Conservatives*. Some members kept the old party name as late as 1911 and it was even renewed as the official party name from 1922 to 1938. For the purposes of this narrative however, to avoid confusion, only the terms *Conservative* and *Tory* are used. This should help to avoid confusion with the *Liberal* (*Grit*) Party of George Brown, Alexander Mackenzie, and Wilfrid Laurier.

Introduction

— ◇ —

A Deluge of Caretakers

ON FRIDAY, MAY 29, 1891, the Canadian House of Commons was holding an evening session, a routine occurrence for that day and age. Most of the debate had centred on the questionable participation of Canada's high commissioner to England, Sir Charles Tupper, in the recent federal election. Liberals objected to what they saw as interference by an allegedly non-partisan official in the democratic process. As the debate droned on, a young parliamentary page slipped down the aisle between the seats of the members and stopped at the front row. He handed a neatly folded note to a front-bench MP from Quebec, Sir Hector Langevin, and then quickly retreated from the chamber. Langevin stared at the piece of paper and visibly paled when he read the message. He passed it to several nearby colleagues and then rose and walked silently across the aisle to speak with the leader of the Opposition, Liberal leader Wilfrid Laurier. As the two held a whispered conversation, the rest of the MPs attending the evening's debate fell silent, knowing that something serious had happened. Langevin returned to his seat on the Conservative side of the aisle and then, obviously shaken, rose to speak.

"I have the painful duty to announce to the House that the news from Earnscliffe just received is that the First Minister has had a relapse, and that he is in a most critical condition. We have reports from the medical men in attendance on the right honourable gentleman, and they do not seem to believe that he can live many hours longer."

Earnscliffe was the home of the prime minister, Sir John A. Macdonald. Langevin was relaying the news that the grand old man had suffered a life-threatening stroke that afternoon and was completely paralyzed down his right side. He'd also lost the ability to speak. The attending physician, Dr. James Grant, had written the note to Langevin. In it, he stated, "I have just seen Sir John in consultation. Entire loss of speech. Haemorrhage on the brain. Condition hopeless."

Within a minute of Langevin notifying the members of Parliament of Macdonald's condition, Justice Minister Sir John Thompson rose to make a motion for the House to adjourn. Langevin, who'd been a member of Macdonald's initial Cabinet in 1867, sat at his desk stunned. He openly wept. Other parliamentarians crowded around him to see the note and try to console the man who was Macdonald's Quebec lieutenant. Liberals and Conservatives alike stood in small groups around the chamber discussing the tragic news.

"For thirty-three years, I have been his follower," Langevin repeated over and over again, both to other politicians and seemingly to himself.

Eventually, the minister of public works pulled himself together. Joined by Quebec colleague Joseph Chapleau, who was the secretary of state, and John Thompson, the Halifax-based minister of justice and attorney general, the men shared a horse-drawn cab to travel to the prime minister's residence. The men discovered that, while gravely ill and unlikely to recover, Macdonald was still alive, but he was breathing rapidly and his heartbeat was irregular.

The governor general was informed of what had happened; he in turn cabled Queen Victoria in London. By ten o'clock that night, telegraph messages had carried the news across the country, from Halifax to Victoria. The front pages of the newspapers the next day blared out headlines about Macdonald's condition. The stories left little doubt in the minds of millions of Canadians that Macdonald, their recently re-elected prime minister, was dying.

The man who'd been a parliamentarian since 1844 and prime minister of Canada since 1867 — with a short span out of office between 1873 to 1878 — was on his deathbed. He lingered for nearly a week, communicating with his wife and son by using his left hand to squeeze out *yes* or *no* answers. On June 6, Macdonald took a turn for the worse. His strength, such an asset throughout his political life, failed him. At 10:15 a.m., Macdonald passed away.

Canada had lost its most dynamic individual: a man whose drive, ambition, and energy had led to nation-building on a scale that was barely imaginable; a man who knew how to handle the reins of power as if he were born to the task; a man who controlled the levers of political office the way an engineer handles a train engine; a man who knew when to stand firm and when to compromise; a man who had become, perhaps, legendary beyond reality and fact. Old Tomorrow. The Old Chieftain. Now he was gone. The chasm that had opened in the political landscape of the nation was more than just gaping. It was stupendous.

The country had barely known another leader. Liberal Alexander Mackenzie, a dour Scot, a man without Macdonald's empathy or common touch, had led the country for five years in the 1870s, after Macdonald had been implicated in what was known as the Pacific Railway Scandal. Mackenzie, however, had never captured the imagination of the country; had never found his way into the nation's hearts. Edward Blake, the Liberal leader who followed Mackenzie, could not match Macdonald's charismatic personality. Nor were there any provincial premiers — even Ontario's popular Oliver Mowat — who captured the public's attention the way the prime minister had.

Not that Sir John was without his critics. The taint of corruption never really disappeared following the railway scandal. In the years prior to his death, he'd all but lost what had once been widespread support in Quebec, thanks to his mishandling of both the Red River Rebellion and the North-West Rebellion; and, more particularly, his decision following the latter to allow the execution of the rebellion's leader, Louis Riel.

Despite all that, the old man had just won re-election — his fifth victory since 1867. The voters were familiar with the Conservative leader; his leadership offered a sense of security, something to trust in. It was not the party brand that mattered. Macdonald was so much bigger than his party.

Suddenly, he was gone.

The next few years would be chaotic for the young nation. As the Conservative Party scrambled to replace someone who seemed irreplaceable, the politics of the nation were transformed. The bookish and underestimated Liberal leader, Wilfrid Laurier, sat across the floor of the House of Commons biding his time, but that time had not yet arrived. Instead, turmoil and uncertainty plagued the governing party as it scrambled to find someone to fill Macdonald's sizeable shoes.

One of Sir John's great failures was that he never anointed a clear successor. There was confusion as to who would follow in his footsteps. King Louis XV of France was said to have uttered the nihilistic "*après moi, le déluge*" to indicate that he had complete indifference to what came after him. To many, it must have seemed that Macdonald led with the same heedlessness for the future of his party: "after me, the deluge."

As it turned out, in the space of the next five years there would be four men who would lead the country. One was reluctant. One was unpopular with his colleagues, his party, and the public. Some critics have even called him dimwitted. One was capable but was restrained because of his religious beliefs. One, a former star on the political scene, found that, having finally achieved the highest political office in the country, he no longer seemed to have the magic touch.

This is the story of those four leaders who followed Sir John A. in the prime minister's office: John Abbott, John Thompson, Mackenzie Bowell, and Charles Tupper.

The years between June of 1891 and June of 1896 were an interregnum that linked the Macdonald era to the Laurier years. But it was an inglorious one. Historian Michael Bliss wrote a 328-page book about the prime ministers of Canada called *Right Honourable Men: The Descent of Politics from Macdonald to Mulroney*. In it, prime ministers Abbott, Thompson, Bowell, and Tupper combined rate less than half a page. Abbott gets his name mentioned in one sentence. Bowell at least gets an adjective beside his name: incompetent. John Thompson is labelled with the pejorative "Sir John the Lesser."

In their 1999 book *Prime Ministers: Ranking Canada's Leaders*, Jack Granatstein and Norman Hillmer concluded that of the twenty prime ministers who had served in office up to that time, Thompson ranked tenth, Abbott seventeenth; Tupper came in at number sixteen, and Bowell was a lowly nineteenth. (Only Kim Campbell ranked lower than Bowell, and she held office for a mere 132 days before the Progressive Conservatives lost all but two seats in the 1993 election.) Those four men share a scant eight-page chapter in the book. Even short-term prime ministers Meighen, Clark, Turner, and Campbell warranted their own chapters.

But is any of this a fair assessment of Macdonald's four successors? In their own ways, each man was remarkable. Each man was successful in other endeavours, often spectacularly so. Each man had great personal energy. Each man achieved great success in life. They all would warrant admiration even if they'd not reached that pinnacle of Canadian political heights. Somehow, though, these men have never received the respect that perhaps they deserved.

Why is that? How was it that the Conservatives had not groomed a suitable replacement for John A. Macdonald? There was an obvious successor: John Thompson. So then why was Thompson, the obvious heir to power, not selected first and given a chance to build the party fortunes? How was it that both Abbott, who was uninterested in the position, and Bowell, who was unsuited for the job, were selected by the party brass to take the reins anyway? Why did the party, as it approached an election nearly thirty years into Confederation, reach back into history and come up with Tupper, a capable man but one who was well past his best-before date? Were there political issues of the day that tied their hands or somehow conspired to deny these men the recognition that they may — or may not — have deserved? Were there forces at play that somehow doomed the Conservative chances in the 1896 election? How was it that four very different men in character and temperament led the country in the short span of years between 1891 and 1896? It is a story that has gone untold for too long.

The early 1890s were years of incredible change. The young country was growing. Immigration and expansion of the nation into the West were a welcome evolution of the young nation — this view was not shared, of course, by the First Nations Peoples who were displaced — but it also placed a strain on the existing infrastructure and resources. Not only was Canada seeing immigration into the country, but there was also a great movement of people within the nation. Already, the migration from the farms to the urban areas had begun, changing the nature of both the rural and urban landscapes. By 1890 nearly one third of Canadians lived in towns or cities. Industrialization was quickly transforming the economy of the country and the lives of its citizens. Factories seemed to be popping up everywhere, and even the smallest towns and villages often were home to at least one type of industry.

And trade unions were gaining a foothold to look after the rights of the workers in those factories. Laws were being enacted yearly to limit the exploitation of children and, indeed, adult labourers. Living conditions in the cities, even for the labourers who were working and earning money, tended to be appalling. Movements were afoot to bring temperance to a country that was plagued by alcohol abuse. There were stirrings for women to be enfranchised, to earn more rights not only at the ballot box but in their homes where most were still under the thumbs of their husbands.

Through all those years, economic uncertainty loomed ever on the horizon. The connection to England and the British Empire overshadowed the politics of Canada in the late nineteenth century. Coupled with that was the tenuous bond with the United States. There was also a measure of fear of the growing behemoth to the south.

Yet, despite all the changes, some things remained the same. The age-old conflict between Catholic and Protestant as well as the one between French and English divisions across the land reared its head all too often.

This was the Canada that Sir John A. had helped to build and manage. By force of personality, he'd led a stretched-out amalgam of farms and scattered villages to believe that it was a united country when in fact it was little more than a loosely knit, fragile patchwork along the northern border of the United States. There was no homogeneity to this new nation. The loggers of British Columbia had little in common with the fishermen of Nova Scotia. The farmers of Manitoba differed from the farmers of Ontario and Quebec. The French-speaking shopkeepers along the St. Lawrence River had little to share with the factory owners or labourers in the cities of Toronto or Hamilton. And of course, the Indigenous Peoples, robbed of their land and, in most places, forced onto reserves, were excluded from society. This was the country that Macdonald passed on to his successors.

Through manipulation, compromise, tenacity and determination, Macdonald not only built but held this loose confederation together in the face of multiple threats and crises. One of his great accomplishments — the building of a transcontinental railway across a vast and unsettled region — was the tangible glue that held this flimsy chain together. And the links in that chain, as diverse as they were, owed their prosperity and independence at least in part to the man who headed the Conservative Party. Now, he'd left things to a Conservative Party that was divided, lacking focus and in dire need of serious leadership. Great industrial and commercial change was in the air. The world was changing rapidly as steamships and trans-oceanic cables brought continents together.

Who could step forward and maintain the regime and legacy left by Macdonald?

Chapter One

The Legacy of Sir John A. Macdonald

TO PROPERLY EVALUATE THE MINISTRIES of Abbott, Thompson, Bowell, and Tupper, it is necessary to first look at the life and career of the man who set the tone for the future prime ministers of Canada. John A. Macdonald invented the job. He accomplished great things. He was brilliant in many ways. He made a number of horrendous mistakes as well. In normal circumstances, those who followed him would have been asked to build on his accomplishments and clean up the messes he left behind. However, the four prime ministers who briefly held office after Macdonald's death did not have the time to properly do so. Each tried, and their efforts are worth considering.

The story of Sir John A. Macdonald has been well-told in outstanding books by historians and authors such as Donald Creighton, P.B. Waite, Richard Gwyn, and Pierre Berton. Volume One of Gwyn's two-part biography is appropriately titled *John A: The Man Who Made Us*. Most Canadians are able to recite at least some accomplishment of our first prime minister. His rugged and unique face, having graced the ten-dollar bill for decades, is familiar to the nation. The myths — especially in regard to his fondness for alcohol — have been told and re-told to Canadians many times. He was a complex man, one with both admirable qualities and unlikeable biases. There is no doubt about his contributions to this country.

In the nineteenth century, no politician dominated his country's public affairs more than Macdonald. His stature was on a par with Abraham Lincoln and Benjamin Disraeli in that regard. He was the first world leader to advocate for women getting the vote. He was accepting of French Canadians and Roman Catholics at a time when bigotry and prejudice controlled many levers of political office. He famously said of the English-French dichotomy in Canada, "Treat them [the French] as a nation and they will act as a free people generally do — generously. Treat them as a faction and they will become fractious." Friendships, such as those he had with Georges-Étienne Cartier and Hector Langevin, were not merely out of political expediency to cement the French-English relationships in government. They were based on genuine rapport. He also welcomed immigration to Canada, although admittedly most of those he foresaw entering the country were of English, Scots, or Irish stock.

He had great respect for Parliament. As he sat in the front bench of the Commons, he was attentive to his own members but equally so to the Opposition members, even as they tried to criticize the work of his government. When Alexander Mackenzie became prime minister in 1874, Sir John demanded that his Tory MPs mind their manners and treat the Liberal government with solemn respect. On the other hand, he indulged in parliamentary mischief that drew outrage from the Grits. He had a propensity for turning his back on the Opposition side and speaking directly to his own party or the gallery that sat behind them. Much of that was for dramatic effect.

As it is with all great figures, special character and a positive attitude gave Macdonald the ability to achieve the things he did. A man who lived a tragic personal life, he nevertheless maintained a positive attitude both in public and privately. His first wife was bedridden for most of their marriage and died young. A much-adored infant son died of crib death. His only daughter was hydrocephalic and unable to care for herself. Yet despite the sorrows of his home life, Macdonald had what one biographer called "irrepressible good cheer."

He worked on his personal relationships, often having humble workers mix with the power brokers of the day at his dinners at Earnscliffe. His photographic memory was a skill that awed those who experienced his phenomenal recall of names and faces. Even his political foes admitted that he was extremely charming. As a joker and mimic, he could lighten the mood of political meetings, parties and even the House of Commons. A natural storyteller, he was often self-deprecating in his anecdotes, turning himself into the brunt of the joke. His quick mind could skewer hecklers in a crowd. Audiences learned to anticipate the humour mixed with the seriousness of his talks. Not that he planned his ad-libs. He was always better at giving off-the-cuff speeches than to drone on from a prepared text.

As well as being witty, Sir John could also be shrewd, cunning, slightly cynical, and devious. And it must be admitted that he could be corrupt, as he depended too much on patronage as his means to control his party and the political landscape of the country. He resorted to nearly any means to win elections, and even as late as his last election in 1891, he was accused of cheating.

Macdonald was born in Glasgow, Scotland, in 1815 and emigrated to Canada with his family when he was only five years old, settling in Kingston, Ontario — Upper Canada, as it was named then. (A side note: Macdonald did not have the heavy Scottish brogue that many modern actors and historical re-enactors adopt when playing the man. One contemporary said that he sounded as if he'd been born and raised in the Bay of Quinte (Belleville) area. He was, however, a natural actor and mimic, so using the Scottish accent was merely part of Macdonald's gift for storytelling.)

Macdonald's schooling included Latin and history and although he learned to read French quite well, he rarely (if ever) spoke it in public. At fourteen, he left school and at age fifteen began an apprenticeship in a law office in his new hometown of Kingston. He was admitted to the bar at age twenty-one in 1835.

Macdonald was not enthusiastic about practising law. He looked further afield and became something of a land speculator during his twenties. He began purchasing properties in the Kingston area and then all through Upper Canada in the early 1840s with varying degrees of success. Although only twenty-four, he became a director of the Commercial Bank of the Midland District in 1839. Even while sitting as prime minister later in life, he sat on the boards of directors of a number of companies. By 1888, he was the president of the Manufacturer's Life Insurance Company. Conducting business outside of politics was much different in those days for elected men. There were few rules or regulations regarding appointments that may have led to perceived conflicts of interest. Few made issue with the questionable practice of mixing business and politics.

Macdonald entered politics in 1843 when he was elected as an alderman in Kingston. The likeable young barrister had found a use for his demonstrable charm. A year later he ran and was elected to the Assembly of the Province of Canada. (Upper and Lower Canada had been renamed Canada West and Canada East by that time and shared a joint legislature.) He declared at the time his fundamental belief on entering politics was that the government needed to focus on developing the young colony's resources and "improve its physical advantages," rather than to waste time on theoretical discussions, which wasted the money of the people of Canada East and Canada West. It was a philosophy that he stuck to for his entire career.

His talents did not go unnoticed in the legislature. Recognized for his intelligence, collegiality, political acumen and administrative savvy, the young man earned promotion to what we now call a Cabinet position. In May of 1847 he became receiver-general and commissioner of Crown Lands. Following the election of a Reform government led by Robert Baldwin and Louis-Hippolyte Lafontaine in 1848, Macdonald found himself on the Opposition benches for the next six years. In 1854, his party returned to power, and he was made attorney general for Canada West.

During this period, Macdonald manipulated and coerced his fellow members of the Liberal-Conservative Party — as his party was officially called at that time — to see things his way and eventually to follow his leadership. By 1857 Macdonald had taken on the leadership of the party and became the leading elected official in the colony of Canada. He learned early on the nuances of cajoling, prodding, and encouraging his fellow politicians. He was well-liked by most of his peers, be they Grit or Tory. He believed in slow, incremental change. Although he was not a reformer — or, heaven forbid, a radical — he was a visionary. That can easily be seen in his key role during the leadup to Confederation and even more so with his National Policy.

The early sixties witnessed stifling political stagnation and years of great indecision. Much of the antagonism between the political opponents of the day and the vacillation that resulted came from the imbalance between the English and French majorities in each half of the colony. While Macdonald and the francophone co-leader — Étienne Taché or Cartier, depending on the election — were able to build a French-English coalition of sorts, they also were mainly focused on running the colony of Canada efficiently. Unfortunately, the political quagmire wouldn't allow for efficiency. Governments fell with great regularity as the ever-shifting alliances struggled with a number of issues; clear majorities were rare.

A movement had been afoot for years to unite British North America into one colony. The Canadas, New Brunswick, Nova Scotia, Prince Edward Island, and Newfoundland were individual colonies, mostly controlled by the Colonial Office in London. There was little trade or even communication between them. In many ways they were almost as separate as the nations of Europe. Each had its own legislative and executive branches of government, its own governors and insular attitudes that matched their independence from one another.

Macdonald had long opposed the idea of a "confederation." As early as 1858 he'd turned his nose up at a plan put forward by his colleague Alexander Galt. (In the legislature, Cartier actually spoke out against Galt's proposal; Macdonald sat with his arms folded, tacitly agreed and said nothing.)

Macdonald, appalled by the situation in the United States, was reluctant to embrace any form of union. That federation was such an abysmal failure in Macdonald's opinion, and he feared a similar result if the politicians of British North America did not exercise caution and care. But the defeat of his government in June of 1864 — yet another switch from the Liberal-Conservatives to the Grits — convinced Macdonald that something had to be done to solve the political stalemate that plagued the colony of the two Canadas. He changed his mind almost overnight. On June 14, a committee report recommended discussion of confederation and Macdonald refused to sign the document. Yet within a mere two days he saw the light and was convinced that something had to be done immediately.

Macdonald's motives for his change of heart were mostly pragmatic. He could see that nothing was getting done, that there was no end in sight for the revolving door of either a Grit or a Tory government falling because of non-confidence votes. And he could read the tea leaves in messages sent from the Colonial Office in London. Britain favoured some sort of union — so long as the Canadian politicians could handle the task.

An unlikely catalyst intervened to move things along. Grit leader George Brown made the courageous first move. Setting aside his distaste (and it is not too strong to actually call it hatred) for Macdonald and the man's politics, Brown stepped forward and offered to enter into a coalition. He can rightfully be called the hero in the Confederation story, even more so than can Macdonald. A fellow Scot, owner of the *Globe* newspaper, and a vocal proponent of representation by population — "rep by pop" — it was Brown who initially led the forces that pushed for union of the British North American colonies. And it was Brown who took that first step by offering to enter into a working relationship with his long-time nemesis Macdonald.

Macdonald and Brown cobbled together what is often referred to as "the Great Coalition." Setting aside their political differences, the two men and their French-speaking lieutenants Georges Étienne Cartier and Antoine-Aimé Dorion ironed out a scheme that was to result in a swift adoption of a plan to unite the British colonies. Both Brown and Macdonald displayed a remarkable flexibility and something else — pragmatic cooperation. Putting their differences aside, they were able to work together and finally get something done.

Word reached the Canadas that the leaders from New Brunswick, Prince Edward Island, and Nova Scotia were meeting in Charlottetown in September of 1864 to discuss some kind union of those Maritime colonies. Macdonald, Brown, Cartier, McGee, and others from the Canadian legislature boarded a ship and sailed east to convince their fellow colonial colleagues that the Canadas and the Maritimes should be part of one union. The politicians from Montreal, Kingston, and Quebec City — especially Cartier and Macdonald — spoke so convincingly that a second conference was hastily scheduled at Quebec a little over a month later where the concept of union was widely accepted. (The delegates from Newfoundland and Prince Edward Island attended the Quebec Conference and signed the documents but did not follow through and join Confederation in 1867.) By 1866 the Canadas, New Brunswick, and a very reluctant Nova Scotia agreed to terms for the union of the colonies under the British North America Act. Their respective legislatures approved the plan for union.

Macdonald was well-suited to take the lead in this endeavour. His role in leading the discussions was at once astute, measured, and convincing. His oratory, always a strength, helped to sell the concept to his fellow politicians and then to the public. Little convincing needed to be done at the Colonial Office. The Brits were more than willing to shed a part of their responsibility for the North Americans who were still loyal to Queen Victoria. Drawing on the positives (as well as taking into account the negatives) of both the British and American democratic models, Macdonald and the other Fathers of Confederation drew up a brilliant form of federalism.

At the so-called London Conference of late 1866, the colonial delegates worked on the British North America Act, dividing powers of the federal and provincial governments. The basis of Canada's constitution, it laid the groundwork for establishing the House of Commons, the Senate, a justice system, and details of things as precise as taxation, banking, the postal system, and the armed forces. The role that Macdonald played in the federation's development and implementation cannot be overestimated.[1] He was the unanimous choice to chair the conference. His insistence on a strong federal government vis-à-vis the provincial authority was easy for many of the other politicians to accept. They embraced a federal system, one where each province looked after specified areas as spelled out in the BNA act. This came at the insistence of Macdonald's Quebec (Canada East) supporters, *les bleus*. It was no surprise that when the dust settled and the colonies found themselves about to become a nation in July of 1867, the governor general asked Macdonald to lead the country's first government.

Although the first federal election was not scheduled to take place until August and September — elections took more than a month at that time — Lord Monck, the governor general, named Macdonald as prime minister well before the election was held. As Macdonald had been unanimously chosen as chair of the London Conference, Monck felt he was the obvious choice to head the government, even though the people had not yet spoken. It was a unique situation to say the least.

Macdonald took on a monumental task. As prime minister, it fell to him to organize not only the federal government but also ensure that the new provinces properly implemented their responsibilities as well. Macdonald and his allies — people like Charles Tupper — had to convert myriad Confederation doubters such as Joseph Howe in Nova Scotia and thereby ensure nationwide support for the new Canadian federation. He continued to push for the inclusion of Prince Edward Island and Newfoundland and even far-off British Columbia.

Almost as enormous an accomplishment as sewing the nation together was Macdonald's success in forging a national party. The Liberal-Conservative Party (aka the Tories or, simply, the Conservatives) had to be woven together from the diverse parties that existed in each colony prior to Confederation. He had to unite Conservatives from all four provinces into a workable coalition that would be not only willing to follow his lead but also adhere to the principles that he himself held dearly.

The amalgam that was created may have included many different groups, but it was definitely conservative in nature. There was not really a substantial liberal element in the Liberal-Conservative Party. Granted, there were some Reformers who had been wooed to join Macdonald in the party, but they were few in number. In his first Cabinet, Macdonald was obliged to include a Reform element, though, so as to keep the illusion of his party being both Liberal and Conservative. He even considered — but ultimately rejected — naming arch-rival George Brown as a Cabinet minister. He himself was centrist, not leaning too radically either left or right. Moderate was a word that Macdonald used over and over again in speeches and letters.

Macdonald, never an idealist, let political pragmatism guide him in his efforts to build the party. He did what he deemed necessary to obtain and hold on to power. He was determined to pull together a disparate group of men to form a modern political party, one with the cohesiveness necessary to ensure that it would remain in power for some time to come.

Macdonald wanted French Canadians to play a major role in the new party. Again, it was political pragmatism that inspired him. Francophones had been the dominant faction in his Conservative governments in the Canadas prior to 1867. There was equal representation between Canada East and Canada West prior to Confederation, and it was Canada East's Parti Bleu that had managed to give Macdonald (and Cartier) their pluralities during those years leading up to union. The support of that party's leaders was still needed by Macdonald after 1867.

They were willing to lend their aid to him because the French-speaking populace had reason to support Confederation. They feared that the Americans would take over British North America if England's colonies did not form their own union. A Yankee takeover would doom French Quebecers, leaving them as a tiny minority in a much larger United States.

Georges Étienne Cartier believed he would be able to save *les Québecois*. Macdonald steered the French Canadian members of Parliament who remained loyal to Cartier into his government by promising them a number of concessions. He saw this in terms of needing to forge a permanent English-French alliance that would assure the party was national in scope as well as recognizing the linguistic duality of the new country.

When the time came to form the government in Ottawa, Sir John had all the Tories from the new province of Ontario in his back pocket. Not that it was a homogenous group. The pro-tariff, pro-imperial preference businessmen of Toronto tended to support him because those were policies he'd long embraced. The Protestant — non-Catholic — men elected throughout the province fell in with Macdonald's party although they had a strong distaste for the ultramontane French Catholics with whom they shared the government benches. The Orange Order, rabid anti-Catholics, backed men like Mackenzie Bowell, a life-long conservative. Macdonald was progressive-minded in a way that the old Upper Canada establishment Tories could never imagine, yet he was able to bring those last few United Empire Loyalist stalwarts under his thumb as well. The Reform (Liberal) policies were far too radical for such a reactionary bloc anyhow.

Wisely, when it came to New Brunswick and Nova Scotia, Sir John relied on the two men who headed the governments in those provinces. Leonard Tilley and Dr. Charles Tupper were to become longtime allies in establishing a national Conservative Party. Both were enthusiastic supporters of Confederation and had worked doggedly to bring it about in the three years since the Charlottetown Conference.

Tilley and Tupper were both like-minded in many respects though very different in personality. Tupper was a scrapper, a fighter with little tolerance for anyone who did not think the way he did. Tilley was a teetotaler. It was his interest in the temperance movement that had initiated his interest in politics. He was a pharmacist by profession and not one given to lofty oratory. Instead, he was a logical thinker with a calm approach to all political arguments. Yet both men were in tune with Macdonald when it came to such things as uniting the colonies, maintaining imperial economic ties, and building railways. Both men brought with them the "conservative" voters of their respective provinces — the fishermen, the loggers, and the merchants.

From all that, Macdonald brought together a team of men from all four of the original provinces to make up what would be the Conservative Party: J.J. Abbott, the businessman's lawyer from Montreal and Mackenzie Bowell, the Orange Order kingpin were two of the originals in that first caucus when it met in the autumn following the 1867 election; Georges-Étienne Cartier, the francophone leader; Thomas D'Arcy McGee, the Irish Catholic poet and fervent anti-republican; Hector Langevin, a capable man whose predilection for patronage would eventually bring him down; Alexander Tilloch Galt, the financial wizard who had been one of the first proponents for union of the British colonies in the 1850s; Sir Francis Hincks, who had been a co-premier of Ontario and an early advocate of responsible government; Peter Mitchell, an anti-prohibitionist from New Brunswick who was famously known for carrying a pistol during election campaigns. It was a group of men who individually varied widely but who thought alike politically.

Once he had succeeded in winning control of the new nation for himself and his party, Macdonald had to ensure that he would be able to maintain control. He relied on what is arguably the greatest tool available to a politician. Throughout history, political leaders have used patronage to obtain support and reward favours. Canada's subsequent leaders have not been averse to using it either. Politicians of all stripes had practised it long before Macdonald was ever elected to office. But he refined it and mastered its intricacies. (Sir Wilfrid Laurier proved to be equally adept at it when he eventually became prime minister.)

At the time of Confederation, nearly every government job in every riding in the country was awarded by a politician. With such discretion, politicians wielded enormous power. Although Sir John tried to develop a system that rewarded merit, the entire nation's civil service was run by men who owed their jobs to someone in political office. It remained that way until at least the First World War. Macdonald, Laurier, and the men who served in the interregnum all recognized this basic fact of nineteenth-century political life.

It was Macdonald's reliance on patronage and the seedier side of politics that nearly brought a premature end to his career.[2] A lesser political animal could not have weathered the storm that ensued.

At the time of Confederation, the Maritime colonies were promised that an intercolonial railway would be built. Many understood this as a commitment to build a line from Halifax to Montreal or Toronto. Macdonald had a grander vision. (He had the enthusiastic support of Alexander T. Galt, his finance minister and, perhaps not coincidentally, the owner of a western coal company that could benefit from a rail line to British Columbia)

Macdonald's "National Dream" envisioned a railway that stretched from eastern Canada all the way to Vancouver and the Pacific shore. It became one of the promises made to British Columbia, a condition for that western province to join Canada.

A Canadian coast-to-coast railway line was a gloriously over-ambitious idea. There was such staggering risk to it. Undertaking such an endeavour could potentially bankrupt the country. To critics, it seemed foolhardy to agree to such a project when the lands to the west of Ontario seemed little populated: a stunted little Scottish and Métis settlement around Red River; a smattering of trading posts; and a few sparse settlements in the mountainous rainforest that was British Columbia; the First Nations inhabitants who occupied the land were largely ignored.

The gains did not seem worthy of the risk according to many. Yet Macdonald showed vision and foresight. He understood that the realization of his plan would not only bring enormous economic benefit to the new country, it would also help to achieve a critical political goal. With the American West filling rapidly — and they already had a transcontinental railway by 1869 — it seemed not only prudent but imperative that Canada build a link to tie British Columbia to the eastern part of the country. Otherwise, what was to stop a Yankee takeover of the British lands north of the 49th parallel? That was a nightmare scenario for the prime minister.

The railway project was undertaken with haste.

The movement to build a transcontinental railway across the rugged Canadian Shield and seemingly endless prairies and then through the Rocky Mountains was an undertaking like no other in Canadian history. An exercise in nation-building, the railway was also a means to counteract the "Manifest Destiny"[3] mindset of Americans to the south.

It began with what we now call a "private sector" accord with the government. Then, as now, investors and corporations were needed to take on the task since the government of the nation could not possibly afford to undertake such a Herculean task. Financiers poured into Ottawa and entered into open — and secret, in some cases — agreements with Macdonald, his political colleagues, and his business partners such as Montreal railway magnate Hugh Allan.

Two companies in particular vied to finance and take on the risk of building the railway. Hugh Allan's Canadian Pacific Railway Company and D.L. Macpherson's Inter-Oceanic (at times spelled Interoceanic) Railway Company. Allan had made his fortune with a steamship line, had then moved on to establishing the Merchants' Bank of Canada, and was heavily invested in railway construction. Allan, as it turned out, had connections high up in the Conservative Party. (His lawyer was future Conservative prime minister J.J. Abbott. More about him later.)

Hugh Allan put together a syndicate that could ensure a railway was built and then set to work to convince Macdonald that his Canadian Pacific was the company to choose. That was done using the good old-fashioned, tried-and-true, if not entirely legal method of bribery. He donated over $350,000 to Macdonald's campaign for the election of 1872. That amounted to over eleven million in 2020 dollars. In turn, Macdonald promised — not explicitly, it seems — that Allan's Canadian Pacific would receive the charter to build the line. Senator Macpherson, resentful of the choice that was eventually announced by the government, called Allan's plans "an audacious, insolent, unpatriotic and gigantic swindle."

Macdonald had said in no uncertain terms that he wanted no American funding of the Canadian railway and the Canadian public had wholeheartedly agreed. Allan had promised to abide by this provision, but he lied to the prime minister about his sources of funding. In fact, some of the money came precisely from American investors. The American backers, though, upon learning that they'd have little control over the Canadian Pacific, were understandably angry. Their unhappiness with the deal sifted into the smoking rooms of the business elite in Montreal. Whispers and accusations about the unfairness did not remain secret for long. Soon, Liberal Party operatives heard of the background corruption and illicit money arrangements.

The Opposition in Parliament jumped all over the Conservatives for their dishonourable business dealings. Macdonald's grasp of power in Ottawa was tenuous to begin with following his narrow minority win of 1872. It would not take much to wrest control of the reins of power away from the Tory government. To deflect the attacks from George Brown, Edward Blake, and the Grits, Macdonald used various tactics that he'd learned over the years.

He obfuscated; he spoke for hours at a time in the House of Commons; he told the partial truth, hoping that that might dampen the Liberal attacks; he braved it out and let the Opposition rant and accuse; he set up procedural roadblocks that delayed and kept the problem temporarily in the background. All of which only served to delay the inevitable.

On Friday July 18, 1873, three influential newspapers simultaneously published damning evidence that Macdonald had committed an unthinkable political error. His culpability was brought to the public with the publication in those newspapers of a telegram from Macdonald to J.J. Abbott, Hugh Allan's lawyer (also a Conservative MP).

Immediate. Private. I must have another ten thousand.

Will be the last time of asking. Do not fail me. Answer today.

Even with that, the prime minister soldiered on. He arranged to prorogue Parliament early in August. He appointed a royal commission to investigate the scandal. When the House of Commons met again in late October of 1873 — this time with representatives from the new province of Prince Edward Island — members of all political stripes felt the affair had gone far enough and something must be done to end it.

Macdonald bravely stood in the House the night of November 3 and, in an eloquent speech that lasted for five hours (fuelled by gin and water), he denied corruption and denied that Hugh Allan had been promised the charter in return for his political donation. However, the struggle to maintain power became too difficult; he couldn't keep up the fight any longer. Two days later, Macdonald went to Rideau Hall and tendered the resignation of his government.

Sir John A. Macdonald, at age fifty-eight, was no longer prime minister. It seemed that his political career had come to an abrupt and ignominious end. The *Globe*, an admitted opponent, declared in an editorial that his role as a Canadian politician had "played out."

Rather than let their leader fall on his sword, however, the Tory Party rallied behind him. The Conservative caucus met on November 6, 1873. Stepping to the front of the hall and facing the men in the room, he addressed them in a calm voice that barely hid his disappointment. He implored the caucus members to select someone else to lead the party going forward. Macdonald was more than a little surprised when the caucus gave him a rousing ovation and stood as one to clap for their leader. In the end, they backed him unanimously, vowing to fight on with him as head of the party. While the "Old Chieftain" claimed that he wanted to find a younger leader, he'd not done much in the way of mentoring anyone in particular. Nor would he in the near future. The party chose to stand behind the only person that they could imagine as leader.

In the election of January 1874, Alexander Mackenzie and the Liberals won a convincing majority, outnumbering the Conservatives by sixty-four seats. Macdonald won his Kingston riding (although even that result was challenged on the grounds that the Conservative leader had used bribery and other illegal means to eke out a narrow victory). Once more, he threatened to resign, believing that his party could never again win power as long as he was its leader. He did not follow through on his ultimatum, however. Instead, he adopted an uncharacteristic approach to handling the party in the House of Commons. He advised his members to be less partisan than usual and to support the good measures brought forward by Mackenzie. It was as if Macdonald could foresee the troubles that were about to land in the laps of the Liberals and wished for his Tories to stay squeaky clean.

Just as the Mackenzie-led Liberals took office, a general depression hit Canada and the United States, throwing many Canadian factory labourers out of work as American protectionism hurt Canadian businesses nation-wide. Mackenzie's Ontario MPs rebelled at some of the concessions granted to the new province of British Columbia. Mackenzie struggled to keep rebellious elements in his party, such as the irascible and eccentric Edward Blake, in line. Despite Mackenzie's accomplishments, the Liberals gradually lost favour in the country. His free trade agreement with the United States did not alleviate the economic misfortune that had hit both countries hard, and it was Mackenzie's Liberals who took the blame. In the election of 1878, the Liberals retained only sixty-three seats in the 206-seat House of Commons.

Macdonald was back in office as prime minister of Canada. He had quietly watched Mackenzie's government collapse. Now he was ready once more to carry on the job of governing the country that he'd cobbled together.

How he had weathered the five years out of office is an interesting study in political shrewdness, savvy, and endurance. At the beginning of this political exile, Macdonald was repeatedly ready to quit politics altogether. Forces within his party resisted dumping their leader despite the Pacific Scandal. The truth of the matter was, Macdonald was indispensable. There was no ready successor, and the party still rode the coattails of a man whose intellect, political acumen (touched as it was by cynicism and guile), charm, and sagacity had no equal on either side of the political aisle. Out of office, Sir John had cemented his relationship with francophones in Quebec, charmed the people of British Columbia, doled out favours to elected Conservatives, and sat in the bushes, waiting for Mackenzie to ultimately fail.

Going into the 1878 election, Macdonald saw the need for a policy that would not only ensure the Conservatives' victory but also see the country move forward economically. He developed just such a plan during his time in Opposition, and his party ran in the 1878 election on the promise of an innovative "National Policy." It consisted of a plan to encourage Canadian manufacturing by placing high tariffs on manufactured goods coming from the United States. The push to finish a transcontinental railway (the "National Dream") was a showcase part of the policy as well. And then, tied to that part of the plan was a scheme to encourage immigration so that the West could be developed and populated.

Once elected, the Tories set about to implement their National Policy; they were, in the long run, successful. The transcontinental railway, despite many crises, financial and technical, was built by 1885. That success reflected well on the party and on the leader. In the elections of 1882, 1887, and 1891, Macdonald's Conservatives won consecutive majority governments by substantial margins. The voters of Canada (i.e., the men, since women did not yet have the vote) showed a preference for the policies of Macdonald over those offered by the Liberal Party.

But much of that success was thanks to the personality of the man. That was what drove his popularity.

Not everything went according to plan, and it was far from smooth sailing. Apart from the fallout from the Pacific Scandal, perhaps the biggest issue to plague Macdonald was his handling of the Métis rebellion of 1885.

The Métis, a people of mixed French and Indigenous heritage, had been living in the Red River settlement near present day Winnipeg for generations. By the time of Confederation, the number of Métis living near Fort Garry numbered an estimated ten thousand. The Hudson's Bay Company administered the area until 1870 and severely limited the number of non-native inhabitants.[4] The fur traders and those supplying the fur trade were largely the English-speaking Scots or Irish; a few, scattered French-speaking labourers also worked for the company.

The Métis were not pleased when Canada prepared to take over their territory in 1869 with plans on making Manitoba a province in 1870. Surveyors from Canada were sent to the region and given orders to divide the countryside in a grid-like fashion akin to the surveying that had been done in Ontario. This plan would displace and potentially carve up the farms that existed there, such was the insensitivity to the people native to the area. The Métis, who had no title to the land they inhabited, saw the threat that these surveyors represented. They naturally resisted. Not only had they not been consulted properly, but now there was a threat that many Métis homes and farms might be lost. Louis Riel, their charismatic young leader, declared a provisional government in Red River in order to properly negotiate the terms of the takeover. The Canadian lieutenant governor, William McDougall, was stopped as he tried to enter the new province.

Riel, during that short term as head of a provisional government, had made the misguided and fatal mistake of executing a trouble-making Ontario Orangeman named Thomas Scott. Macdonald and the government in Ottawa saw these actions as unlawful rebellion. The Orange Order in Ontario fired up anti-Métis rhetoric.[5] Propaganda in the form of newspaper stories and editorials fomented the anti-French, anti-Catholic, and anti-Indigenous sentiments that already existed in most of the province.

Troops were sent to Manitoba to deal with the Métis. Riel fled to the United States, though he maintained contact with his people at Red River. He was even elected by them in three federal elections, though he was never able to take his seat in the House of Commons.

Macdonald's handling of the Red River Rebellion was not completely heavy-handed and insensitive. He took the matter seriously, mostly because he suspected American subterfuge and feared that any kind of upheaval in the West could lead to takeover by the United States. He interviewed people from various walks of life regarding the situation at Red River and saw that the Canadians who'd arrived on the scene were likely as guilty as anyone when it came to stirring up trouble.

The surveyors who'd come from Canada to assess the land in Manitoba were English-speaking Orangemen by and large, and it was clear that they were completely inconsiderate of the Métis' rights. The surveyors' attitudes and actions resulted in them being detested by the people at Red River. The prime minister could see that the Hudson's Bay Company was somewhat complicit in fomenting the unrest also. The London head office of the company never let the settlers at Red River know the details of the Canadian takeover. In a letter to Cartier, Sir John explained that the "poor people" in the colony were being turned over to Canada as a "flock of sheep."

Yet in the long run, Macdonald showed little consideration of the rights and history of the Métis people or the other Indigenous Peoples living in Canada. He trudged forward with adding Manitoba to Canada despite many protests from the people who actually lived in the new province.

The outrage in Ontario at Scott's so-called murder, fuelled by the Orangemen's hatred of all things French and Catholic — of which the Métis were "guilty" — created a political dilemma for the government and the prime minister. The Conservatives needed the support of the Protestants in Ontario, and a huge number of those voters were part of the Orange Order. Macdonald acted hastily to secure the province by sending troops to take back the colony. In doing so, he sacrificed Indigenous rights; political considerations were clearly of greater importance to him. Macdonald made many such gambles and calculations over the years.

Fifteen years later, a second Métis rebellion took place. This time, the Indigenous Peoples in what would become Saskatchewan joined in the revolt. Although the causes for this second uprising were similar to those that spawned the earlier uprising, the consequences were very different.

By the mid-1880s, many of the Métis had moved farther west (into present day Saskatchewan). There were a number of reasons for this move. The open racism displayed by the Canadian settlers in Manitoba was an important one. Perhaps more important was the fact that their principal food source was disappearing. The diminishing number of bison, still a mainstay of Métis life, also served as a spur to their migration. The Métis were following what remained of the great bison herds. Within a decade and a half, the Indigenous Peoples of the Plains had suffered incredible hardship. They had been deprived of their land. Great numbers had fallen to disease brought by the Europeans. Their traditional nomadic way of life was being eroded by repressive treaties, many of which were never honoured. Crowfoot, a Blackfoot chief, had seen the future as early as 1876 when he stated, "the day is coming when all the buffalo will be killed and we shall have nothing more to live on."

The Métis called upon Riel to come back from his exile in the United States and help them to resist any further destruction of their way of life. With Gabriel Dumont serving as the military leader, warriors from the Blackfoot, the Cree, and the Assiniboine First Nations joined in what came to be known as the North-West Rebellion. Once again, surveyors were a source of discomfort and distrust. The situation in Saskatchewan[6] seemed to be a repeat of what had happened in Manitoba. Poverty and starvation motivated the Indigenous groups. Armed conflict marked the difference between the two rebellions. This time, however, the recently completed railway across the Plains enabled Ottawa to get both army troops and the North-West Mounted Police to Saskatchewan rapidly and efficiently. Several bloody battles took place. In the final one, the Battle of Batoche, which occurred near present-day Prince Albert on May 9–12, 1885, the Métis fighters, along with their Cree and Sioux allies, were defeated and Louis Riel was captured.

Riel was put on trial for treason two months later in Regina. The jury was white, English, and Protestant. There was a question about whether or not Riel was fit to stand trial. Although some of the doctors who examined Riel at the time concluded that he suffered from mental illness — he had spent time in a mental health hospital — others who examined him rejected that claim. (The issue remains a subject of debate.) In any case, Riel refused to plead insanity. Instead, he twice addressed the court and spoke eloquently about the rights of the Métis people. Within five days, proceedings wrapped up and the jury found the Métis leader guilty. They recommended mercy.

Macdonald found himself in a dilemma, perhaps the most serious and consequential of his political life. In a letter to Charles Tupper, the prime minister mentioned that, on one hand, he considered the successful return of the rebellion's military volunteers a nation-building success but, on the other hand, the trial's outcome posed a difficult question. What should be done with the Métis leader? If the federal government commuted his sentence and sent the rebel to a mental asylum, they would face the wrath and political rejection of the Protestant Orangemen of Ontario. On the other hand, allowing the hanging of Riel, a French-speaking Catholic, might alienate a good portion of the French population of Quebec.

Macdonald sought the advice of people familiar with the details of the rebellion as well as the conditions of the Métis and Plains First Nations. While Orange Ontario cried for revenge for Scott's so-called murder fifteen years earlier, the plea in Quebec was for clemency. Despite lobbying from both sides, Macdonald held to a belief that the trial had been fair; its outcome had been just; the sentence — hanging — was appropriate; and that there was no need for the government in Ottawa to interfere with the judicial process.

A less-examined reason for Macdonald's cynical decision was his belief that Catholic Quebecers would perhaps approve of his inaction. He gambled his Quebec support on the fact that prior to the outbreak of the rebellion, Riel had ranted about divine revelations and seemed to have developed a near-messiah complex. He had rejected the Roman Catholic Church and was even barred from taking sacraments during Mass. Sir

John was aware of Riel's feelings, so he felt that the resolutely Catholic inhabitants of Quebec probably wouldn't be all that upset if this so-called heretic was executed.

Macdonald was seriously wrong.

By allowing the hanging of the French-speaking and Roman Catholic Riel, the prime minister alienated a good number of Quebec's francophone voters. Those men (and their non-voting wives, one assumes) saw the execution as a symbol of English Canada's hatred of all things French and Catholic. The parish priests ranted against the execution from their pulpits. Honoré Mercier, a charming and capable Liberal politician in Quebec, exploited this sentiment to the detriment of the Conservative Party.

Macdonald, in the wake of the Riel fiasco — although not because of it — told both his political confidantes Charles Tupper and Lord Carnarvon, that his work was over, and the time had come to retire. He had carved out a country from a disparate set of colonies and far-flung territories. He had developed political institutions that followed a constitution he'd brought into being, and he'd weathered several political storms. His National Policy — building a transcontinental railway, settling the West, and developing eastern industry — was gradually being realized and would pay great dividends in the near future.

But Macdonald also saw that there were a few things that still needed his attention, his leadership, and his energetic *esprit*. In the late 1880s, the effects of a great depression were still being felt. Immigration was, in reality, still mostly just a plan. The prejudice and racism illuminated by the North-West Rebellion needed to be handled very carefully. The threat of American Manifest Destiny never seemed to fade too far into the background. Each province seemed to have some gripe or other with Ottawa. Nova Scotians continued their perennial complaints about their poor economic status in Confederation and their threats to leave Confederation never seemed to completely go away. The nascent nationalism that had boiled to the surface in Quebec, thanks to Riel, threatened to be mirrored by an equally divisive nationalism among the Protestant Orange supporters in Ontario. It seemed impossible that Macdonald, with all these issues needing to be managed, could resign. He couldn't leave the nation in the hands of an untried Conservative leader. And of course, it was still not clear if there was a successor to the Old Chieftain.

In the 1887 election, Macdonald's Tories defeated the Liberals led by Edward Blake. It seemed that, in the words of historian Donald Creighton, "Canadian politics ... were apparently proceeding in their accustomed way. Things were surely as they always had been. And was not the re-election of John A. Macdonald for Kingston a significant proof of the fact?"[7] Despite his victory, Macdonald again, as he seemed to do with some regularity, sent a letter to his close associates in the Tory Party proposing his resignation. And once again, the Conservative Party insisted that Sir John carry on, citing that his National Policy had been endorsed by the electorate and that he should be the one to lead the nation as it developed that ambitious blueprint. He was persuaded to stay on. It was as if Macdonald did not trust anyone else to handle the job and the party could not bear to be led by anyone else.

In truth, no one else could handle the job as well as Sir John. Much like Atlas holding up the world, Macdonald was the giant upon whose shoulders the rest of the Conservative Party sat. He kept them together by force of personality. His wit, intelligence, and charisma could not be matched on either side of the House. He had an incredible number of contacts in every part of the Dominion. Some were friends, some wished to be his friend, and some were friendly to the man, whether they liked him or not, because they needed to be on good terms with him. The promise of patronage demanded that they court his favour. The thing was, though, most people found him likeable, whether or not they were Tory supporters. His skill at charming people of all political stripes kept everyone on their toes. He knew government rules and procedures better than anyone else. In addition to all that, he was a quick study. He was able to assess a situation and come to a decision — or non-decision — quickly. (He hadn't earned the nickname "Old Tomorrow" for nothing.) He worked harder than most men who had less work to do.

Well-liked as he was, Macdonald was by no means without his critics. He now faced a whole new generation of antagonists. Honoré Mercier at the provincial level in Quebec and Laurier on the federal scene argued both old Liberal grievances and new nationalist beliefs. From his premier's office at Queen's Park in Toronto, Oliver Mowat, Macdonald's one-time law partner, was a constant thorn in Macdonald's side. Thomas Greenway from Manitoba proved to be a nuisance to the prime minister as he argued for greater provincial rights, reforms in the province's school system, and what he saw as unfair railway rates. Nova Scotia was a perpetual whiner in the economy of the nation.[8]

But it was in that province that Macdonald found two of his staunchest and most reliable allies. As it turned out, the two would also be members of the group of four men who served as immediate successors at the head of the Tory Party.

His friendship with Sir Charles Tupper, the rakish physician from Cumberland County, had been a long one. The two had worked side by side since 1864, helping to bring about Confederation and then working together to unite the new country, and although they had a brief falling out in the early 1880s, their correspondence was prolific. At one time, Tupper had been seen as the obvious successor to Macdonald in the prime minister's role, but the likelihood of him following as PM had diminished over the years. Tupper was in his sixties by the late 1880s, and although Macdonald was even older, everyone assumed that a much younger man was what the party needed when Macdonald eventually gave up the reins of power. There was no doubt about Tupper's intellect, loyalty, energy, and political skills. Shortly after the election of 1887, Macdonald met with Tupper as the latter prepared to return to England, where he revelled in his role as Canada's high commissioner.

"I wish to God you were in my place," Macdonald said.

Tupper answered, "Thank God I am not."

The other Nova Scotian who seemed to be waiting in the wings for Macdonald to hand over the reins of power was John Thompson. A Haligonian with a brilliant legal mind, he had had a wide-ranging career over the years, serving as a lawyer, judge, and premier of Nova Scotia. Thompson was young, competent, and capable of being prime minister.

Yet he had one thing that was held against him, and it was a serious matter in those days. He was a Roman Catholic. (He'd actually been born Protestant but converted later in life.) That did not sit at all well with the influential Orangemen in Ontario, who went so far as to call Thompson, on the basis of his ecclesiastical affiliation, a "pervert." Lady Macdonald had used the same epithet. That was a mild sobriquet in those days of heated religious fervor and was not a reference to any sexual depravity. Ardent Protestants simply disliked Catholics, holding on to centuries-old prejudice carried over from England, Ireland, and the days of King William of Orange. Anyone with the gall to convert to the Pope's religion was on the wrong course and, in the collective opinion of the staunch Protestants who held sway in English-Canada, unworthy.

And so, Macdonald stayed the course and led the party into the election of 1891, against the newly installed leader of the Liberals, Wilfrid Laurier. The National Policy, protective tariffs, and a repudiation of the Liberal's proposed policy of reciprocity[9] with the United States dominated the election debates. Macdonald called for and offered stability. A poster for the Tories showed Macdonald on the shoulders of a farmer and a baker with trains, factories, and farms pictured in the background. The caption read, "The Old Flag. The Old Policy. The Old Leader." Macdonald played on the fears of annexation with the United States. The campaign issues worked for him and for his party, and he retained power, winning with a slight majority over the Liberals.

That election has never been held up as a model for any democracy. While the secret ballot had been in place since the 1870s, there were still far too many examples of voter suppression and intimidation, as well as other illegal practices. The 1891 election was a particularly troublesome one. Men were openly offered food or alcohol to purchase their votes. Sometimes they were blatantly handed cash in exchange for a vote. Personation, voting in someone else's name, was rampant, especially in cities where the population was more likely to be itinerant, moving from house to house. Close to the American border, a common practice was to import Canadians. Former citizens who were residing in the United States were brought back to ridings to vote in the election. In March of 1891, two trains arrived in Quebec carrying over two thousand textile workers from the United States, all allegedly former Canadians who were entitled to vote.

Falsification of the voters list was common. The lists were drawn up by people appointed by the party in power. They were not updated often. The data on the list might change the status of a person, making that eligible voter suddenly ineligible. It was not uncommon to add the names of deceased persons to a list, have a party lackey assume that name, and then allow that person to vote. Sometimes they would vote more than once, casting a ballot in different constituencies. A comparison of the 1889 voters lists in Ontario with census information from 1891 shows a discrepancy of over thirty-four thousand voters. That huge difference signalled the fact that there were floaters, people who voted using dead person's names or voted in place of someone who had moved away. Because that Ontario list, for example, had not been updated just prior to the election, there were tens of thousands of new citizens who may have moved location but were denied the right to vote as their names were not on the official lists.

Intimidation remained the most common strategy to manipulate the election. Parish priests in Quebec regularly told their parishioners how to vote. To a lesser extent, the same thing occurred in New Brunswick, Ontario, and Manitoba. Employers were known to order their employees to vote a certain way, threatening loss of wages or even loss of a job if they didn't do as they were told.

Parliament was dissolved at the beginning of February 1891. The Conservatives were ready with a slogan that resonated with the population of the country. "A British subject I was born. A British subject I will die," said Macdonald and it became his most famous election catchphrase. According to Macdonald's secretary, Joseph Pope, "the old man" fought the contest "almost single-handedly." The Ontario Tories, for instance, were too busy scrambling for support in their own ridings to be of much service elsewhere. Pope's statement was an exaggeration but demonstrates the "one man team" thinking that so often revolved around Sir John A. Macdonald.

Among the Canadian populace, sentiment toward England ran deep. The country, beyond the borders of Quebec, was at that time predominantly British in nature; most of the largely agrarian society was of English, Irish, or Scottish descent and Canadians revered their connection to the British Empire and to Queen Victoria. The Anglo-Saxon Protestant majority easily outnumbered any other cultural group. The National Policy's immigration platform had yet to bring in a great number of the eastern European immigrants who eventually came to Canada's open Prairies.

The Indigenous Peoples there and elsewhere in Canada were marginalized, driven off their land, given little regard by their contemporaries. The destruction of Indigenous culture was advanced by means of the creation of residential schools. (Macdonald was intimately involved in their creation and as a result his reputation is under increasing attack today.) The few Canadians of African or Asian descent who lived in Canada were treated dreadfully. In many instances, the laws and systemic racism they experienced were beyond unforgiveable. Sadly, that is another story.

Fear of annexation by the republicans to the south was equally resonant from Nova Scotia to British Columbia. Americans were portrayed, rightly or wrongly, as greedy, covetous, and unyielding in their aspirations to take over Canada or at least large swaths of Canada's territory. While the Liberals obviously had no intention to hand over the country to the Americans, it was an argument that their political rivals, the Tories, made. Laurier's party believed that with closer economic ties to the United States, prosperity would be the order of the day. The Grits felt that everyone in the Dominion of Canada would benefit. Conservatives disagreed.

At one point during the campaign, Macdonald obtained a copy of a pamphlet being prepared by a Liberal named Edward Farrer. The propaganda sheet was intended to give Americans advice on how they could pressure Canada into political union. During a Toronto rally on February 17, the prime minister revealed what he labelled deviousness on the part of the Liberals. The revelation took much of the wind out of Laurier's sails for the rest of the campaign. Adding to the Liberal leader's problems was a denunciation of the reciprocity treaty by none other than former leader, the maverick Edward Blake.

Macdonald, a man who had worked with such energy throughout his life and who insisted upon carrying the party on his shoulders one last time, was beginning to fail physically. At a rally on February 25, he left the stage weak, pale, and unable to remember what he'd said. It may have been a slight stroke although he was not given any diagnosis at the time. He simply did not appear at any further rallies for the duration of the campaign.

A global depression had seized the world's economies. Underlying the 1891 election was the fact that Canada, under Tory rule, was weathering the worldwide economic hard times relatively well compared to the United States. The late 1880s and 1890s were a time of industrialization, growth in the timber and mining industries, and virtually no unemployment. Nearly 70 percent of Canada's exports went to Britain while less than 30 percent of trade was with the United States. Macdonald's "old policy" seemed to be faring well for the farming communities just as much as the industrializing towns across the country. The Liberals faced an uphill battle to convince the electorate that they could do a better job of managing the economy.

Sir John A. Macdonald was tired and often ill despite the facade he managed to put on most of the time. At seventy-six, he had weathered many political and personal battles. During the stump speeches, he acknowledged that this was his last campaign and pleaded with the voters to throw his party their support one final time under his leadership.

The election was held in March. The Conservatives won 117 seats; the Liberals took 90.

Sir John spent many weeks afterward at Earnscliffe, dashing off memos and receiving visitors to his bedside. He roused himself to open Parliament on April 29. Dressed in his familiar frock coat, stovepipe hat, and flashy red necktie, he sat in the Commons and addressed Liberal leader Wilfrid Laurier, boldly saying, "We are going to stay here, and it will take more than the power of the Honourable Gentleman and all the phalanx behind him to disturb us or to shove us from our pedestal."

Less than two weeks later, Macdonald scheduled a meeting with the governor general to discuss the nature of a dispute between Canada and the United States over waters in the Bering Strait. During the meeting, he found that he could no longer speak properly. An alarmed Joseph Pope ran to get Thompson, who rushed to the prime minister's office. Thompson, Pope, and Lord Stanley all noticed that Macdonald's mouth was drooping and twisted, an obvious symptom of a stroke. Somehow the men completed the meeting, but the moment Stanley left, Macdonald admitted to Pope that "I am afraid of paralysis. Both my parents died of it, and I seem to feel it creeping over me." He had, in fact, suffered a small stroke, but by that evening, the symptoms had miraculously eased, and his speech returned to normal. That way, he was somehow able to keep the whole matter secret from his wife, Agnes.

He returned to his parliamentary duties and although weak and tired, carried on with business as usual. The night of May 23, he and Lady Macdonald hosted a dinner for several Conservative MPs at Earnscliffe. In the middle of the night, Agnes heard him crying out from his bedroom that he had lost all feeling in his left leg. Then came the devastating stoke of May 29. He stubbornly clung to life for more than a week. Finally, at ten o'clock on the morning of June 6, Joseph Pope emerged from the Macdonald home to speak to gathered reporters. "Gentlemen, Sir John Macdonald is dead."

Macdonald was not perfect and often his flaws — his drinking, his conniving, his opportunism, and his cynical approaches get less analysis than do his positive traits. His role in the destruction of Indigenous culture has only recently received widespread attention. For most of Canada's history, Macdonald has been considered a giant, his strengths far outweighing whatever failings he had. Focus has been placed on his achievements, "the ends." The "means" have been largely ignored. Today, that opinion is increasingly being questioned, but whatever position is taken, it must be acknowledged that the legacy of the man is undeniable. And it was his personality that drove him and the country for its first decades.

He was devoted to the country he helped to birth. His actions in establishing the new nation were at once calculated, ambitious, shrewd, and pragmatic. His performance on the political trail demonstrated his wit, charm, and charisma. Both admired and despised, he had a political intelligence that few men or women throughout history, let alone Canadian history, could match. His ability to manoeuvre the political waters was unmatched. He knew how to compromise and knew when to give in to the will of the people or even his political opponents at times. Macdonald had an innate understanding of human nature that he exploited often. He had an impressive ability to convince people to follow him or to at least see his side of a given issue. His most redeeming feature and the characteristic that kept him near the top of the political greasy pole for over four decades was his likeability. Most people — George Brown and Oliver Mowat were notable exceptions — liked the man. Laurier admired him so much that he emulated the old man's style to a certain degree. It was Laurier who gave the most eloquent of eulogies. "The place of Sir John Macdonald in this country was so large and so absorbing that it is almost impossible to conceive that the political life of this country, the fate of this country, can continue without him ... as if indeed one of the institutions of the land had given way."

Such a man was not easy to replace. In the five years following his death, four other Conservative leaders tried and failed to sustain the kind of leadership that Macdonald brought to Parliament and to Canada. This is their story.

Chapter Two

◇

Sir John Abbott:
The Reluctant Prime Minister

ONLY DAYS BEFORE HE ASSUMED office as Canada's third prime minister, Senator John Joseph Caldwell Abbott sat at his desk in his Ottawa office writing to a friend in Montreal. He wrote, "I hate politics.… I hate notoriety, public meetings, public speeches, caucuses, and everything that I know of that is apparently the necessary incident of politics, except doing public work to the best of my ability."

He wrote those words as Prime Minister John A. Macdonald lay dying. Everything was in limbo; no clear successor was ready to take the reins of power. It was possible that the job would go to Abbott, but that was far from certain. He did not want to be prime minister, but there was pressure from within his party for him to step up to the plate. The role was about to be thrust upon him.

Macdonald had held the prime minister's post for nineteen of the twenty-four years since Confederation. He'd won his final election in March of 1891 as a very ill seventy-six-year-old who was both physically and mentally exhausted. For him to have held office for so long and to win one more electoral contest at his advanced age were great accomplishments.

As noted earlier, historians have claimed that one of Macdonald's great failures was his inability — or unwillingness — to anoint a successor. Over the years prior to his death, there had been some contenders, but many had either drifted away from the party or chose not to vie for the leadership. Dalton McCarthy, a central Ontario MP, had at one time been touted as a potential successor. He'd been close to Macdonald as a legal advisor but was quickly supplanted by John Thompson when he arrived in Ottawa from Halifax in 1885. The two rivals disagreed on a number of issues but especially the rights of French speakers and Catholics. McCarthy's open antagonism toward the French and toward Roman Catholics in the country doomed any ambitions he might have had. He drifted away from Sir John A.'s inner circle, then finally broke with the Conservatives altogether (although a number of Tory insiders held out hope that he would be lured back into the party fold).

Hector-Louis Langevin and fellow Quebecer Joseph-Adolphe Chapleau were considered at one time potential successors to Macdonald; however, both had fallen out of favour with the party powerbrokers. The governor general had a face-to-face meeting with Langevin during which he told the Quebec minister outright that he would not be calling upon him to form a ministry.

Two others warranted consideration, and indeed both eventually took on the role, although reluctantly and only after twists of fate. John Abbott was well liked but was not considered a leader in the Macdonald mould. Belleville newspaperman Mackenzie Bowell managed his department with efficiency, but his personal gruffness and inability to inspire meant that he was not in the running. Another strike against them was the fact that both Abbott and Bowell were senators, removed from the daily political action of the House of Commons. It was a convoluted route that led both men eventually to the highest office in the land.

With the old man's sudden death in June, only weeks after the 1891 election, the Conservative Party faced a fractious leadership crisis. It also was a predicament of sorts for the sitting governor general, Lord Stanley of Preston, the person who would ultimately name the successor.

Messages flew back and forth. The streets of Ottawa were witness to fancy carriages and a steady parade of hansom cabs whisking about the capital as prominent Conservatives lobbied, cajoled, and arm-twisted their colleagues in their efforts to determine who should be named head of the party.

Charles Tupper, the Nova Scotia Father of Confederation who was respected by some rank-and-file Tory MPs, was being seriously considered. He was, however, thought to be a man whose time had passed. His son, Cabinet member Charles Tupper Jr. (often referred to as C.H.), naturally pushed for his father to be given the position, but it was simply not going to happen, at least not yet. John Thompson informed his wife, Annie, in a letter written June 10 that C.H. was "mad as he can be at the cold shoulder which the old goat has got in many quarters."

Tupper himself believed strongly that the leadership should go to a French Canadian. At the time, he was serving in London as Canada's high commissioner to Britain and was reluctant to leave his post, a position that offered the pleasure-seeking Tupper ample opportunity to lead the good life. When finally convinced that his father preferred that someone else take on the job, C.H. was ultimately persuaded by Tupper Sr. to back Thompson as leader.

Macdonald had made it known that John Abbott, the seventy-year-old leader of the government in the Senate, had "none of the qualities needed in a prime minister." A few years earlier, during his summer holiday of 1888 in New Brunswick, Macdonald had had a conversation with his friend George Stephen, who kept pressing the prime minister to retire. Stephen felt that Langevin was the logical successor to the party leadership.

"There is no one else," he told Macdonald.

Macdonald's secretary, the ever-present, reliable, and sycophantic Joseph Pope was also present. As he was wont to do, he spoke up. "I have a candidate — one who lives on the borderline between the two provinces, speaks both languages with facility, and is equally at home in Quebec and Ontario."

"Who is he?" asked Macdonald.

"John Abbott," Pope said.

"John Abbott," said Macdonald, "why he hasn't a single qualification for the office."

It was a harsh and unfair assessment. Abbott was organized, energetic, and a very good speaker. But the old man's words resonated with some Tories. Abbott was liked and respected but was as reluctant to take on the leadership as Macdonald had been to hand it to him. The party could see no other way forward, though.

While Macdonald never put into writing that Thompson should be the next leader, it seemed that the old man had, in many ways, groomed the Nova Scotia minister for the role. On the very day that he suffered his debilitating stroke, Macdonald had spent the entire afternoon with Thompson discussing public policy and party tactics as the Conservatives worked to solidify their national support. Abbott never shared that kind of close confidante role with the aging Macdonald.

Not all Conservatives were quick to throw support behind Thompson, however. That was for one reason and one reason alone — his conversion to the Roman Catholic religion.

Sam Hughes, one of the loudest of Ontario's particularly vocal breed of Orangemen, was a rising figure in the Tory Party. (He would go on to serve as Robert Borden's minister of militia and defence during the First World War.) His frequent odious comments about Catholics and French Canadians would be utterly intolerable and career-destroying in a more enlightened time, but in that era of widely accepted, systemic racism, his words were taken to heart by many of his followers. An opinionated newspaper publisher from Lindsay, Ontario, he was an abrasive fellow given to strongly held opinions. Those opinions made their way into his widely read newspaper, the *Victoria Warder*. He had written at various times over the years that French Canadians were "little better than brutes." Bizarrely, he blamed Roman Catholics for the smallpox epidemic that hit Montreal in the mid-1880s.

He believed that industrialization and urbanization would lead to the loss of masculinity in the country, as men left the physical labour of farming for the softer life of city dwellers. He inundated Ottawa with requests on behalf of his Victoria County residents. Sir John A. Macdonald more than once complained to Joseph Pope that Hughes pestered him with scads of letters demanding patronage appointments for his friends. Coming from the man who showered the country with patronage, that was a telling comment.

Although the influential Hughes could objectively see the merits of Thompson's skills of leadership, he could not — in fact, would not — back the Catholic justice minister as leader. He rallied a number of the Ontario caucus members to his way of thinking. He infamously wrote, "Sir John [Thompson] is the right man but it is a ... pity that he is a pervert."[1] Unfortunately, too many men of influence in the party sided with the Orange Order and saw Thompson in the same light as Hughes.

In Quebec, there was ample support for Thompson and very little for the Quebec anglophone Abbott. Although some of the francophone Tories would have preferred to have Langevin as the new prime minister, there was too much controversy in supporting a man with a corruption scandal looming — he was accused of accepting kickbacks from those seeking contracts from the government. Another prominent Quebec Tory, former premier and Macdonald's secretary of state Joseph-Adolphe Chapleau, was not a friend of Thompson's. The two had been at odds over multiple issues, especially the Riel fiasco. On the other hand, Chapleau strenuously opposed supporting Langevin, rightfully thinking there would be too much controversy once his illegal actions were investigated. Chapleau let it be known in *La Presse* that he supported Thompson as leader. Chapleau admitted to the talents that Thompson brought to the prime minister's office, stating in a letter dated June 12, "I regard Sir John Thompson as the only man who can give the quality of stability in the re-organization of the government."[2]

In the succession to Macdonald, it ultimately fell to Lord Stanley to name the next prime minister. His duty was to pick a man who could lead and form a government that would follow that leadership. A number of Cabinet members and influential Tories paid formal visits to Rideau Hall in the days following the Old Chieftain's death. The governor general heard the arguments for the few candidates and interviewed Abbott, Langevin, and Thompson. He weighed the merits of each man. It wasn't an easy decision to make, but it needed to be made quickly. Notwithstanding, Stanley waited until the funeral of Sir John A. was over before making any public pronouncement.

During his own private meeting with the governor general on June 12, Thompson acknowledged the difficulties the Ontario wing of the party would have with him as their leader. With the Tories out of favour with Catholics and French Canadians in Quebec, the party could not afford to alienate the Protestants of Ontario as well. At some point in their hour-long conversation, Thompson turned down Lord Stanley's invitation to form a government. Thompson left Rideau Hall to meet with Abbott. The two of them then returned to the governor general's residence. In the meeting that followed, Thompson used all his courtroom skills to convince both Stanley and Abbott that the latter was the man to take over as prime minister, if only for a short time. Thompson chose to do what he thought was best for his party, sacrificing his own personal inclination.

It seems that in his last days, when he could still talk, the Old Chieftain had also come to the conclusions that Abbott was the best man for the position. He admitted to Thompson that they needed to accept Abbott, as he was the "least offensive" of all the possibilities. Abbott himself admitted to being the least divisive during a self-deprecating speech in the Senate.

There were many in the Conservative rank and file who found Thompson's actions admirable. It served to build his reputation among the Tory power brokers and set the stage for his eventual turn in the prime minister's chair. David Creighton, the managing editor of the *Toronto Mail* newspaper, the Conservative voice in Ontario, wrote to the younger Sir John, "I will never forget the unselfish way in which you have sacrificed yourself for the Party. I believe it was unnecessary, for as I told you, we could have carried things through with you as Premier, even though men such as Dr. Douglas[3] exhibited bigotry, for you would soon live down any prejudice."

Sir John A. Macdonald's widow, Lady Macdonald, reiterated the commonly held opinion about Thompson when she wrote to Tupper in November that year. "Sir John Thompson was right to refuse the Headship of the Government. There would have been, I am sure, a stampede of Ontario supporters. It is not so much his religion, as the fact of being a pervert — but he is a tower of strength in his post & really our very best debater."

John Abbott, who'd actually been contemplating retirement from active politics, accepted the position as leader of the party, fully aware that it was a temporary, place-holder sort of honour. Abbott, who for nearly half a century had been pulling strings behind the scenes on behalf of the party, reluctantly took the job as a stop-gap measure. He would be sitting in the Red Chamber, away from the daily give and take of the Commons. The debates and daily business of the House would fall to Thompson. It was not out of laziness that Abbott let the burden rest on Thompson. He knew who the leader of the party should be, so he tacitly let much of the responsibility lie with his justice minister — Thompson added the unofficial title of leader of the government in the House of Commons to his portfolio.

Not only did Abbott know his position was provisional, he openly acknowledged his temporary role. Speaking in the Senate shortly into his brief time as prime minister, he stated, "I am here [as prime minister] very much because I am not particularly obnoxious to anybody.... Something like the principle on which it is reported some men are selected for the Presidency of the United States ... that they are harmless and have not made any enemies." Abbott, though a member of the Orange Order, knew that it was just a matter of time before a Roman Catholic could be accepted as leader. Like Thompson, he acted out of regard for his party, not out of personal ambition.

John Abbott (known to many of his friends and associates as J.J. Abbott or simply J.J.) had been a stalwart in the party in Quebec for some time, although his reputation was more as a member of that province's English business elite. He'd had a long run in elected politics. At the same time, he chaired the law school at McGill and continued to work as legal advisor to Montreal's St. James Street business leaders. He had eventually been elevated to the Senate by Macdonald in 1887. He was also named at that time to the Cabinet as the government leader in the Red Chamber. He seemed destined to end his days as a member of the Upper House. His knowledge of constitutional law made him an invaluable resource for the Conservative Party. A survivor of the Pacific Scandal — he'd been Hugh Allan's lawyer — Abbott knew the corridors of power and where many of the bodies were buried.

Interestingly, for a man who avowed a distaste for politics, during the first two years of his Senate tenure he was also the mayor of Montreal. These accomplishments and his connections had placed Abbott at the heart of the Conservative Party's hierarchy, so it was not totally surprising that he was selected to become leader in the wake of Macdonald's death. He seemed to know everyone in Ottawa.

Born in the Laurentian village of St. Andrews East, Lower Canada, on March 12, 1821, the son of an itinerant missionary, Abbott was destined to be the first Canadian-born prime minister. His youth was spent travelling with his family around the colony of Canada East. One benefit of that peripatetic life was that the young Abbott became fluent in French (and therefore, eventually, Canada's first bilingual prime minister).[4] The family home was well stocked with books, and the young Abbott educated himself by voraciously reading all that he could. His more formal education came from tutors, and for a short time he lived with an uncle, attending classes in a private school. One of his teachers was a retired sea captain who taught him about astronomy, mathematics, and use of a compass.

At age seventeen, the young Abbott went to work in a "mercantile house," the dry-goods business Laurie and Company. There he learned such business trivia as how apples were to be packed and how one dealt in materials such as calico. He travelled around the colonies of Canada East and Canada West, buying and selling things on behalf of his employers. Because of a serious but undisclosed illness, Abbott had to quit his shop-keeping work and move back home. His parents had by that time settled in Montreal. His father had given up the missionary work in pursuit of something more stable and less transient. Abbott Sr. took on the position of bursar at McGill College.

In 1843, while living with his parents, John began studies at McGill. Thanks to his father's faculty position, the family likely got some kind of financial break on the tuition fees. John simultaneously attended his university classes and helped his father with the accounting duties of the school.

Located at the base of Mount Royal, the college had been founded the year Abbott was born. It was to play a major role in his life. Much of his life eventually revolved around the university and, in particular, its law school. He was dean of the McGill law school from 1855 until 1880. Following his retirement as dean, he served on the university's board of governors until his death.

Abbott completed his law training and was admitted to the bar of Canada East in 1847. To become a full-fledged lawyer, he had to appear before a panel of judges who examined his knowledge of the law. Passing that test easily, he partnered with William Badgley, who doubled as a lawyer in the city and as a law professor, teaching privately and then later at McGill College. Badgley's family had been part-owners of the North West Company, the fur trading rival of the Hudson's Bay Company. From his lofty position as one of the city's leaders in business, law, and politics, Badgley mentored Abbott in how to balance those concerns. The tutoring turned out to be valuable for the young man. Their law firm specialized in commercial and bankruptcy law. Abbott eventually made his reputation in those fields.

Badgley, a man of ambition, was elected to the provincial assembly in 1851 as the member for Missisquoi. In the election of 1851, he defeated the renowned (and often reviled) Louis-Joseph Papineau, leader of the 1837 *Patriote* rebellion. Subsequently, Badgley became attorney general. He later was named as a judge in Montreal.

Abbott's first foray into political activity was somewhat misguided, something he regretted for the rest of his life. In 1849 the recent graduate from law school signed the *Montreal Annexation Manifesto*. Over three hundred businessmen in Canada East put out the document that called for American annexation of Canada. When Britain declared its intention to end its preferential Corn Laws, the entrepreneurs in the colony feared that Canada's small population could not survive economically without similar preferential customs duties. The only answer, as they saw it, was to join the American republic to the south so as to benefit from its ever-expanding transportation networks. These entrepreneurs admired the capitalist spirit so prominent in the United States. Abbott later referred to his signing of the document as a "youthful error." Yet it demonstrates the young man's business mindset and the prime role he saw for businessmen in the life of the country.

He was not alone in his misguided support of the idea. Sir Alexander T. Galt, a Father of Confederation and future finance minister of Canada, had also signed the document, as did Abbott's political colleague of later years, Sir David Macpherson.

In 1853, with the sponsorship of Badgley, John began lecturing at McGill law school. He thrived in the position. He demonstrated remarkable energy and ambition. Always confident as a speaker, he had a steel-trap mind when it came to understanding the law. At the same time that he worked as a lawyer and as a college lecturer, he also studied for a degree in civil law. He earned a Bachelor of Civil Law degree in 1854 at a time when few lawyers earned degrees. (Most earned their standing through apprenticeship.) The very next year, he became the dean of the faculty of law, where he implemented a revised, practical curriculum. The dean's position at McGill was not that taxing a proposition though. Since there were only a few students enrolled and even those students received most of their training in assigned law offices, there was not an onerous load of administrative work to manage. The position was prestigious, however, and it paid well. Abbott's university salary was £500 annually plus a portion of the students' fees. He taught a number of able young men during those years, one of whom was Wilfrid Laurier, who graduated in 1864.

Abbot's extraordinary grasp of the law did not go unnoticed. In 1855 he was offered the post of deputy judge of the Canada East Superior Court, a position he declined as it was a financial step-down. He'd have had to work for about one fifth of the money he was making in his law office. He was then offered a chief justiceship; he turned that down as well. Instead, he continued working as a lawyer, establishing a reputation as having the Canadas' finest legal mind in matters of bankruptcy and commercial law, as well as constitutional law. He was considered an excellent administrator, whether in his law office, in his university department, or working with Montreal corporations.

In 1862 he was named Queen's Counsel, an honorific bestowed on lawyers, something that held considerable sway in the mid-nineteenth century. The awarding of the title was highly political. Being a "QC" was recognized as a perk for one's political contributions. He continued his own studies at the same time as he lectured and practised law. In 1867 he earned his doctorate. He was then entitled to place the initials "DCL" after his name.

During his legal career, Abbott became the advisor to many of the most influential men of his day — brewing mogul John Molson, for example. Another client was Duncan McIntyre, a future founder of both the Canadian Pacific Railway (CPR) and the Bell Telephone Company of Canada. Donald Smith, who eventually became Lord Strathcona and is forever remembered for being photographed driving the famous last spike in the CPR, was not only a client but also a close friend. The Hudson's Bay Company and the Bank of Montreal were among the corporations that J.J. represented.

With such a wealthy clientele and an abundance of business, Abbott prospered through those years. His law firm grew in size and reputation. At one point, he reputedly enjoyed the largest professional income of any lawyer in Quebec. He had a number of partners in his law firm, associates that eventually included two of his sons. He even felt the need in 1870 to establish a second law firm, this one in Toronto, to facilitate "business relations between the merchants of Montreal and the people of Ontario."

Abbott was an entrepreneur who could see the need for action and innovation where others did not. Transportation difficulties presented just such opportunity.

Inter-city roads in Canada at the mid-point of the century were abysmal. Travel from Montreal to Quebec or Montreal to Ottawa meant negotiating mud, ruts, tree stumps, and assorted hazards. Corduroy roads were a poor means to traverse wet, swampy ground, as they were a hazard to the horses and excruciatingly bumpy to the rider of any cart or carriage. Wherever possible, taking a boat — even if it was as primitive as a canoe — was preferable. There were no hotels along the way, no places to obtain food, nor would there be for decades to come. Rural roads were necessary for farmers to get goods to market in towns, but there was little appetite in political circles to spend money on transportation other than railways. That was the means of travel that flourished, much to the consternation of the majority of Canadians, who lived in the rural areas. Those ordinary folks had little stake in building railways.

John Abbott applied his knowledge of business and used his numerous contacts to invest wisely in railways. His father had been fascinated by the developments in railway transportation when trains first appeared in Canada. He passed on that interest to at least two of his sons. John's brother Harry Abbott became a well-respected railway construction engineer. John invested in many railway companies during his time.

He and Harry joined their father in putting money into the Carillon and Grenville Railway, an 1847 venture along the Ottawa River. In January of 1859, the Montreal and Bytown Railway went into receivership. Abbott and a few associates purchased the line for a mere twenty-one thousand dollars. The line had cost its initial investors over four hundred thousand dollars to build. In 1867 Abbott and friends turned around and sold the line for what he once described as a "handsome profit." That was only the start of his investments in rail.

In 1862 he was named president of the Canada Central Railway, a line owned by his friend Duncan McIntyre. Together, they began to merge rail lines. Early on, Abbott saw the value, if not the need, for a railway that crossed the entire continent. He even gave speeches where he espoused the idea of a transcontinental line stretching from Montreal to the Pacific Ocean. In the early 1870s, it was Abbott who urged his friend Sir Hugh Allan to pursue the contract to build that very railway. During his lifetime, Abbott led the way by continually putting money into new lines as the country saw phenomenal growth in the transportation sector.

From the 1850s on, Abbott's reputation as one of the country's finest lawyers grew as he took on high profile court cases. That only helped to add to his substantial wealth.

His most famous case involved the defence of the Confederate agents who carried out the infamous 1864 St. Albans Raid. Abbott, as the most renowned lawyer in the colony of Canada, was the barrister called upon to defend the troop in court, despite his being known more for his work on civil cases rather than criminal ones.

Twenty-one Confederate soldiers, members of the 8th Kentucky Cavalry, had made their way to Canada with a plan to cross back into the United States to create havoc. If successful, Union troops would have had to divert to the Quebec border. The leader of the group, Bennett Young, developed a meticulous scheme. He and his small band of men crossed into Vermont in small groups. They settled into local hotels in the Vermont border town of St. Alban's. On October 19, 1864, in a well-synchronized attack, the Confederates simultaneously robbed three of the city's banks. Some of the townsmen resisted, with one citizen being killed. The raiders then took their quarter-million-dollar haul and fled back across the border into Canada. Union officials naturally protested to the government in Quebec City. The Southerners were arrested by Canadian authorities.

As it turned out, Abbott's former partner William Badgley was the judge trying the case. Abbott argued successfully that the raiders were Confederate soldiers under military orders. He argued that they were not criminals. They were military personnel. Therefore, they could not be extradited to the United States.

The raid and the subsequent court decision became an international incident that inflamed relations with the United States. Britain and its colony of Canada were seen as aiding and abetting the secessionist Southern states in the American Civil War. The tense relations between the British colonies and their American neighbours became heightened and remained so even after the North won the war.

At the same time that Abbott was engaged in defending the Confederate raiders, he was involved in numerous other activities. "Very busy" hardly touches on how hectic and productive those years were for John Abbott. Somehow, with a law practice, a law school to manage, varied business interests, not to mention his duties to his constituents and family, he managed to publish a book in 1864.[5] The title alone reveals its rather esoteric nature: *The Insolvent Act of 1864: With Notes Together with The Rules of Practice and the Tariff of Fees for Lower Canada.* Hardly the makings of a bestseller, it was aimed at the legal profession in a tiny corner of the British Empire.

Law and business were not his only interests by any means. He was, for instance, fascinated by all things military. As early as 1847, he had served in the local militia of Argenteuil. He made friends among the military establishment of Montreal. In 1862, when it appeared that the American Civil War might have repercussions in British North America, he raised the 11th Regiment Argenteuil Rangers, installing himself as its commander. At one point, he spent three weeks roughing it in the Quebec wilderness as his troops patrolled the U.S.-Canada border south of Montreal. The unit was called upon twice to answer Fenian threats. Abbott was the regiment's honorary lieutenant-colonel from 1862 until 1884.

He had an abiding interest in music. Abbott possessed what was publicly described as "a fine tenor singing voice." He even took singing lessons at one point. He was the director of the Christ Church Cathedral choir for six years. The church was only steps from his Montreal home, and he was regularly there on Sundays and other evenings each week whenever he was in the city, leading the choir or practising the hymns to be sung at weekly services. The organ at the cathedral had 2,778 pipes, so the well-trained choir needed to belt out the songs to be heard above the impressive instrument.

Abbott's energy was boundless. He was, at various times, a director on the boards of numerous companies, including the Merchants Bank, Standard Life Insurance Company, the Bank of Montreal, the North Shore Railway, the CPR (of course), and Globe Woolen Mills. He was president of the Canada Investment Company and the Citizens Insurance Company. He chaired the board of trustees of the Guardian Fire and Life Insurance Company. He was a harbour commissioner for the Port of Montreal in the late 1880s.

When Donald Smith and George Stephen (Lord Mount Stephen) pledged one million dollars for the construction of the Royal Victoria Hospital in Montreal, they selected Abbott as the first president of the board of governors. He also acted as its legal advisor, chose the initial building's architect, and supervised the building of the hospital. It can be assumed that he donated a hefty sum to the building as well.

On the personal side of things, he met and married Mary Bethune in 1849. The Bethune family of Montreal was heavily involved in both the spiritual life of the anglophone Protestants and in the university life of the city. Mary's grandfather was Reverend John Bethune, the Principal of McGill College for eleven years.[6] Reverend Bethune and J.J. would have crossed paths many times during their terms at McGill. It can be speculated that perhaps John met Mary through the relationship the two men had but there is no proof of this. Abbott and his young wife started a family that eventually included eight children. They lived in an impressive home on Sherbrooke Street in Montreal. Five years after his death, it sold for over sixty-four thousand dollars, the equivalent of more than two million 2021 dollars. The Abbott's neighbours included the railway mogul William Van Horne.

For many years John took his family to a log house on a small lake in the Laurentian foothills. He was an avid fisherman who enjoyed the peace and solitude of being alone on a quiet body of water, something that allowed him a measure of respite from his overly hectic daily schedule. In 1865 he took a bold step and purchased a country estate on the Lake of Two Mountains in present-day Senneville, at the western extreme of the island of Montreal. It was at the time a rural enclave for wealthy Montreal anglophones. The property had once been the seigneury of Sieur de Boisbriand.[7] The Abbott family in turn called the newly purchased property Senneville Grange and then the equally elegant Boisbriand. Long narrow fields covering over three hundred acres stretched back from the lake. The stone house that the Abbott family built was as opulent as it was sturdy in its design. It had several conservatories and an impressive library. Ivy climbed the outer walls. The sloping lawn was carefully maintained and provided ample room for the children to play or the adults to sit and enjoy the surroundings. The Abbotts cultivated elaborate gardens and orchards. On his farm, John became one of the first people in Canada to import Guernsey cattle, a breed new to North America. Abbott found great solace in his time spent at Boisbriand, although with his frenetic schedule he probably wished he had more time to spend there cultivating his beloved orchids.

Abbott had a busy social life. It is clear, though, that his cultivation of many relationships had much to do with his financial and political interests. He became a member of the St. James Club of Montreal, arguably the centre of the country's economic elite. The club building stood on the corner of Dorchester and University Streets in downtown Montreal. Lunches, dinners, and evenings in the club were undoubtedly political in nature. Abbott — adorned with great bushy sideburns that were the facial fashion at the time — and his colleagues gathered in the smoky sitting rooms, chatting over aperitifs, smoking imported cigars or well-stuffed pipes. It was there that the future prime minister befriended most of the powerful business leaders of his day. An avid card player, Abbott spent many an evening squinting through the tobacco smoke, playing euchre or whist with other club members, swapping stories, and sharing information about business, politics, and the day-to-day life of Montreal.

J.J. was a member of both the Masonic Lodge — conveniently headquartered in the same building as the St. James Club — and the Orange Order. Many of the contacts he made in those organizations spilled over into his professional life. Montreal was really the only major city in Canada at the time and was undisputedly the business centre of the new country. Most businesses tended to be local in nature but any that spanned the other colonies (provinces) were generally headquartered in the St. James Street centre of Montreal. Abbott acted as either the attorney or advisor to many of the influential merchants of his day in Canada. Most of those entrepreneurs were also members of "the club." His contacts there — Hugh Allan, Duncan McIntyre, Hugh Fraser[8] — helped Abbott, the lawyer/politician, to establish lifelong connections with the kingpins in the Canadian business and political worlds.

John eventually became "president for life" of the Fraser Institute (not to be confused with the modern conservative think tank). These men promoted free public libraries in Montreal. Eventually this became the Fraser-Hickson Institute, an organization that continues to promote literacy to this day. In 1882 it was Abbott who purchased, with his own thirty thousand dollars, the land upon which the institute was to be built.

Working with Bishop Francis Fulford, Abbott helped found the Art Association of Montreal in 1860, which eventually morphed into the Montreal Museum of Fine Arts. Arguably the first museum of art in Canada, Edwin Holgate of Group of Seven fame, would become one of its well-known alumni many years later.

Although Montreal was the largest city in Canada and its business hub, like any urban centre it had destitute and needy inhabitants by the score. Abbott, although a privileged, rich man, generously established aid for the poor and people with visual and hearing impairments. Although charity was seen at that time as the job of the churches, Abbott pioneered a movement to set up associations that could help the needy. He also had a hand in establishing the Society for the Prevention of Cruelty to Animals in 1869. (Incredibly, that was set up prior to a Children's Aid Society.)

Abbott's interest in something as radical for its day as a humane society is indicative of his wide range of passions beyond law, politics, and business. He also devoted time and money to art, humanitarianism, music, and literacy. Together, his many pursuits demonstrate the complex nature of Abbott the man.

It was politics, though, that came to dominate much of his activity. He'd long had an interest in seeking elected office. In 1857 Abbott ran for the seat of Argenteuil, a constituency north of Montreal, in the legislature of the Province of Canada (i.e., Canada East and West). He lost the election. But, in those days of open voting — the secret ballot was not introduced for another seventeen years — elections were often challenged because of irregularities. Gifts of liquor, intimidation, bribery, and the admonitions of one's parish priest could all play on men's choices as they stood up before their peers to say who they were supporting. Abbott challenged the results of his first election. Although it took nearly three years, the results were eventually overturned, and he was able to claim the seat in the legislature. He became solicitor general in the 1862 Reform Party government led by John Sandfield Macdonald and Louis-Victor Sicotte.

Initially, Abbott did not embrace the Confederation plans that were drawn-up in 1864, as he felt the rights of anglophone Quebecers might be weakened. He remained, however, a member of the provincial legislature through those tumultuous years leading up to Confederation in 1867. Eventually, he was won over by John A. Macdonald and ran under the Liberal-Conservative banner when the country began voting on a federal basis. He became the MP for the federal riding of Argenteuil. In that first Canadian Parliament, he became chair of the banking committee, a role he held until 1874. One of his least known but most significant accomplishments was the implementation of the Bank Act of 1871. It was Abbott who ushered that bill through Parliament, basically establishing the Canadian banking system, a system that is admired worldwide and has helped Canada weather such economic storms as the Great Depression and the financial crisis of the early twenty-first century.

John lost his seat in the federal election of 1874. That particular contest, fought in the wake of the Pacific Scandal, was basically a plebiscite held to determine if voters still supported the Conservatives. It turned out to be an unmitigated disaster for the ruling Tories. Abbott's candidacy was tainted by his close ties to both Macdonald and Sir Hugh Allan. Although they should take the blame for being the two major conspirators in the bribery scheme that ended up, when exposed, as causing what became known as the Pacific Scandal, Abbott played no small part in the backroom conniving and deal making. The crisis revealed the dark sides of all three men.

J.J. Abbott played a pivotal role as the go-between for Macdonald and Allan. Serving as one of Sir John's elected MPs while at the same time acting as Allan's legal advisor, the normally fair-minded Abbott was caught in the web of patronage and conflict of interest that doomed him to eventually lose his seat in the Commons. He had no compunction about using (and receiving) bribes and patronage. He believed in both and used them openly.

The quest to obtain the rights to build the railway to British Columbia was especially complicated. As mentioned earlier, two railway conglomerates vied for the contract to build a railway across the continent, uniting British

Columbia with the rest of Canada. Hugh Allan, heading up Canadian Pacific Railway, had publicly promised to build the transcontinental line using only Canadian funds. His rival, Senator David Macpherson of the Toronto-based Inter-Oceanic Company, made no such vow. Macpherson said it both publicly and in private to Abbott. He didn't believe Allan intended to keep his vow, and as it turned out, Allan didn't. It was eventually revealed that he had secretly courted New York and Chicago investors. In public however, Allan's promise of an all-Canadian financed line made his proposal more palatable to the Parliament of Canada that eventually had to approve one or the other company's proposal.

To overcome the problem of having to choose between the two bids and get the project started, it was proposed that the two corporations be combined. An amalgamation attempt ended in a dismal failure, despite the prime minister's personal intervention. It all boiled down to one tiny detail. To agree to a merger, Hugh Allan demanded the presidency of the merged company. He would settle for nothing less. Macpherson was equally stubborn in refusing to give unbridled power to his chief rival.

Allan went looking for support. The two leading Conservatives at that time, Macdonald and his French Canadian lieutenant Georges-Etienne Cartier, were both desperately in need of funds to pay for their election campaigns. Allan lobbied the leaders by mail and telegrams, openly begging for his company to be the chosen one. He even made personal "social calls." Allan, accompanied by his lawyer — none other than John Abbott — made at least one personal visit to the home of Cartier to implore him to settle the amalgamation of the railway companies to his benefit, i.e., granting him the presidency. Cartier showed Allan (and Abbott) a letter from Macdonald that promised Allan could head-up the company. "I [Macdonald] authorize you to assure Allan that the influence of the Government will be exercised to secure him the position of President…. The whole matter to be kept quiet until after the elections."

Allan demanded that the government commit that promise in writing. Cartier then asked Allan blatantly for one hundred thousand dollars — a monstrous sum in those days — for the election campaign. The two turned to Abbott to draw up the agreement. Two letters were written and one of them became infamous for its unsavory nature. It stated: "The friends of the Government will expect to be assisted with funds in the pending elections, and any amount which you or your Company shall advance for that purpose shall be recouped by you."

The funds to be doled out showed Macdonald getting twenty-five thousand dollars; Cartier twenty thousand dollars and Abbott ten thousand dollars. They were just three of the many names listed to receive payments from Allan. In modern dollars, the total added-up to millions. All the players in this drama knew what remained a secret — Allan would receive the contract to build the railway as either head of his own company or one that merged with Macpherson's so long as Allan generously gave money to the Conservatives in their election campaign.

It was Abbott's parliamentary clerk, George Norris, who eventually revealed the scandalous actions of the backrooms. Perhaps the man was offended by the greed and corruption that he saw. Perhaps he had personal reasons. Whatever his motivation, he subsequently made himself scarce. Documents were leaked to the Opposition benches, where L.S. Huntingdon, the Liberal member for the Eastern Townships riding of Shefford, revealed the secretive deals of Messrs. Macdonald, Allan, and Abbott.

Abbott, a man who'd already proved his mettle as a law school dean, a judge, a successful and powerful politician and was recognized as one of the most astute businessmen in the country, acted like one of Hugh Allan's fawning minions. He trailed Allan around, not only Canada but across the ocean to England and into the United States as the railway magnate worked on deals, negotiated loans, and alternately made threats and pleas to politicians. Abbott seemed to be always serving the magnate, working either at Allan's side or attending meetings to plead the case for his boss.

Abbott was not without skill at what he did. Macdonald admired J.J.'s talent for sugar-coating the actions of others. That was particularly true of the Pacific Scandal. Once the papers let the cat out of the bag, exposing all Allan's backroom manipulations, someone had to come to the defence of not only Allan but the Conservative government too.

Enter J.J. Abbott. With all the legal expertise he could muster, the future prime minister helped Hugh Allan to prepare an affidavit that, in the long run, took a lot of the stain off Macdonald and his actions. The document explained that, yes, Allan had donated funds to get his friends elected, but stated that, no, there weren't any conditions — such as promises of contracts — attached to the donations. The affidavit also clarified that the money had not come from American sources, such as George McMullen and the American Northern Pacific Railway Company.

Macdonald said of Abbott, "He has made the old gentleman [Allan] acknowledge on oath that his letters were untrue. This was a bitter pill for him to swallow but Abbott has gilded it over for him very nicely."

Nonetheless, Allan was finished as a force in Canadian politics. He had no more to do with building the transcontinental line and railway building.

A royal commission was set up to investigate the Pacific Scandal, but it was not what one might call diligent in the performance of its duties; no counsel was assigned to advise the three commissioners. The statements of the witnesses were taken at face value; there was never any delving further into what people like Allan, Langevin, or even Macdonald said under oath. Abbott was questioned. His answers included a lot of "not likely" answers. At one point, he was called back to clarify his statements and was so long-winded that one of the commissioners fell asleep and a secretary was seen reading the magazine *Canada Monthly* as the lawyer droned on. In the end, Abbott's actions were not judged to be criminal or even inappropriate by the commission, as it was unclear if he had committed any impropriety. Amazingly, there was no report generated, and the statements were simply published without comment. It was left for the public to make their own conclusions.

In the 1874 election, Abbott was narrowly re-elected as their member of Parliament, but he was subsequently removed from office by petition, on charges that the election had been doctored by irregularities in the voters' list.[9] Abbott was merely a lawyer and law professor once again.

Macdonald's reputation, so sterling up to that point, was forever tarnished. Many thought that his political career was over. Cartier, gravely ill, left politics a broken man. Allan survived the scandal but with a hit to his bank account and with a reputation that was forever tainted by what had happened.

The Conservatives found themselves on the Opposition benches, and Alexander Mackenzie, a stern and unimaginative Scotsman, took over as prime minister.

A political crisis in Quebec City occurred at the end of the Liberal's term of office that drew Abbott back into the political action. In 1876, Prime Minister Mackenzie advised the governor general to name Luc Letellier de St-Just, a former Liberal senator and more recently the minister of agriculture, as lieutenant governor of Quebec. In March of 1878, after he'd been in the vice-regal office for just over a year, Letellier dismissed the Conservative government of Quebec, charging that Premier Charles-Eugene Boucher de Boucherville was guilty of corruption regarding recent railway construction. As the provincial Conservatives held a twenty-seat majority at the time, the move was unprecedented and controversial to say the least. De Boucherville protested stridently, claiming that this was not only highly partisan in nature but was in fact a "*coup d'état.*" Both houses of the Quebec legislature — the province had an upper house at that time — passed motions of censure against the lieutenant governor.

That same year the Conservatives returned to power in Ottawa. One of the first things that the Tory government had to manage was the Quebec vice-regal problem. Macdonald's Cabinet was quick to agree with the Quebec legislature and Senate in condemning Letellier's actions. The prime minister turned to John Abbott to help solve the problem.

The Montreal law dean obviously had enormous legal talents; it seemed, as well, that he knew the ins and outs of every piece of railway business in the country. Abbott had failed in his bid for election that year so he could at least appear to be independent. His reputation as an expert in the law and as an experienced politician made him a suitable, if not wholly disinterested, arbiter.

Abbott was sent to Quebec City to sort out the details. He brought his findings back to Macdonald in Ottawa. The two men agreed that Letellier had erred. Abbott then visited the governor general, the Marquis of Lorne.

Lorne refused to make any decision on his own, preferring to hand the matter to the British government in London. To ensure that their grievance was answered, Abbott and Hector-Louis Langevin travelled all the way to England to consult with officials in the Colonial Office regarding the legalities of not only Letellier's actions but the process of removing him from office. The colonial secretary emphatically told the two emissaries and then the governor general to follow the advice of his ministers. Letellier was ordered to step down immediately.

Abbott's investigation not only raised his profile but stirred his desire to return to active politics.

While in Britain, Abbott conducted other business on behalf of the Canadian government. In talks with the American delegation in London, he brokered a deal that would allow American cattle to be imported to England via transit through Canada. Abbott had once again proved useful to Macdonald working behind the scenes and out of the political spotlight. J.J. needed to be rewarded for his efforts.

In 1880 Abbott ran for office in a federal by-election. He won but once again had his election declared void, this time because of charges of bribery brought against his campaign officials. He finally won in a different by-election in 1881 and then was acclaimed in the general election of 1882.

During his years out of office, Abbott dabbled in myriad railway pursuits. He purchased more shares in the Canada Central Railway and served as its president for a number of years. He then became a director of the Montreal Northern Colonization Railway Company. When Macdonald returned to the prime minister's office in 1878, Abbott immediately began to formulate plans for a railway that was to be built as far as Winnipeg. He worked on details for at least two years before submitting it to his political friends in Ottawa. Macdonald asked him to further revise the plan and bring in a larger core of wealthy investors. Abbott did as he was asked, speaking to Duncan McIntyre and others. This meshed nicely with Macdonald's plan to drive the railway even farther west, as far as British Columbia.

The construction of the railway had gotten off to a rocky start. When Macdonald was thrown out of office in 1874, Hugh Allan's Canadian Pacific Railway Company ceased to be the builders of the line. The Liberals were not nearly as keen on seeing the line built across the Prairies and into British Columbia as the Conservatives had been. Alexander Mackenzie focussed instead on small portions of the railway, all under the aegis of the Department of Public Works. Most Liberal initiatives to bring in private sector financing fell flat. Renowned engineer Sandford Fleming was put in charge of the enterprise but not much happened until the Tories returned to power.

When the Conservatives returned to office, Abbott entered into discussions with his friends George Stephen and J.J. Hill (an American railway mogul) and American banker John Stewart Kennedy about the line that was to be built going west across the Prairies and through the Rocky Mountains. One of the other men Abbott discussed the scheme with was Donald Smith, a man out of favour with most Tories. (Smith had been appalled by what had gone on in the Pacific Scandal. Indeed, it had been his decisive vote that had seen the government fall.) His participation was generous but, because of the man's recent political history, it was kept secret from Macdonald and Tupper.

Abbott probably knew more about rail lines, building contracts, suppliers, engineering, and construction than those other well-known railway builders. Having worked as an executive, a hands-on investor, and a political figure, he had experience with all the issues that could arise in railway construction. Plus, with his experience in the Pacific Scandal, he knew what could go wrong and what pitfalls to avoid.

George Stephen, as head of the syndicate, approached the minister of railways, Charles Tupper, with their proposal. Abbott was in on the discussions as the syndicate's legal advisor. Stephen negotiated with both Tupper and the prime minister. Eventually, a contract was drawn up that was overly generous to the financiers. The CPR[10] was given twenty-five million dollars in cash, twenty-five million acres of land to the west of Winnipeg, and 713 miles of already finished railway. They also received lavish tax exemptions, relief on duties of building materials, and a twenty-year monopoly on railway building south of their western Canada mainline. Such was their desire to get the construction project completed that Tupper and Macdonald gave Stephen's syndicate far more than they required.

Abbott was fully committed to doing whatever he could to make this happen. He played a large role in the eventual construction of the transcontinental line. In 1880, as the group's solicitor, it was Abbott who drew up the provisional contract that established the Canadian Pacific Railway Company — identical in name but not the same company Allan had set up nearly a decade earlier. Eventually, J.J. became the sole author of the final charter of the CPR. Such was his legal expertise and the precision of his work that the document has been called the most perfect contract of its kind ever written in Canada.

In 1884, at the same time as the railway was simultaneously making its final push west over the Prairies and eastwardly through the Rockies, Abbott accompanied Stephen, McIntyre, and R.B. Angus to England to secure funds necessary to complete the construction work. J.J. was re-elected to Parliament that same year. Significantly, Abbott remained active in not only the financial arrangements but also in preparing legislation and contracts related to the byzantine railway deals of that economically turbulent decade. Furthermore, he returned to England with George Stephen (the future Lord Mount Stephen) to negotiate with Queen Victoria's government a deal where the CPR provided steamers to open up trade with Japan and China. Abbott could see the potential for bringing goods from Asia across the Pacific, then eastward by rail to Quebec or Halifax, and ultimately across the Atlantic to Britain. English goods could potentially follow the same route in a westerly direction.

Abbott served as a member of the board of directors of the Canadian Pacific Railway company. Behind closed doors, he urged Macdonald to financially prop up the corporation through the fiscally tight years of the 1880s. In late November 1883, Abbott and a delegation from the CPR visited Macdonald at home to beg the prime minister for a new loan. At that low point in the work, CPR stock had fallen to less than fifty cents per share, a disastrous situation for the company as it struggled to complete the railway across the Prairies and through the mountains. Abbott pleaded with his old friend.

"The CPR needs this loan. You must find a way to force Parliament to approve it," Abbott said.

Macdonald replied, "You might as well ask for the planet Jupiter."

In the end, the money was eventually found, and the CPR construction work continued.

It was to his own financial advantage to press for federal aid, but, in a larger way, it showed Abbott's belief in the transcontinental dream of uniting British Columbia with the rest of the nation. While a sitting member of Parliament, Abbott showed political wisdom, however, by abstaining from any railway-related votes in the Commons, since he was ethically forbidden from owning stock in the railway business and promoting it through government devices. He'd perhaps learned some ethics lessons coming out of the Pacific Scandal. Macdonald was not always happy that his MP, the lawyer for the rail syndicate, remained mute during discussions about the railway in the House of Commons. But Abbott remained aloof, staying away from partisan interference. He had also wisely refused to buy any stock in the CPR, although he did make a great deal of money when the Canadian Pacific purchased his Canada Central Railway in 1881.

When the railway was officially completed in 1886, a souvenir timetable was printed. In it was a photograph of the company's first general counsel: John Joseph Caldwell Abbott. There were few if any men in North America who had a better grasp of railway law than did Abbott. The day that Donald Smith drove the last spike at Craigellachie, Abbott was in the crowd of spectators, mixing with the navvies and the top-hatted officials.

In 1887 the Conservatives, with their rail line completed across the Prairies all the way to Vancouver, won their fourth federal election majority. Tired of the day-to-day squabbling, questions, and debates in the House of Commons, Abbott decided not to run in the election that year. Instead, after lengthy talks, the prime minister named Abbott to the Senate. He was given two jobs: minister without portfolio and government leader in the Senate. Those positions put him at the Cabinet table, part of the inner circle of power but also freed him from the daily grind of the House.

Abbott had other reasons to give up his federal seat. He had retired from his law practice that same year. Although ostensibly busy with political duties in Ottawa as a senator and Cabinet minister, he ran for the office of mayor of Montreal and won. Even for a dynamo such as Abbott, he took on an incredible workload that left him with little time for family, his men's clubs, or his beloved rural estate. As well, he was now an elderly man.

Abbott was highly regarded as a mayor. At the end of his one-year term, he was presented with a petition from the entire city council asking him to stay on at the head of the municipal government. He was, therefore, acclaimed to the office for 1888. He made his way to England that year as part of a three-man delegation to obtain a loan to consolidate the city's debt. He headed so many committees and organizations that wags in the city nicknamed him the "Great Pooh Bah" or "Lord High Everything." As in the previous year, he was again petitioned at the end of his term to stay on for another, third run as mayor, but he declined that invitation, deciding to focus on his federal duties instead. His ultimate plan was to gradually ease out of the political arena, though fate had something else in store for him.

In 1888, Abbott agreed to act as "chief commissioner" on a mission to Australia. It was a venture to develop trade with what were still known as the Australian colonies (Australia did not become an independent nation until January 1, 1901). Abbott started preliminary talks when he was in England in 1889. He never made the actual trip Down Under, but his work as a commissioner gave him added experience in international affairs. Considering his position at the head of the municipal government in Montreal, it was surprising that he had time for any of his Ottawa responsibilities.

Abbott was driven by remarkable energy throughout his life. In many ways he was ambitious, but that drive did not include rising to the highest office in the land. He never pined to one day succeed Macdonald. He did not yearn to sit at the head of the Cabinet table, doling out orders and proclaiming policy initiatives. His ambition had its limits.

When Macdonald died, Abbott ardently supported Thompson as the choice for the top office and only accepted the role himself with the proviso that he be a caretaker prime minister, seeing the party and the country through a brief period until a new leader could be named. Although he was a prominent member of the Order, Abbott did not hold with the Orange distaste for having a Catholic at the helm of the country. As a bilingual, lifelong Quebec resident, he harboured no ill feelings toward French Canadians or Roman Catholics. He believed in merit. He asserted that Thompson was truly the worthiest member of the Tory Cabinet to succeed Macdonald. In a letter he wrote to a friend two days before Macdonald's death, Abbott stated, "My own impression is that Thompson is the man to be sent for, and I should think he could carry the work through."

The respect was mutual. Thompson knew that his own elevation to prime minister would bring about dissent, disruption, and a loss of a sizeable amount of voter support. He made the case during those hot summer meetings following Macdonald's death that it was not quite his time to lead the party and therefore the country. He and his colleagues knew how difficult it would be to sell the idea of a Catholic at the head of the government to the country's fervent Orangemen.

In the immediate days following Sir John's death, Thompson deferred to Abbott and greased the wheels for J.J. to take over as leader. In one of the numerous letters Thompson wrote the week of Macdonald's passing, the justice minister responded to a prominent Conservative colleague who was urging him to take on the mantle of prime minister,

> I fear, however, that you have conceived the idea that I aspire to lead the party, now or in the future. No greater mistake could be made. I am not willing to take that position now, or to enter a period of probation with a view to that end. I hope that the party can be much better led, and I am willing to serve or to retire as may seem best to the man who shall take up the reins which have fallen from the hands of Sir John Macdonald.

The letter is overly modest in tone. Thompson knew he was the best man to take over the job. He also knew that eventually he'd be offered the leadership of the Conservatives. He was willing to bide his time, build up support, convert the naysaying Orangemen, and await his turn. And so, he initially supported the push to make Abbott prime minister.

Thompson's esteem for Abbott was demonstrated a few years later at the unveiling of a statue to Sir John A. Macdonald in 1894, a year after Abbott's death. By that time Thompson had eventually taken on the role of prime minister. In his speech at the unveiling in Hamilton, Ontario, the young prime minister said of Abbott, "The man who succeeded [Macdonald] was worthy to be his successor. Sir John Abbott's great qualities of brain and heart, his great qualities of statesmanship, his great abilities and great desire to serve this country will never be thoroughly understood by the Canadian people because his career as First Minister was so short."

In a bitterly divided party, Abbott was the compromise choice to fill the vacant office. In a letter, he described himself as the "least loathsome" of the available candidates: Thompson, Langevin, Mackenzie Bowell, and Charles Tupper.

Despite the disparaging comments he'd made, Macdonald himself would likely have reluctantly approved of Abbott as his successor. He held the Montreal businessman in high regard as a person, as a parliamentarian and as a legal expert. Abbott, according to Sir John A., a dispassionate member of the House, was always well-informed, prepared, and dignified. Abbott was considered one of the best speakers during debates. Macdonald noted at one time that he was "distinguished for his lack of animosity and personal bitterness." He thought so highly of Abbott that he offered him the post of president of the Privy Council when setting up the 1891 Cabinet. Abbott deferred to the prime minister. Most telling of all, though, was what Macdonald said to Thompson, shortly before he died. "When I am gone, you will have to rally around Abbott; he is your only man."

At age seventy, Abbott felt deep down that he was getting too old to handle the day-to-day challenges that came with the job of prime minister. In addition, being a senator, he was physically removed from the daily proceedings in the House of Commons, where he believed the government leader needed to be in order to debate issues and answer to Her Majesty's Loyal Opposition. That was a remarkable admission from a man whose vibrancy far surpassed men who were much younger. How many public figures could boast the incredible number of interests, projects, committees, and tasks that Abbott had juggled expertly all through his life?

Well-read, articulate, and erudite to a degree that few could equal, he had seemed a good choice to lead the governing party in the Senate. Then, with the death of Macdonald, he seemed a suitable — if not the best — choice to lead the country.

Abbott brought to the prime minister's office a lengthy resumé in the politics of both Quebec (Canada East) and Canada when it became a country. His business acumen, his international experience, his knowledge of law, his political contacts all combined to put him at the top of the political pile, whether he ever wished for that or not.

The governor general's task to name Macdonald's successor was not an easy one. After consultation with Conservative Party officials and Cabinet members, he took the advice that Abbott was the best choice at that moment. Everyone, including the man himself, acknowledged that it was a temporary job for the Montreal lawyer.

On the morning of Sunday, June 14, Abbott had breakfast at the Rideau Club, where he confessed to his friend J.D. Edgar his reticence to take on the monumental task of governing. Yet the office was thrust upon him, and he reluctantly accepted. Abbott agreed to remain in the Senate and direct the Cabinet from the Red Chamber. He insisted that Thompson lead the caucus in the House of Commons. He made the former Nova Scotian judge responsible for answering to the Official Opposition, which was led by the wily, highly competent Wilfrid Laurier. Thompson and the equally brilliant Laurier were a good match for each other as they battled across the aisle.

A curious little incident that very same day, June 14, illuminates Abbott's modest demeanour. As described by Joseph Pope, Sir John A. Macdonald's personal secretary, an elderly man came to Pope's door in Sandy Hill, a fair distance from downtown Ottawa. Pope was not home, so the man asked if he could come in to rest, stating to the servant at the door that he was tired and it was hot outside. The servant was reluctant to let him in but finally allowed it. When Mrs. Pope came downstairs to see who was resting in her hallway, she was shocked to find that it was none other than the new prime minister, who'd come to ask Pope to stay on as secretary.

The Conservative Party that Abbott inherited was in many ways in shambles. Despite its recent electoral triumph, it was divided by language and religion. Without Macdonald's firm grip keeping things together, the party quickly splintered into its very divisive component parts. The French-English discord would not go away. Religion was a bigger issue than ever, as there were so many groups: French Catholics from Quebec, Irish Catholics in New Brunswick, Orange Protestants in Ontario and Manitoba. Each of these had their own interests, and each desired different things from their party and from political life in general. Then there was the business coalition to consider. Cobbling together support from the merchant and agricultural sections of the country was nigh on impossible when so many of the issues each group held sacred were at odds with what the other group wanted.

In addition to uniting the party, Abbott faced the issues of determining the legality of religiously funded schools in Manitoba. He had to stickhandle the dispute between Britain — and therefore Canada — with the United States over the Bering Sea. Significantly, he would be tasked with managing yet another economic recession that had settled over the country's economy.

Abbott was sworn into office on June 16, 1891, ten days after the death of Sir John A. His first chore was to name a Cabinet capable of carrying on the work started by Macdonald. He studied the list of recently elected members of Parliament, looking especially at those in the Cabinet that had recently been selected. Anyone who had been a member of Sir John A. Macdonald's final Cabinet lost that membership on June 6, 1891, the day that Macdonald died. Conspicuously, and not surprisingly, Abbott chose to keep those exact same ministers as his Cabinet, simply re-installing them in their same ministerial posts. Did he mean to show he was following Macdonald's path? Did he wish to not rock the boat by upsetting those who'd already started to work at their particular departments? Was it an example of not being able to find more capable ministers? In the end, keeping the same people in place was a tactic that allowed him to avoid any controversy that might further split the party ranks. A change in the Cabinet roster might also indicate that he was at odds with Macdonald's choices. He couldn't risk that.

As he was no longer a member of the House but a senator in the Upper Chamber, he sent a message announcing his ministers to the House of Commons, where it was read into *Hansard*. Abbott took on Macdonald's positions as not only prime minister but also as president of the Privy Council. He continued as leader of the government in the Senate.[11]

The men who gathered around the table in the Privy Council Office were an interesting mix. John Carling, of the London brewery fame, was the minister of agriculture. Abbott's fellow senator, Belleville newspaper publisher Mackenzie Bowell, was named minister of customs. Bowell was also appointed as minister of railways and canals, a key job that Macdonald had for years stubbornly kept for himself because of its importance. George Eulas Foster, a New Brunswick classics professor, retained his role as minister of finance. Thompson of course was at the Cabinet table as minister of justice and attorney general. Nova Scotia's Charles Hibbert Tupper, who was the son of Charles Tupper, retained his post as minister of marine and fisheries, a department reserved for a Maritime member of the governing party. Sir Joseph Caron, who'd been Macdonald's minister of militia and defence during the North-West Rebellion, kept that position under Abbott. John Haggart from Perth, Ontario was the postmaster general. His claim to fame would ultimately be his long-time service in Parliament. First elected as an MP in 1872, he remained in the Commons until 1913. Hector-Louis Langevin, a member of Sir John A.'s 1867 Cabinet, a Father of Confederation and a one-time potential successor to Macdonald, began the session as the minister of public works. It turned out to be a very short-lived appointment. He was forced to resign by August of 1891 as a consequence of an ongoing scandal. He was replaced by Frank Smith, a man who fought for the rights of Irish Catholics at a time when there was great prejudice against that group of immigrants. Joseph-Adolphe Chapleau served as both secretary of state and registrar general. Chapleau and Thompson had a grudging respect for each other, but it was an open secret that they had nothing close to a friendship.

The Cabinet was not a strong one, and it was not by any degree a cohesive group. The same could be said for the 117-seat Conservative caucus.

Too many of the men disliked each other for the group to function optimally. The deep religious schisms and the underlying racial tensions were mostly to blame. There was some ambition among the group but most of it was disproportionate to the men's talents.

The East Block office where the Cabinet met had a number of uneasy sessions, as the MPs wrangled over religion, language, party tactics, and the best policies moving forward as a government. The new prime minister's serene presence helped to cool tempers somewhat. He did not abide open hostility between caucus members and admonished anyone who carried grudges out of the meetings. Abbott's ministers had to deal with a backlog of pressing business, bills, and motions that had been put on hold during the election campaign and the pause in action following the death of the prime minister.

Perhaps the most vexing thing Abbott faced during his time as prime minister was the kind of politicking that, within days of taking office, had the new premier regretting his decision to accept the position. Abbott despised listening to deputations. Yet it was the method of doing business that Macdonald had used for years. Representing every interest group in the country, nearly every MP came to him with claims and petitions.

"Anyone who thinks that I could be influenced by a deputation is a damned fool," Abbott said to Hugh John Macdonald, Sir John A.'s son.

The scandals that kept erupting did not make his work any easier. An early biographer of Sir John Thompson labelled the Abbott ministry's brief period in office as "the scandal session."[12] There is no doubt that Sir John A. Macdonald led a party that had learned to manipulate, cajole, patronize, bribe, and orchestrate. Building a new country from a small collection of colonies to a transcontinental nation, second only to Russia in size, had necessitated much manoeuvring of people and resources. It was a fact of life in the politics of the day, not unique to Canadian affairs. Accomplishing that nation-building seemingly could not be done without some examples of inappropriate behaviour.

A series of scandals dogged the Conservatives in the spring of 1892, though none of them were linked to John Abbott. The Rykert Scandal, which involved questionable grants of timber permits in Cypress Hills, was already two years old but still riled the Liberals. Hector-Louis Langevin and his affair in Quebec involving kickbacks from contractors led to his resignation from Cabinet in the late summer of 1891, but as expected, the Liberals would not let the matter rest. They seemed to want blood.

Abbott faced a dilemma when dealing with the Langevin patronage scandal. Langevin had a reputation as a nation-builder. He'd been in on the talks about Confederation from the start. Over his years at Macdonald's side, he'd been loyal and a source of strength when dealing with the French element in government. Although Abbott was a long-time associate of Hector-Louis Langevin, he could not allow the kickback schemes of Langevin's relative-through-marriage Thomas McGreevy to fester and stir up trouble for the party in Quebec. McGreevy had been handed contracts by Langevin's Public Works Department, but the blatant patronage — indeed the outright theft of public money by McGreevy — was simply too great an instance of corruption for the prime minister to ignore. Not that the Opposition allowed him to ignore the matter. Despite Langevin's lofty position as the leader of the French Canadians in the government, Abbott asked for his resignation as minister.

A secret deal was worked out. McGreevy would take the fall; the official report would gloss over Langevin's role, and a new position would be found for Macdonald's old friend. It was hoped that an inquiry would clear Langevin of any wrongdoing. Suspiciously, though, documents related to the affair that might compromise other Conservatives were secretly destroyed.

Langevin later maintained that Abbott had offered him the lieutenant governor's post in Quebec, but that position went to Joseph-Adolphe Chapleau instead. Why Abbott reneged on his promise to the disgraced minister is uncertain, but it is likely he did so because of pressure on him to name an unsullied Tory to the vice-regal office in Quebec.

Abbott was not alone in his condemnation of the McGreevy-Langevin business. Justice Minister Thompson made a public speech in Halifax where he declared that the government would not defend McGreevy nor excuse him if he was found guilty. As it turned out, McGreevy was eventually expelled from the Commons and was charged with defrauding the federal treasury of over three million dollars. He went to jail because of those charges. He ended up financially ruined as well. The one positive from the affair was that Parliament was forced to pass legislation that demanded fair dealings between contractors and the government. Even in a time of rampant graft, there were limits to what people could tolerate.

No sooner had Abbott settled the Langevin affair than further questions were brought forward by the Opposition concerning the actions of other prominent Conservatives. The postmaster general, Sir Joseph Caron, was accused of influencing subsidies to a railway that he partly owned. Another accusation was made that the election of John Carling in London, Ontario, had been improper. Almost daily in the Commons, Thompson had to answer to charges from prominent Liberals such as Israel Tarte, Richard Cartwright, and James Edgar concerning allegations of Conservative wrongdoing.

Governor General Lord Stanley called the House back under Abbott's advice on June 16, 1891. Considering his short time in office, in reasonably short order Abbott managed to clear the legislative backlog. Through the fifteen months of his time in power, his government proved to be competent and hard-working, just like the man himself. Abbott was a decisive leader, sure of his opinions and not afraid to act upon those very beliefs. Abbott's term as prime minister can be whittled down to three important things: he tried to reform the civil service; he made a number of important revisions to the Criminal Code of Canada; and he worked on a reciprocity agreement with the United States in an attempt to solve the economic difficulties that plagued North America at the time.

Even before Parliament returned in that summer of 1891, Abbott saw that there was a need to review and reform the civil service. Although he had been a backroom negotiator who was no stranger to nepotism or the pork barrel, Abbott saw that the civil service in Ottawa was in dire need of change. Too many incompetent, unqualified people held positions that affected the day-to-day efficiency of the government. Too often the prime jobs went to political appointees who were more energetic in seeking promotion than men who were better suited to handle those very positions. A royal commission seemed to be the best way to look into how the bureaucracy of government in Ottawa could be revamped.

Abbott established the commission to study the matter in 1891. Named to the group were George Hague, the general manager of the Merchants Bank of Canada. He was well known to Abbott, since the two men were directors of that same bank. J.M. Courtney, another banker who doubled as the deputy minister of finance,[13] was a commissioner. E.J. Barbeau, the manager of the Montreal City and District Savings Bank, took part as did Mr. Justice G.W. Burbidge, an Ontario judge of the Exchequer Court of Canada. These men were tasked with examining the irregularities that were seen to exist in the public service in Ottawa. Their findings were presented in a thoughtful volume of work that recommended, among other things, the establishment of "a permanent Civil Service Commission and the adoption of the principle of appointment by open competition." Members of both the Conservative and Liberal parties, however, were loath to give up what they saw as their right to grant positions by means of patronage. (Laurier, it turned out, would be as adept as Macdonald in doling out such favours.) A.H.U Colquhoun, writing in the *Canadian Magazine* in 1896, made the comment that "there is reason to suppose that if Sir John Abbott had lived to occupy the premiership for a longer term than his health permitted him to do, more would have been heard of the proposals of the commission."[14] In the end, although it was a gallant, far-sighted attempt in a time of rampant favouritism, nothing much came of Abbott's initiative to change the public service.

As for Canadian-American relations, so much of that area fell under the aegis of the British Colonial Office. When it came to international dealings, Canada remained in a near-colonial position — under Britain's control, despite the Dominion's supposed status as an independent nation. But it rarely was left for Canada to negotiate with the United States on its own. Boundary issues — especially those regarding fishing territory disputes — had plagued the two countries for years. In many of these discussions, the Canadian delegations were quite often relegated to observer status or attended as one small part of the British contingent. A fitting example involved the negotiation of the 1871 Treaty of Washington. The prime minister of Canada, Sir John A. Macdonald, was simply a member of the British delegation. Much to his dismay, he was given very little say in the matters discussed.

As has happened repeatedly in American history, the 1890s saw a time of "America First" protectionism, where tariffs were imposed by the United State to grow its own economy. Little regard was given for the impact of these measures on the country's trading partners. Both countries were evolving. Canada was transforming itself, changing from a land of fishermen, fur trappers, miners, loggers, and farmers to a more industrialized and therefore urbanized society. In 1851, 90 percent of Canadians in what was then British North America lived in rural areas. By 1891, only 70 percent did so. The trend was much the same in the United States. As industries blossomed, as the move to the cities accelerated, both countries sought ways to protect their new factories, the products that were being produced, and the jobs of their workers.

It fell to Sir John Abbott to seek ways to maintain a trade balance that benefitted the people of Canada. The 1891 election had been fought over the issue of trade, with the Liberals promising to negotiate a reciprocity treaty with the United States. Now, Abbott and the Conservatives took up an altered version of that very same policy. They tried to work out a trade deal with the Americans. Not exactly reciprocity, the new plan simply called for a loosening of the rules for goods crossing the border.

The ruling Tory Party had laid the groundwork for the first Canadian Department of Trade and Commerce in 1887. Abbott oversaw the creation of that portfolio in 1892. (It took a number of years for the department to fully get up and running — the first trade commissioner was not named until 1895.) Until that ministry was fully functioning, negotiations were difficult to coordinate.

The Conservatives began consulting with representatives in Washington about ironing out some sort of trade deal between the two nations. Prime Minister Abbott sent Charles Tupper to the American capital to speak with

Britain's ambassador to the United States about the possibilities of reciprocity. Tupper — who was at that time high commissioner to Britain — met with U.S. secretary of state James Blaine. Blaine was a man who believed that the time for American isolationist policies was over, favouring, instead, expansionism. He was a key figure in American incursions into Latin America, the Pacific, and the Caribbean. Whether his sights were set on his northern neighbour is unclear. Blaine was amenable to further talks, but what followed turned out to be a farce.

Tupper returned to Ottawa, met with then-Justice Minister Thompson and Finance Minister George Foster. The three ministers then boarded a train in Ottawa for the long trip south, travelling with the purpose of entering into talks with Blaine and his people. The Canadians unfortunately missed a telegram from Blaine informing them that he would not be available for the scheduled discussion, since President Harrison, who had insisted on attending in person, could not make that specific meeting. Communications were such that the trio of Canadian politicians arrived in Washington only to find that their meeting had been cancelled. Nevertheless, Tupper, Thompson, and Foster marched into Blaine's Capitol Hill office. The American politician met with them but for only a few brief minutes. Then, seeing the futility of their mission, the trio was obliged to head home the same day. The only positive outcome of their fruitless excursion was that they at least laid the groundwork for more meetings later in the year.

After lengthy delays, a conference was eventually held in Washington in February of 1892. Thompson, Foster, and Mackenzie Bowell represented Canada; Blaine and U.S. secretary of state General J.W. Foster were the Americans; and Sir Julian Pauncefote, Britain's envoy to the United States,[15] was there to oversee whatever the Canadians could negotiate with the Americans. The agenda was a full one. Among the matters discussed were the Alaska and Passamaquaddy Bay boundaries, fisheries, and salvage rights. General trade relations between the two countries were also on the agenda.

A few years before, in the late 1880s, an international problem arose when the Americans began seizing Canadian sealing vessels in the Bering Sea. The Canadian ships were operating in what they considered open waters, but the Americans viewed the seal hunt near their recently acquired Pribilof Islands as an incursion into American territory. It fell to the new Abbott government in Ottawa to negotiate, through the British Colonial Office, a settlement of what was essentially a Canada-U.S. problem. Little came of the talks.

Canada's stance was that it was entitled to international access to the Bering Sea. Canadians also felt that the Americans needed to make financial reparations for the seizures of the Canadian ships. Thompson argued on Canada's behalf, insisting that the two issues were not to be negotiated separately. The outcome of those talks resulted in a settlement that was favourable to both sides. Although Abbott was prime minister, it was really considered a success for his justice minister, John Thompson.

Another issue facing the government in their term under Abbott was an examination of the country's Criminal Code. Abbott's background as a law professor prepared him well for the actual drafting of laws. He was knowledgeable about procedures for changing the Criminal Code where it was thought to be necessary. Along with his brilliant minister of justice, John Thompson, Abbott can lay claim to making a standardization of the Criminal Code of Canada. It was an ideal partnership for an enterprise that both Thompson and Abbott had prepared all their lives for. The judge from Halifax and the law dean from Montreal: who better to improve the criminal laws of the Dominion? Using their expertise, the new Criminal Code was drawn up with the advice of legal experts from across the country.

Two of the changes that were implemented were quite radical in nature. The alterations became important to the Canadian legal system. The culpability of juvenile offenders was changed so that children were no longer subject to the same rules as adults. This meant that the age at which a young person could be held accountable was standardized. No child under the age of seven could be convicted. Those seven to thirteen could be tried and convicted only if they competently knew of the nature and consequences of their actions. Secondly, the bill that Thompson sponsored and Abbott confirmed made the provision that offences under an act of British Parliament were no longer applicable in Canadian courts unless the act was something specific to Canada or to Her Majesty's Dominions and possessions. It was a step toward further independence from British control.

Amongst other provisions: No one could be convicted of a crime if that person was found to be insane or "labouring under natural imbecility." Crimes that had previously been defined by local courts were uniformly defined: murder, treason, sedition, theft, libel, corruption.

While most Canadian legal minds were supportive and pleased with the codification of the country's laws, there was one notable dissenter. Mr. Justice Jean-Thomas Taschereau of the Supreme Court published a public denunciation of the new code. Yet his criticism was somewhat tainted because he had refused to offer legal advice during its writing. His critique offered nothing in the way of suggestions for improvement either.

The Manitoba Schools Question was undoubtedly the issue that plagued the federal government more than any other problem in the years between Macdonald and Laurier. In a step that was taken from the playbook of Sir John A. Macdonald, Abbott made the unilateral decision to let the courts handle the issue, a bitter dispute over language and religious rights. Macdonald had dodged in the same fashion, though it continued to torment his Tory successors in the prime minister's office.

Essentially, the Manitoba Schools Question was a case of the Manitoba government altering the rights of the minority population of the province. The Manitoba Act of 1870, the federal legislation that created the province, guaranteed the rights of Catholics, francophones and anglophones in courts and the legislature. It also guaranteed that there could be French schools for Catholics and English schools for Protestants.

In 1870, the mostly French-Catholic Métis were the majority in the province; by the late 1880s, however, the anglophones were far more numerous, and more were due to arrive in the province. That English speaking majority, many of whom were from Orange Ontario, resented paying for publicly funded French schools.

The Manitoba Schools Act 1890 created a single, non-denominational system with English as the sole language. This provincial statute broke the provisions of not only the Manitoba Act but also the British North America Act, Canada's essential constitution. Both had provisions for protecting denominational schools. Catholic and French leaders in both Manitoba and Quebec protested to the federal government. Macdonald was reluctant to implement disallowance, a federal ability to overrule provincial legislation. His feeling was that since education was a provincial matter, there should be a less formal way to solve the issue. Instead, the federal Tory government punted the issue to the courts.

As the Manitoba Schools issue made its glacial move through the court system, Abbott and his government moved ahead in other areas.

A mark of any prime minister's effectiveness is how well his party does in by-elections during his term of office. Remarkably, there were fifty-two federal by-elections during Abbott's brief tenure. (There were only 215 seats in the House of Commons at the time; many of the contests were re-runs of the 1891 contest thanks to close votes, corruption, questionable electoral practices, or petitions from the voters in constituencies.) The Conservatives won forty-two of those electoral battles. The party's majority in the House rose from a somewhat shaky twenty seats to well over sixty. Such results can only be seen as a significant approval rating for Abbott as prime minister.

That being said, through all the issues and events that transpired in the year and few months that Abbott sat at the head of the Cabinet table, it was really Thompson who carried the party on his broad shoulders. As Abbott sat in the Senate chamber on the east side of the Parliament's Centre Block, a few metres down the hall, in the House of Commons chamber, the leader of the government in the House faced the Opposition daily as that group hammered away at Tory policies. For instance, when Laurier and the Liberals made a fuss about Tupper participating in the 1891 election although still serving as high commissioner to London, it was Thompson who upheld Sir Charles's reputation and refuted any charges of corruption or scandal. Brilliant lawyer that he was, he handled the Liberal accusations easily and their criticism was summarily repudiated.

Abbott's term in office was shorter than most people expected. Although he saw himself as a caretaker prime minister, temporarily holding office until a better candidate could be accepted, it was tragically cut even shorter than expected by illness. Working in the East Block one afternoon in late July 1892, he was overwhelmed by a sudden attack of dizziness. One of the parliamentary messengers helped him stagger to a nearby office where he rested for a time, exhausted and extremely anxious. At first, he staggered back to Earnscliffe. Then, later the following week, he travelled to his mansion at Ste. Anne de Bellevue, where doctors told him that he was suffering from bad circulation and a weakened heart. He was advised to rest. He wrote to Thompson, saying, "I shall have to give in, I suppose … and shall try to keep things running somehow until we can make other arrangements, and in the meantime will shirk all I can."

Following a Cabinet meeting held in Montreal for his convenience, he took a brief boat trip down the St. Lawrence. Although it was meant to give him rest and relaxation, his symptoms of weakness would not go away.

With his health failing, Abbott tried to turn over the leadership to Thompson. He called in his party faithful to explain that he was not well enough to continue in office. The stress of the work was too much for him. Abbott's failing strength was affecting how well he could carry out his important duties. Thompson should take over, he argued. The younger man was reliably leading the government in the Commons, and with no other acceptable flagbearer in sight, it seemed the right thing to do. Yet, even at that stage there was opposition among Conservative Party members to the succession plan. Some of the opposition came from the overly modest Thompson himself. The Manitoba Schools Question, with all its ramifications for Catholics in the province was a huge roadblock. Too many Tory Party members felt that, as judicious and upstanding as Thompson was, the average Protestant voter might be skeptical that the Roman Catholic

Thompson could act fairly to settle any problem that had religious ramifications. The power of the Orange Order drove the thinking of many
Conservative caucus members.

Abbott's appeal to turn things over to Thompson was rejected. Party
stalwarts from Ontario, even those who did not necessarily side with the
Orangemen, still could not accept a Roman Catholic leader — even when
faced with a prime minister who was obviously faltering.

Discouraged and somehow trapped in an office he no longer wished to
occupy, Abbott set off for England in October of 1892, hoping to find some
kind of answers to his deteriorating health. Before he left, he dictated and
signed his resignation letter. He did not officially submit it, but he seemed
to know what was coming. Doctors in London advised him to take a long
rest to recover from what they called, "brain congestion and consequent
exhaustion of the brain and nervous system." It was, in fact, an incurable
brain tumor. There was nothing that could be done for his cancer. It was a
death sentence. Abbott set off on a tour of Europe, visiting Genoa, Rome,
and Naples in hopes of reviving his failing health. Sadly, he simply got
weaker and more ill. His return voyage across the Atlantic was a dismal one.
Returning to Montreal, he began to put his affairs in order, signed documents that were awaiting his return and notified his closest political friends
of his medical and political status. He informed the closest of his Ottawa
colleagues of his grave diagnosis.

As if to formalize matters, within days of his return to Canada, letters
arrived from the London doctors addressed to Abbott, the governor general,
and Thompson explaining that the prime minister needed to leave office
immediately. The Cabinet was notified of the serious condition of their
leader. On November 23, the governor general summoned Thompson to
Government House, where he informed the Nova Scotian that he was the
only choice to replace Abbott. The party had to accept him, like it or not.
Abbott's resignation was confirmed the next day and Thompson was officially sworn in as prime minister on December 4, 1892. Abbott was only
prime minister from June of 1891 until November of 1892 — 526 days.

The energy that kept Abbott going as a businessman, lawyer, mayor, MP,
Cabinet minister, diplomat, prime minister, director on a number of boards,

law professor emeritus, musician, philanthropist — not to mention father and grandfather and husband — began to flag markedly. A dying man, he returned to Montreal to spend his final days at his beloved Boisbriand.

John Joseph Caldwell Abbott, the dynamic polymath, died October 30, 1893, in Montreal.

Since he spent such a short time in the prime minister's office, Abbott has been given short shrift in Canadian history. What has been lacking in the assessment of the man is the work that he did beyond his brief term at the helm of the country, especially outside of electoral politics. He was the country's pre-eminent lawyer in the second half of the nineteenth century. He had a hand in much of the backroom manipulation — for good or bad — that dominated the actions of the Tory Party during the Macdonald era. His enterprises in Montreal were not only enriching to the man and his family but also to the less fortunate people of that city. As a lawyer, he reputedly fought hardest when representing the poorest and most ill-advantaged of clients (though his clientele tended to be the rich and powerful). His encouragement of the arts, his philanthropy toward the disadvantaged, the blind, and the deaf are praiseworthy.

On the other hand, perhaps Abbott can share some of the blame for multiple problems within the Conservative Party in the last three decades of that century. The party was divided along language and religious lines. The support that the Macdonald-Cartier leadership had forged in the sixties dissipated, largely because of the myopic handling of the Riel rebellions. The ascendancy of the Orange Order's power within the Tory ranks undercut their support in ridings where Catholics and francophones were found in sizeable numbers. Abbott had been one of Macdonald's advisors throughout those decades. As a Quebecer, perhaps he failed to advise his leader appropriately about the needs and idiosyncrasies of that province. Abbott was truly influential among the highest ranks of the Conservative Party; therefore, he must share the blame for having failed to develop a process for nurturing younger, fresh leadership. Other than John Thompson, the party relied on its old guard.

Abbott did not want the job of being prime minister. It seems that he could have put up a stronger fight to arrange that Thompson take over from Macdonald. It is unlikely that Abbott harboured any negative feelings toward Thompson or had any strong prejudice against his religion. More likely, the opportunistic lawyer saw the Orange Order, with its camaraderie and benevolent work at the time, as suiting his ambitions and needs. Abbott's membership in the Montreal Orange Lodge likely weakened his legitimacy with French-speaking Quebec voters and with Catholics across the country. He — although not alone by any means — missed an early opportunity to unite the disparate Catholic and Protestant factions within the party.

In no way, however, was Abbott a failure as prime minister. He was competent, assertive, and calm at a time when those qualities were needed. He meant well. His loyalty to his party and his desire to do what was best for the country drove him to accept the position he did not want. Ultimately, his own unexpected illness and subsequent resignation left the Tories no alternative but to select, unexpectedly in some ways, the Roman Catholic Thompson as the next leader, the man who should have succeeded Macdonald in the first place.

Chapter Three

◈

Sir John Thompson: "The Great Might-Have-Been" Prime Minister

SIR JOHN A. MACDONALD WAS once overheard to say, "My one great discovery was my discovery of Thompson." From a man who had been at the apex of Canadian politics for over fifty years, that was quite a compliment.

Much the same as his predecessor in office, Sir John Abbott, John Thompson was a reluctant politician, a man who played the political game but disliked making speeches, although he was very good at it, and who hated spending time away from his beloved family.

Living in Halifax, John Sparrow David Thompson was a man well-respected for his brilliant legal mind. He had served as a lecturer at Dalhousie Law School and, more importantly, sat as a judge on Nova Scotia's Supreme Court. He was hailed as a success. The position suited his temperament as well as his ambition. He found reward in his professional activities and was content amid the tiny capital's society. At home, he was blessed with the love of his devoted wife and family. Never rich, he nevertheless enjoyed a comfortable life.

Despite the comfort he found in his position, Thompson couldn't resist the attraction of the political life. He had joined the provincial Conservative Party and quickly rose in its ranks. He had even been premier of Nova Scotia for a brief time in 1882. So, when Sir John A. Macdonald began searching that province for quality candidates to represent the Tories in the national election of 1885, he was advised to strongly consider Thompson. Macdonald called upon emissaries such as the editor of the Halifax *Morning Herald* to woo Thompson. Dangling the minister of justice portfolio in front of the Nova Scotia judge, Macdonald used his considerable guile to coax Thompson into making the move to Ottawa. The ultimate catalyst, though, in persuading Thompson to uproot himself and his family was his devoted wife, Annie. When he informed her of the overtures he had received from the national capital, she boldly told him to accept the Cabinet position: "Go. Now you can show the world what you can do."

Born in 1845, John Sparrow Thompson was the youngest of seven children in a working-class Irish family. His father was a well-read man in a time of widespread illiteracy. He held a number of respectable jobs. He worked for Joseph Howe's *Colonial Herald* as an assistant editor. He was also a secretary of the Halifax Mechanic's Institute. For a time, he was the Queen's Printer in Halifax. Then he held the post of superintendent of the money order department of Nova Scotia's Post Office.

Thompson Sr. was a man with definite opinions and views. Although generally liberal in his views, he was a strict temperance advocate, having experienced the ills of alcohol in his native Ireland and then in the unruly behavior of sailors along the Halifax docks. He was also very much against Confederation, taking the side of his mentor, Joseph Howe, the great Nova Scotian advocate for responsible government. He was a man who abhorred the idea of uniting British North America and no doubt would have found it ironic that his youngest son eventually became the leader of what were in effect those united British colonies.

Tragedy struck the Thompson family often. John's two older sisters died in the 1840s; his brother William died in 1857 in South Africa of alcoholism; and his brother Joseph died in Texas in 1867 of yellow fever. One of his remaining two sisters married and moved away from Halifax. Thompson Sr. died the same year as Confederation, leaving John, at age twenty-two, to support his mother and one of his sisters.

As a teenager, John had begun an apprenticeship in the law firm of former Halifax mayor Henry Pryor. In 1865 Thompson, aged twenty, was called to the Nova Scotia bar. At the same time, he reported on the debates of the Legislative Assembly, where he used his skill as a writer of shorthand — learned from his father — to become "reporter-in-chief." The experience taught the young man the nuances of the legislative process. He also made the acquaintance of the major political actors of the province. Four years later, Thompson joined in a partnership with flamboyant trial lawyer Joseph Coombes. From his colourful partner, Thompson learned to overcome his inherent unassuming, reserved manner. John began to speak confidently and boldly, in a voice that carried to the back of any room. His newfound eloquence would serve him well in both the law courts and eventually on the political stage.

At the same time as he was starting his law career and supporting the remains of his family, John met a young Halifax woman named Annie Affleck. A sea captain's daughter, she was a spirited woman at a time when females were expected to be demure. The couple's first date was to attend a cricket match. She admired his intellect and quiet yet feisty nature; he was drawn to her beauty and intelligence. Something that appealed to him was the passion that she openly displayed for life. Where Thompson was patient, calm, and self-disciplined, Annie was impulsive and exuberant. A girl who'd grown up in a severe, strait-laced household that demanded an enforced self-discipline, she yearned for freedom. John's open kindness instantly appealed to her. She felt that he was the only person in the world who cared for her. With him, she felt that she could "let go" and behave in a less restricted fashion. He delighted in the vivacious way she approached nearly everything. In some ways, it was an example of opposites attracting.

In order to be with her as much as possible, John spent hours in the Affleck home, where he ostensibly tutored her in French.[1] Eventually, he was there five or six times a week. What's more, he taught her how to write in shorthand. She used that skill when keeping a journal that kept prying eyes from knowing too much about their love affair. The two communicated in their unique shorthand for years. The couple wrote normal letters that any prying eye could read; on the other side of these, however, was a code known only to the two of them. Some of the messages were, by Victorian standards, rather suggestive. (For years, the letters were examined in schools that specialized in shorthand, but no one could decode the messages. In 1978, a cryptography expert in England finally discovered that the code was a British one formulated in the eighteenth century.)

Neither family seems to have been happy with the young couple's relationship. Annie was a Roman Catholic while John's family included Presbyterians and Methodists. In a time where religious denominations mattered profoundly and prevented many a wedding from taking place, their religious differences required much of their courtship to be carried on in secret. Hence, the shorthand correspondence.

Thompson's family may have been Protestant, but as mentioned, his father had been quite liberal in his philosophical leanings. He had preached tolerance of Roman Catholics. He even went so far as to forbid his children to have anything to do with the Orange Order, that dogmatic brotherhood known for its anti-Catholic sentiments. His father's lessons in tolerance likely explained the fact that young John displayed a total lack of religious bias.

Inevitably, the young couple wished to marry. However, because of the bias that existed at the time, which effectively prevented inter-faith marriages, the couple could not wed in any church in Halifax. Instead, they had to travel across the border to Bangor, Maine. There, with a bishop's special dispensation, since John was still a Protestant, the young couple exchanged vows. The newlyweds moved into the Thompson home in Halifax.

A year later, with Annie four months pregnant, John was formally christened as a Roman Catholic. His decision would have an impact on his political career for the rest of his life. He had considered the move for more than a year and had waited to clearly demonstrate that he was not simply converting in order to marry. His sincere belief in Roman Catholic tenets was both genuine and self-determined. The couple allegedly never discussed religion, although that seems highly unlikely given the ramifications of his decision to switch denominations.

As a practising barrister in a predominantly Protestant city, Thompson knew that the prejudice of the day toward Roman Catholics might cost him dearly. Just before he converted, Thompson wrote to a friend, "I have everything to lose from a worldly standpoint by the step I am about to take." Yet that did not happen. He did not lose a single client after his switch of religious affiliation. That can probably be attributed to his growing reputation as a talented, up-and-coming lawyer as much as anything.

Annie was a perfect match for John. Throughout their marriage, she was a presence in both his legal and political careers. Where he could be naive about people, always thinking the best of individuals, she was realistic and a good judge of character. She was less likely to think well of others. She prodded him to take action when he wavered. She chided him for his absentmindedness, knowing that there were people who might take advantage of that personality quirk. Above all, she believed in his talent and was ambitious for him to rise as high as possible in whatever field he chose.

His generosity was a well-kept secret, something known usually to only his closest friends. He gave money to religious causes, to the poor, and even to his legal clients. He once gave a woman advice on how to manage her money. She came back to him several years later, complaining that her investments had failed, and she'd been left destitute. Thompson, although he could ill-afford it, paid the woman the original amount out of his own bank account, apologizing for his poor financial advice. He was destined to never be a rich man.

Thompson became active in the community during his early years as lawyer in the provincial capital. He was president of the Young Men's Literary Association in Halifax and active in the Charitable Irish Society. In 1871 he entered electoral politics when he ran successfully as an alderman for Halifax's Ward 5. As a municipal politician, John demonstrated early on his aptitude for organization. He liked to examine a matter, then simplify it. For example, along with fellow alderman Lawrence Power, he set about to categorize the laws of Nova Scotia that applied specifically to the city of Halifax. It was characteristic of what Thompson brought to each of the positions he attained throughout his life, including that of prime minister. He abhorred confusion or obfuscation, so he made it his duty to clarify, codify, and organize matters that pertained to whatever he oversaw.

As a city councillor, Thompson familiarized himself with the issues that existed in not only Halifax but in the province of Nova Scotia in general by serving on a number of committees. For example, he worked on the Board of School Commissioners, where he played a part in reforming public education throughout the province. Specifically, he was able to work out a policy that enabled schools to function capably with both Catholic and Protestant supporters combined in a single system.

Thompson's reputation grew to such an extent that he was persuaded in 1877 to run for the provincial legislature. A vacancy existed in the riding of Antigonish. Thompson was parachuted into the by-election race to represent that area. With the vital assistance of the local Catholic bishop, John Cameron, Thompson was able to wrestle the county from the Liberals, despite being initially seen as an outsider.

Lectures and speeches were an integral part of nineteenth-century entertainment. Gifted speakers were much appreciated. The local paper in Antigonish praised Thompson's oratory. "Mr. Thompson is the most perfect public speaker we have ever listened to. In fluency and ease, and grace and vigour of expression, he is without peer in this country." Although he lacked the warmth, humour, and open geniality of the likes of John A. Macdonald, he brought to political speeches a directness and understandable rhetoric that appealed to the voters. With Bishop Cameron's help, guidance, and especially his influence, Thompson's cool manner and intellectual superiority won the election in the overwhelmingly Catholic county. Cameron was to play a role in Thompson's career for many years to come.

Within a year, the provincial Liberal government fell. In the election of 1878, John maintained his seat by acclamation. Now part of the governing party, Thompson was appointed to Cabinet as attorney general. That made him, at age thirty-three, the chief of law enforcement for the province. It was an area that had suffered from incompetence over the years. Thompson set about in his characteristic way to reform, modernize, and make efficient a badly neglected system. He took on several tasks at once: he had to steer proposed legislation through the provincial parliament; visit with officials and members of the public throughout Nova Scotia; and he had to keep in touch with his constituency in Antigonish. At the same time, his major role as attorney general was to personally take part in prosecuting the major criminal cases in the province. Annie Thompson complained in her diary that he worked into the "wee hours of the morning" far too often.

The premier at the time, Simon Holmes, became increasingly unpopular with both his caucus and with the voters. His undoing was his singular obsession with unifying all the railways in the province. It seemed to the men around him that he was too focused on that one issue and was ignoring the plethora of other matters that plagued the province. A caucus rebellion resulted. In May of 1882 he resigned, citing ill health. Thompson was drafted by a movement that named him the next leader. In a matter of days, he took on the dual roles of premier and attorney general.

There was some duplicity involved in his assumption of the premiership. Thompson's acceptance was based on a secret promise. If things did not turn out well in the June election, it was understood by the local powerbrokers that he would be offered a recently vacated position on the Supreme Court of Nova Scotia.

The new premier of Nova Scotia took his party to the polls that June but was narrowly defeated. An early biographer, John Castel Hopkins, alluded to religious bigotry as one of the reasons Thompson's government went down to defeat, although that cannot, of course, be verified. Following an unsuccessful attempt to cobble together a coalition government, Thompson resigned July 18. His secret agreement kicked in. Nine days later, he was appointed to the provincial Supreme Court by none other than Sir John A. Macdonald.

At age thirty-six, Thompson became the youngest judge in Canada at the time. He quickly came to be known as someone who was, above all, courteous to members of the bar when they tried cases in his courtroom. His legal decisions were considered to be liberal, fair, and quite charitable. He was extremely intolerant, however, in cases where cruelty to women or children were involved. In those verdicts, his sentences were as harsh as the law permitted. He once gave a severe prison term to a woman who'd been especially cruel to a child. Years later, as federal minister of justice, he had the occasion to visit the penitentiary where the woman was brought to him to plead for a more lenient sentence.

"So, you expect to be let out?" Thompson asked.

"I hope so," the woman replied.

Thompson answered, "Well, if in a hundred years you were living and I was still minister of justice, I would not let you out."

While securely established as a judge in Halifax, Thompson enjoyed his home life and, free from political duties, was able to comfortably give time to other interests. He visited the law schools at Harvard, Columbia, and Boston universities. He then came back to Dalhousie in Halifax with plans to emulate those American institutions whose law departments were turning out well-trained attorneys. Working with what he'd seen and researched, Thompson helped to establish the Dalhousie law school, where he lectured during its first terms in 1883 and 1884. Such was the respect for his legal mind that many of the barristers in Halifax enrolled in Thompson's lectures on "Evidence." He played a large role in building up a first-rate law library at Dalhousie.

Seeing the efficiency that he brought to both the courtroom and to political office, the provincial Liberal government asked him to reorganize the Supreme Court of Nova Scotia. That assignment culminated in the Judicature Act of 1884, which led to a reform of the provincial court system. So diligent was his work that the act remained unchanged until well into the twentieth century.

Those who knew him intimately speculated that Thompson would have been content to remain a judge in Halifax for the rest of his days. He and Annie had a happy, solid marriage. He claimed that he harboured no political ambitions, as he neither liked nor wanted the public speaking nor the travel that politics demanded. And yet, as a man of such intellectual capability, he felt some urge to make a difference in the wider world. His wife encouraged that sentiment. So, when John A. Macdonald came dangling the federal Justice portfolio, Thompson took the bait. He resigned his seat on the Nova Scotia bench and prepared for the move to Ottawa.

The Cabinet of the federal Tory government badly needed a re-set in the mid-1880s. Sir Charles Tupper, a former premier of Nova Scotia and a renowned Father of Confederation, was a confidant of Macdonald. Yet he was tired of Ottawa and electoral politics. He asked for and accepted the post of high commissioner to the United Kingdom in 1883. New Brunswick's Sir Leonard Tilley, another of the Founding Fathers from the Maritimes, had done his time as finance minister in Ottawa. He retired to take on the role of lieutenant governor of his home province in 1885. Sir Alex Campbell of Ontario handled his portfolios in the government from his seat in the Senate. He too wished to retire. As a reward for his years of service, Campbell was eventually handed the ceremonial position of Ontario lieutenant governor in 1887. New blood was needed to revive a government that had been in office since 1867 with just the short hiatus of the Alexander Mackenzie Liberal years.

Events of 1885 moved swiftly. Local Conservatives such as Tupper and, eventual Supreme Court judge Robert Sedgwick, had advised Macdonald about the political scene in Nova Scotia over the years. They urged Sir John to tap Thompson on the shoulder for a position in Ottawa. Although Macdonald knew Thompson in only a cursory manner, the prime minister was impressed with the Nova Scotia judge's first-rate credentials. That such a young man had accomplished so much in a brief number of years impressed the prime minister. Macdonald began a brief correspondence with the Nova Scotian. Initially, Thompson refused to take the bait. Macdonald, never an easy man to be discouraged when he'd made his mind up, sent his final solicitation in September. Thompson caved in, responding to Macdonald's plea mostly out of a sense of duty to his party, although there may have been some personal ambition at play in the decision. As happened frequently, Annie Thompson was behind the scenes with pointed comments and prodding. She poignantly asked John if he wanted to spend the remainder of his life among the "sere old crows" on the Nova Scotia bench.

Meanwhile, behind the scenes, the patronage that Macdonald wielded craftily greased the wheels for Thompson to make the move. On September 26, even before he had won a seat in Parliament, Thompson was appointed as minister of justice. At the same time, the sitting MP in Antigonish — a

Liberal — was offered and accepted a county judgeship. His resignation required a by-election to be called in the riding.[2] Liberal papers such as the *Yarmouth Herald* were offended by the "disgusting shuffling of judgeships," but most of the vitriol was aimed at the prime minister, not the parachuted candidate for the Tories. Thompson agreed to accept the nomination for the Conservatives in what had been his old provincial seat. On October 16, 1885, the voters of Antigonish sent him to the national parliament. That autumn, John made the long train trip to Ottawa, where he set up an office in the Parliament Buildings and prepared for his term as the minister of justice.

Thompson found himself warmly welcomed to the national capital. Although pining for Annie and his children, he fitted himself into the city's social scene, what little there was. One of the very first events that he attended was a lavish dinner at Earnscliffe. Thompson wrote to Annie about the party. He made the rather catty and ungrateful comment that the prime minister's wife was "as ugly as sin." Nonetheless, he found her pleasant and enjoyed the cuisine: oysters, consommé soup, fish, lamb, Charlotte Russe (a cake topped with whipped cream,) lemon ice, and fruit. As one might expect in the Macdonald home, abundant claret and sherry bottles were cracked open. Also on Thompson's social calendar were dinners or meetings with Sir Alexander Campbell, a fellow Cabinet minister, and Lord Lansdowne, the governor general. Most of his time, however, was spent in his lonely boarding house room or in his office on Parliament Hill. He took occasional walks but spent most of his off-work hours reading.

Although Parliament was not sitting, the Cabinet met a number of times. According to at least one source, the single topic of discussion was Louis Riel and the North-West Rebellion.

A heavy burden fell on the new minister immediately. Only weeks before Thompson's arrival in Ottawa, Riel had been summarily tried in a Regina courtroom before a jury of all-white, Protestant men for leading the Métis and assorted First Nations in the North-West Rebellion. Found guilty, he'd been sentenced to hang. The Macdonald Tories refused to commute or delay the execution. The political fallout of that execution, especially in Quebec and in francophone parts of the country, was disastrous for the Conservative Party. Macdonald was burned in effigy; an estimated thirty thousand people marched in protest to Champs-de-Mars in Montreal; rhetoric in the leading newspapers of the day put the issue front and centre for months. Once a Conservative stronghold, the province of Quebec appeared to be turning its back on the Tories.

In Ontario, the Conservatives faced a problem of a different nature. Among the Orangemen of Ontario, there were many who recoiled at the appointment of a Catholic justice minister. They feared that the demonized Riel might avoid the hangman's noose because of Thompson's influence. It was the contention of many that a fellow Catholic might somehow manipulate the outcome of the trial. That apprehension turned out to be totally unfounded, of course. The rebel leader was led to the gallows on November 16, 1885, without interference from the federal government. Minister Thompson made no move to save his fellow Catholic.

The furor over the execution, however, would not die down. Outrage on both sides of the issue dominated the political life of the Dominion over the winter. It was hoped that the matter could be settled in the House of Commons by spirited but rational debate. When Parliament resumed in the early spring of 1886, the Opposition used their response to the Throne Speech to address the Riel issue. The Liberals could see the opportunity to build up their support in Quebec. Embarrassing the government with what they believed was the inept way the rebellions had been handled, they insisted upon keeping the problem front and centre in Parliament.

The French-Catholic resentment across the country toward the government's actions was exploited by the Opposition Liberals. In the words of Phillipe Landry, the MP from Montmagny, Quebec, "the wonton sacrifice of the life of a French Canadian Catholic upon the altar of sectarian hatred and bigotry" needed to be addressed publicly. The House of Commons became the natural arena for such a discussion.

A heated debate consumed weeks of Parliament's time. The back-and-forth arguments demonstrated quite clearly the opposite positions of the two political parties. At one point, Wilfrid Laurier rose and, adding to Landry's charges, plainly stated that the execution was both "unwarranted and un-justified." Liberal leader Edward Blake, one of the finest orators in Canadian history,[3] argued that the trial had been an unfair one. He pointedly accused the government — but especially Macdonald — of being guilty of a great miscarriage of justice. Hector-Louis Langevin, Macdonald's Quebec lieuten-ant, responded with a tepid speech about the great difficulty the government had faced, how Riel was tried under the law, and how Riel had attacked the authority of the queen. He reiterated the belief that Riel had revolutionized the country, deceiving his own people by "destroying their faith."

Finally, it came Thompson's turn to speak in his role as the minister of justice. The rookie MP had never risen in the House up to that point. With his inaugural speech before the House of Commons on March 20, 1886, he established a reputation as not only a magnificent speaker but as a new leading light in the Conservative Party. Although a virtual unknown outside of Nova Scotia until that moment, Thompson's defence of the government's actions raised his profile and earned him a sterling reputation. According to sources who heard that important address, he spoke quietly, in a courteous manner, and with a low, clear voice. The new justice minister, wrote one observer, possessed a "full, deep and satisfying voice."[4] This was an import-ant thing in an age when eloquence in one's oratory was as much public entertainment as political necessity. He did not use the flowery language that often filled the pages of *Hansard* in those days. Instead, he spoke like a sensible lawyer or judge. It was the first reasonable, convincing argument that the Tories had been able to mount following the death of Riel. His address established Thompson as a force to be reckoned with in the House of Commons. It gave him a national presence outside of his native province.

In a two-hour speech that was remarkable for a newcomer to the House, he stunned the sitting members and the parliamentary gallery. A contem-porary account stated that one could hear a pin drop during the speech, a rarity in that usually raucous chamber. Thompson eviscerated the Liberal arguments. He drew parallels with American abolitionist John Brown and his traitorous behavior; he referenced British prime minister Gladstone and his dealings with the Fenian brotherhood; he quoted the Marquis of Salisbury's contention that treason warranted the death penalty. He even addressed the insanity defence that Riel had turned down. In his summary, Thompson declared that the Indigenous Peoples in Canada needed to know that the federal government was there to dispense not only protection but also punishment. At the conclusion of his speech, he was greeted with wild cheering from the Conservative MPs in the House. He also had the grudging respect of Her Majesty's Loyal Opposition. The subsequent vote saw the Conservatives win 146–42.

One of the first things that he did in his role as justice minister in the wake of the Riel fiasco was to make a month-long trip through the Northwest Territories and on to the Pacific coast. The trek west was meant to be a working holiday. Annie and the children arrived from Halifax early in August, and the family set off for Vancouver in a private railway car. One of the things he was able to do during stopovers, in what is now Saskatchewan and Alberta, was to inspect the prisons in that region. Thompson visited Indigenous communities, where he spoke to the leaders and ordinary citizens, cementing the notion that their federal government was there to protect them and uphold the law.

That autumn, Macdonald exploited Thompson's new-found fame by taking him on a speaking tour of Ontario, shoring up support in that province in order to counteract the votes they'd lost in Quebec. Along with several other notable Conservative members, the prime minister and justice minister boarded Macdonald's private railway car *Jamaica*. They travelled from one end of the province to the other. Their train crisscrossed Ontario, where they were met with huge crowds and torchlight parades in places such as Renfrew, Orillia, Stratford, Sarnia, Peterborough, and Port Hope. To the cheers of their supporters, the Tory speakers roasted Blake, Laurier, Quebec premier Honoré Mercier, and former Conservative Sir Richard Cartwright.

John wrote to Annie about how impressive Macdonald was at charming the crowds. He told her how the prime minister would "shake hands with everyone and kiss all the girls." Thompson played second fiddle to the ebullient Macdonald. The Nova Scotian's speeches were more subdued and undoubtedly less humorous than the prime minister's. The people of the province did see, though, that their new minister of justice was a young man who was as capable as he was articulate.

As in his other positions, Thompson quickly earned a reputation as a steadfast, diligent worker. As he adjusted to life in Ottawa, he looked at the department under his watch. He saw where he could make appropriate changes. The civil servants in his ministry offices knew that their boss demanded that they do their best. Slackers were not to be tolerated. Not that Thompson was authoritarian. He was generous with his praise when accolades were merited. He ran his own department efficiently. The minister (or his deputy minister) read every piece of provincial legislation that was passed in the country and sifted through each one for any sections that were controversial or questionable. Before the end of the year, he ushered legislation through the House that amended both the banking laws and codifications of criminal law in Canada.

Official portraits of Thompson show a pudgy, straight-faced man, not quite middle-aged and with no hint of a smile. Yet family photos, taken in more relaxed circumstances, revealed a man who could grin from ear to ear. It made him far more handsome than the staid studio photos. (One of the photographs shows Mackenzie Bowell also caught grinning widely, something that seems uncharacteristic of snapshots from that time. Or of these particular men.)

Joseph Pope, Macdonald's personal secretary, related how Thompson had a dark, caustic wit. One day, Thompson and the prime minister were asked to witness a new railway contraption set up by an over-zealous inventor. The man frantically ran around a room in the East Block where he'd set up train models but more or less wasted the politicians' valuable time with his ineffective device. When asked what he thought of the eager inventor, Thompson sardonically replied to Sir John A., "He deserves to be killed on a level crossing."

Another time, while dining with governor general and Lady Aberdeen, the dinner party was plagued with a horde of mosquitoes. Lady Aberdeen suggested that the windows be closed. Thompson replied, "Oh, thank you. Pray, don't trouble; I think they are all in now!"

Over the years spent in Ottawa, Thompson became a master of the parliamentary order-paper, where he knew exactly what was going to be discussed, who was going to speak, and what the government's position would be. Macdonald was pleased with his earnest justice minister. He came to rely more and more upon his knowledge, competence, and skills as a parliamentarian. It became obvious to nearly everyone that Thompson was becoming the number two man in the Old Man's ministry.

Thompson was never a sycophant. Although Cabinet secrecy was and is a sacred part of the institution, word got around that Macdonald and his justice minister disagreed at times during Cabinet meetings. The two men argued during the closed sessions over a variety of subjects. Neither backed down, but neither took the other's words personally to the extent that they held spite or grew apart. Indeed, the prime minister's respect for Thompson grew over the few years they worked together. It developed, in part, because of the backbone the younger man displayed.

Thompson never seemed to be in a hurry. As one early biographer noted, he had "like most really great men, a wonderful capacity for work." When he argued the government's case on the many issues that arose, his fellow MPs of the day noted that he possessed a sharp, analytical mind. He made himself thoroughly aware of the minutiae of issues being debated. He was patient and thoughtful before he spoke, whether in private conversations or when rising in the House of Commons. In the press, he was described as being unselfish, devoted, loyal, and a true statesman. Although an eloquent speaker, he rarely tried to convince his listeners by resorting to prejudice or by inflaming passion. Instead, he debated with logic. His intellect was unquestioned. Few men on the other side of the House could match him for those powers. Early on, he took a seat on the front bench alongside Macdonald where more and more often he spoke on the Tory government's behalf.

In the February election of 1887, the Conservatives once again won re-election. Thompson won Antigonish by a mere forty votes over his rival Angus McGillivray. John returned to Ottawa prepared to set his legal mind to a new task, this time in Washington.

In November of that year, Thompson, in the role of legal advisor to the official Canadian delegate Sir Charles Tupper, travelled to Washington to negotiate a treaty with the United States regarding the ongoing fisheries dispute. The two Nova Scotians were part of a joint Canadian-British delegation. Tupper was a physician by training, so he needed the advice of a lawyer to sift through the legal details. Thompson was the obvious choice, although it meant that the nation's justice minister was relegated to advisor status in Washington and New York for several months.

The American demand for fish, disdain for the customary three-mile limit, and seizure of Canadian/British sealing vessels had put an end to the landmark sealing agreement of 1818.[5] As Maritimers, Tupper and Thompson were more than aware of the serious nature of the dispute and argued that Yankee fishermen must honour the three-mile limit for fishing off Canadian shores. They were also tasked with defending the international right of British or Canadian vessels to seize intruding American fishermen. Both men knew the intricate details and demands on both sides of the border. Discussions dragged on from November of 1887 until February of 1888, during which time Thompson submitted many legal opinions. The American lawyers had met their match and were unable to defend against the two irrepressible Maritimers. Finally, thanks in large part to Thompson's diligent work, a treaty meant to clarify the dispute was signed March 15.

Although it was not something the public knew, Thompson was praised by both Canadian and British insiders for the crucial role he played. But, in a more public acknowledgment of his contribution, he was named Knight Commander of the Distinguished Order of St. Michael and St. George "in recognition of his eminent services on the Commission." Ottawa was about to have another Sir John. On the morning in September when he received the honour, Sir John A. Macdonald poked his head into the justice minister's office.

He said, "How is Sir John this morning?"

Thompson looked up from his desk, and, forgetting for an instant that he now had that designation, replied, "You ought to be best able to answer that question."

This turned out to be characteristic of Thompson. Self-effacing, he did not seek the spotlight the way many of his colleagues did. Instead, he seemed to pride himself on his intellectual skill, legal expertise, and his efficient use of time. Serving the public and his party gave him all the satisfaction he needed. Upholding the law was his driving force. Whenever an issue arose that needed someone to sort out the legal details, it was Thompson who could be counted upon to deliver clear, exhaustive arguments that the government could then present in the Commons or apply to legislation. Amid any gathering of lawyers on Parliament Hill, Thompson sat on the top of the heap.

The travel, especially in that frantic year of 1887, never suited Thompson. He complained about it incessantly. Nor did he enjoy living alone in an Ottawa boarding house while his family stayed in their Halifax home.

John and Annie wrote to each other continually whenever they were apart, and their letters provide probably the most interesting writing of any politician in Canadian history, save for the enigmatic diaries of Mackenzie King. The correspondence shows a couple who were totally enthralled with each other. What they wrote is interesting for both its salacious personal nature as well as a political document. John relied on Annie to bolster his ego, to calm his anxieties, and to confirm his opinions. She, in turn, urged him to pursue things he may have been reluctant to do. She chided him for his eccentricities and bad habits. They used numerous nicknames for each other: Pet and Kitten were two. He was "Grunty" and she was "Baby." He teased her with threats to "beat her" if she did not do what he said. In several letters to Annie, Thompson ended his message with the promise to give her a "whipping" or a "warming" when he got home. It is clear, however, that their relationship was a tender one. It is also clear that it was passionate. In one letter, he told her, "I am so fond of you that I want to give you a good licking." He was known to inquire if her menstruation would be over before he arrived back from a trip.

Not all their letters were erotic by any means. They openly communicated their feelings and were not afraid to say what had to be said. In 1886 when John wrote from Ottawa to Annie in Halifax, complaining about how lonely he was without her and their children, she wrote back to chide him, "Don't mope. Go out to dinner with the men. Stop acting like such a poor child out in the cold with such a 'nobody-to-care-for-you tone.'"

In 1888, his family finally joined Thompson in Ottawa. The stress of being apart was somewhat alleviated. Everyone in the family was happy with the reunion. During the years between 1888 and 1894, they rented four different houses in the area near Metcalfe and Lisgar Streets in Ottawa. While prime minister, they lived at 181 Lisgar Street, a red-brick home defined by its curlicue eaves and pale corner brick work.

Thompson regretted that he had never received what he considered a well-rounded education while growing up in Halifax. His law credentials had been earned through an apprenticeship rather than formal schooling. He was determined that his children be brought up differently. The Thompsons had nine children, though only five survived infancy. He sent his two sons, John and Joseph, to the highly regarded Stonyhurst School in Lancashire, England, a Jesuit institution. His two oldest girls, Mary Aloysia ("Babe") and Mary Helena, were sent to an academy for young ladies run by the Religious Order of the Sacred Heart in the northern suburbs of Montreal. He was determined that they learn French properly. His youngest daughter, Frances Alice ("Frankie"), was a constant source of worry for her parents. She suffered from a chronic condition with her hip joints and required a number of expensive operations and treatments. A great deal of the family's money went to pay for treatments for Frankie.

When William Alexander Henry of the Supreme Court of Canada died in May of 1888, there was speculation in the press and on Parliament Hill that Thompson might be named as the replacement. He may have been tempted but ultimately chose to stay the course, remaining a loyal member of Macdonald's Cabinet. His devotion to the Conservative Party often outweighed his personal preferences.

Thompson continued to both promote and defend party policies in his role as justice minister. He was at the centre of the inflamed debate raised by the Jesuit Estates Act. In this case, too, he had to calm the passions of both Catholics and Protestants across the country.

The Jesuits had played a major role during the French regime, i.e., New France. After the English took over in 1763, their considerable land holdings were taken over by the British government. In 1831 Britain gave those lands to the Government of Lower Canada. When the Jesuits returned to Canada in the 1840s, they petitioned the government, demanding either the return of the land or compensation for the confiscation of it. Neither proposal was granted. Finally, after years of negotiations and pleas and, eventually, intervention by the Pope himself, the legislative assembly of Quebec passed the Jesuit Estates Act. It promised a payment to the Jesuits of $160,000, a one-time payment to Laval University of $140,000, and a further $100,000 to be paid to various dioceses in the province. The Orange Order saw the intervention of the Pope as an intrusion on Canadian affairs. They caused such a furor over the matter that a fiery debate took place in the House of Commons, seriously challenging French Catholic-English Protestant relations in the country. Thompson, as justice minister, had been asked to disallow the provincial bill but he'd refused. In the debate, both Macdonald and Laurier supported his stand, and the Orangemen were defeated in the Commons. Thompson was seen as the peaceful arbitrator who'd smoothed the waters.

Macdonald declared, "What would be the consequence of a disallowance? Agitation, a quarrel — a racial and a religious war would be aroused. The best interests of the country would be prejudiced, our credit would be ruined abroad, and our social relations destroyed at home."

One result of the debate was that in order to decrease the tension but recognize the group's increasing political clout, the Conservatives meekly passed an act in 1890 incorporating the Orange Order in Canada.

Thompson often had to either petition or respond to the edicts passed down from the Imperial Privy Council in London. He was in charge of steering landmark copyright legislation through Parliament in 1889. In addition, Sir John A. Macdonald let Thompson take on more and more of the daily speaking to issues in the House of Commons.

The government's mandate drew to a close in early 1891. The Macdonald Conservatives had been in uninterrupted power since 1878 and the regime was a tired one, a fact that was reflected most dramatically by their aging leader. Sir John A. was seventy-six years old, at a time when a man's life expectancy was fifty. Although someone with incredible physical endurance all his life, he was by that time exhausted from the work and often ill from colds or assorted ailments. Thin and beginning to appear frail for the first time in his life, Macdonald nonetheless was determined to keep going. He was nothing if not stubborn. He remained of the opinion that his work was not yet complete. His revered National Policy was under threat as the Liberals pushed for unrestricted reciprocity with the United States. Close ties to the Americans was something anathema to Macdonald. He was determined to lead the fight one last time. In some ways he was handed a political gift in that he could argue rather convincingly, if somewhat disingenuously, that the Liberal policy would lead to annexation with the United States. Tired or not, Sir John A. was determined to lead the party one more time in the fight against the Liberals. "The battle will be better fought under my guidance than under another's," stated the old man.

During the election campaign, Thompson played an important role in echoing the sentiments of his leader. For years, he too had preached about Canada's role in the Empire. In a speech in London in 1890, he had talked about "the strength of the colonies across the sea." He vehemently opposed the preference for American goods. He felt that any independence from Britain was "dangerous." He believed that it was in Canada's interest to maintain the imperial bond on economic and cultural grounds as a nation, separate but forever tied to England.

Contrary to Pope's claim that Macdonald was fighting "alone," Thompson bustled about the country, speaking in different ridings in defence of the Tories' policies. Tupper and Thompson visited their native Nova Scotia to speak on behalf of the Conservatives in the Maritimes.[6] John then returned to Ontario, where he gave a rousing speech in Toronto on February 6. Although his text was absurdly self-deprecating ("Let me say at the outset that I am no orator ..."), his delivery was not only well-received, but it expressed the Tory election platform in clear, precise language that the average voter could easily comprehend. Using the age-old political manoeuvre of appealing to one's wallet, he spoke about how the Liberal reciprocity plan would necessitate a tax increase of fourteen million dollars annually.

It was imperative, of course, that John visit his own riding of Antigonish, where he was facing strong opposition once again from his perennial rival, Angus McGillivray, a former Speaker of the House in Nova Scotia. McGillivray had held the provincial Antigonish seat in several elections, then lost by the narrowest of margins to Thompson in the election of 1887. John — now "Sir John," — remained a popular figure among the farmers and fishermen of the region. To many of them, he was better known as the man who'd been a judge in Halifax before becoming the federal minister of justice. This time Thompson won by a majority of 227 votes.

Catholic Bishop Cameron had once again intervened, stating his preference for the sitting justice minister to weekly church attendees. The bishop's influence did not go unnoticed. The far-away Toronto newspaper the *Globe*, a Liberal organ if ever there was one, made the snide comment that the justice minister had won his seat because of the "strenuous intimidation" of the local bishop.

The old man, the old flag, and the old policy — the captions on the Conservative campaign poster — carried the day. The Tories won the election by another majority and Macdonald remained prime minister. The night of March 5, 1891, his supporters in Kingston celebrated the victory of the only federal representative most of them had ever known in their lifetime.

But all was not well with the new government. The leader was visibly in poor health. The MPs who had been elected were predominantly the same tired crew that had occupied the House of Commons prior to the election. There was a definite lack of new blood to revive the ruling party and give it the boost that it needed to carry on effectively. Corruption plagued the Tories on many fronts. Added to all that internal turmoil was that a sizeable portion of the public had supported Laurier and the Liberals' call for reciprocity with the United States. The Conservative majority had gone from thirty-three in 1886 to only twenty-one in 1891. Forty-seven percent of the public had voted Tory; forty-three percent went Liberal.

Macdonald's new Cabinet was the same one that had sat around the East Block table prior to the election. No new ministers were added. No new ministries were created. Thompson was one of the few young men in a group that included a seventy-six-year-old prime minister, a seventy-year-old leader in the Senate (Abbott), and several others, such as Mackenzie Bowell, who were well into their sixties. How vigorous could one expect such a Cabinet to be?

In the hours after Macdonald's death, Canada's federal government — politicians and bureaucrats alike — were at a loss as to what to do. No one truly knew what was supposed to happen when a prime minister died in office. The Cabinet, most certainly was dissolved but did that mean that those ministers had to go back to their constituencies and run in by-elections? Another serious issue that needed attention was the fact that all money votes from 1890 expired at the end of June, and as justice minister, Thompson would have to determine what should be done for all those federal salaries. Those constitutional questions filled a lot of Thompson's time.

Many of the meetings to argue the merits of the next leader took place in Thompson's home in Ottawa. Many French Canadians in the party were cool to the idea of Abbott succeeding Macdonald. They argued that Abbott had always represented the powerful anglophone big business interests of the province, never fully appreciating the francophone needs and concerns. A small minority felt that Abbott would simply act as a short-term place holder until Charles Tupper could find the appropriate moment to return with his usual flair from London and take over. Thompson himself was not in favour of his fellow Nova Scotian. In a letter to Annie, dated June 9, 1891, he mentioned how angry C.H. Tupper was when his father — "the old tramp" in Thompson's words — was given a cold shoulder by many of the Conservative brass.

Added to the confusion was the rather strange idea held by Lord Stanley, the governor general, that Macdonald had left a will which named his successor. Nothing came of it other than unnecessary delay and futile searches through Earnscliffe desk drawers.

It was eventually Thompson himself, with his cool, legal-minded demeanour who guided the talk toward accepting Abbott. Several times he repeated Macdonald's final conversation about Abbott: "He is your man."

Abbott was indeed chosen as leader and as prime minister and handled the job efficiently. The fact that he had Thompson as his chief, if unofficial deputy, most certainly facilitated the smooth running of the Abbott ministry for the next year. Thompson led in the House, set the agenda for most of the debates, held departmental meetings to clear up issues (such as the supply bills) and it was Thompson who appeared to be the face of the party to the public and to the press. He and Abbott were quite close in their dealings with one another, as from the start Abbott made it clear that he had neither the ambition nor the personality to lead the country for any length of time. The already diligent Thompson took on more and more of the burden of running the country, filling much of the role that should have fallen to Abbott. For example, it was Thompson who appointed two superior court justices in Quebec to a royal commission to investigate alleged misdoings by Sir Adolphe Caron, the Postmaster General.

The refusal of the Conservatives to fully embrace Thompson never was a cause of bitterness for the forty-six-year-old Haligonian. In a typical show of character, he was more concerned with the practicalities of the day-to-day business of Parliament. He truly believed that his time would eventually come when he would take on the leadership, but he solidly and emphatically backed Abbott as Sir John A.'s immediate successor. There appears to have been no bitterness or resentment that his party couldn't accept a convert Catholic as premier. He said to Annie, "their [Conservatives] new Premier will have the devil of a time and yet they fancy it is a vast honour."

When Abbott fell ill in the summer of 1892, even more work fell Thompson's way. The prime minister confided in Thompson, keeping the younger man updated on any health news. None of it was good. Abbott's cancer, untreatable in that time before chemotherapy or radiation, was a death sentence and both men knew it. Abbott was so weakened by his condition that he barely had strength to walk around the lawn of his Montreal home.

Abbott's excursion to England in the autumn of 1892 confirmed what was most feared. The London doctors, in the vernacular of the time, spoke of the poor blood circulation to the brain and that the condition required

Abbott to give up work. Abbott sent a formal letter of resignation that was to be dated "at Thompson's convenience." Even with that ominous message, Thompson demurred.

He suggested the name Mackenzie Bowell.

"Any of us would willingly follow him while we could agree with his policy," Thompson said to Senator W.D. Perley.

Abbott disagreed. While in England, he discussed the succession with Finance Minister George Foster, who was there on business. Foster agreed that it was Thompson who must lead. Abbott pointedly said to Thompson in a letter from London, "The feeling of the party points directly and unmistakedly (sic) to yourself. No other person could hold the party together. All you need is a strong Ontario Protestant."

Although Thompson did, in the end, agree to accept the dual role of leader of the Conservative Party and prime minister, he continued to express reluctance to take on those roles. Quite apart from the fact that he still felt he'd alienate the Ontario Protestants, he initially demurred when encouraged to assume leadership of the party because he had been seriously considering leaving politics. In his seven years in Ottawa, he had managed for the Conservative team a long list of difficult items: the North-West Rebellion, the sealing dispute with the United States, revamping the Criminal Code, the Jesuit Estates question, leading the government in the House of Commons. He was tired of the incessant work, telling daughter Frankie that he regretted not spending more time with family. A letter to daughter Helena contained the exaggerated description of letters piled as high as his head on his desk. A vacancy was coming available on the Supreme Court. That was exceedingly tempting.

As discussed, it was the illness of their leader cutting short his term in office that prompted the entire federal Conservative Party to face the fact that there was only one man suited to take on the reins of power. For a number of the sitting MPs — particularly the Orangemen from Ontario — it meant swallowing their distaste for Thompson's religious conversion. The vacuum at the top had deteriorated to such an extent that the Tories saw no alternative way forward and no other person to take over from the dying Abbott other than Thompson.

Thompson caved-in to the wishes of his colleagues. He was finally confirmed leader of the Conservative Party, the role he should have been allowed to assume upon the death of Macdonald. He must have known that it was right choice for the party and that despite his own humility, he was the right person to lead the country.

"They will find that they cannot do without you," Annie Thompson said to her husband.

On November 23, at a meeting on Parliament Hill, the governor general officially asked Thompson to form a new government. He accepted. Abbott's resignation was announced on November 25. Thompson was formally sworn-in on December 5, 1892.

At age forty-seven, he was considered a vibrant, relatively young man ready to take charge of the country. Physically, he had a John Bull look about him. Portly, with a double chin and prominent stomach that teased the buttons of his suit jacket, he stood apart from many of his colleagues. Despite his overweight condition, his relative youth gave him an appearance of vitality that many of his peers lacked.[7] His close-cropped hair was parted impeccably. What had once been dark brown was turning into the grey of middle-age.

Since he was a Catholic, Thompson's backers felt that he would be much more acceptable to the party members and to the religiously biased voters if he could simultaneously raise the profile of a staunchly Protestant — meaning "Orange" — lieutenant from Ontario in the House of Commons. That had been Abbott's advice to him.

Such a person was already prominent in the party. William Ralph Meredith, the Conservative Opposition leader in the Ontario legislature, fit the bill. Described as "able, eloquent, popular and genial," he was respected by both Liberals and Conservatives. Naming Meredith to the federal Cabinet would assure the electorate that a Protestant viewpoint would figure prominently in government decisions. John Abbott had made an unsuccessful overture to Meredith when selecting his Cabinet, but Meredith turned him down. The reason is unclear. When it came Thompson's turn to offer Meredith a position, a third party interceded. Hearing that Meredith might wind up as Thompson's lieutenant, the Roman Catholic bishop of Kingston intervened on behalf of most other Catholics in Ontario, effectively vetoing the appointment. He, along with other Catholic leaders, opposed the appointment of the Ontario Tory leader as they felt that Meredith's history of attacks on the Catholic separate schools of Ontario disqualified him as an acceptable choice. Meredith had also quarrelled with Sir John A. Macdonald, going so far as to refuse to participate in the 1891 election.[8] Weighing the backroom advice, Thompson decided to look for another candidate altogether.

The new prime minister turned instead to the man who was the grand master of the Orange Order of British America: Nathaniel Clark Wallace, the member of Parliament for York West.

Despite the political optics, it was not a wise choice. Wallace was unapologetically anti-French and anti-Catholic. He had never been all that effective as a member of the government. Thompson, knowing that he was being saddled with a questionable wingman, was hesitant to grant Wallace too much responsibility so he did not name him to an official ministry. No minister of customs was named; instead, Wallace was appointed controller of customs, a position that did not merit a ministry but one that, because of its importance to the federal treasury, would entitle him to attend Cabinet meetings. Thompson would regret the entire business of including Wallace in his inner circle of associates since the man continued to spend so much of his time in political office fomenting racial and religious bigotry. Like far too many of his fellow Ontario MPs, he openly opposed religious separate schools and the rights of Catholics nationwide. At a time when that precise issue was of such national importance, he was not a man to be given much voice on behalf of the governing party. It was his distrust of francophones, more than his anti-Catholic sentiments, that rankled Tory members who did not belong to the Orange Order.

Interestingly, the enigmatic Wallace made a speech in the Toronto area during a by-election in 1892, in which he praised Thompson as a "more than capable leader." Wallace enunciated that there was no reason to object to a Catholic becoming the prime minister of the country. His comments may have shocked his more zealous friends but perhaps did much to convince those radical Orangemen that they should accept Thompson as a fair-minded, exceptional leader for the country. In addition, perhaps Wallace may have felt a little sycophancy might smooth the political waters for himself and his followers.

The Ontario MP was said to have conducted the administrative business of customs competently; however, over the course of his term in office, Thompson was inundated with complaints about Wallace and his openly prejudiced viewpoints.

J.J. Curran, the solicitor general, was not fond of Wallace. He thought that the man was a bigot who bullied his way through life with the support of "unsavoury" Ontario Orangemen. His comment to the prime minister was one that would not be out of place in the twenty-first century. Curran wrote to Thompson that Wallace did not have "the art of making his Yahoos (sic) cheer without putting his foot in it."

Nonetheless, as he took office, Thompson continued to suffer personal attacks from a number of sources regarding his personal religious beliefs. In addition to the "pervert" charges, he was labelled a "Papist" by leading Protestants such as Reverend Dr. Carmen, the superintendent of the Methodist Church of Canada. As a practising Roman Catholic in an era where religious denomination played such a major role in the political zeitgeist, Thompson had to balance his religion with his political decisions. What so many opponents failed to realize was that being the principled man that he was, Thompson would never conceive of favouring his church in any political decisions that needed to be made. His fellow MPs would simply not stand for any such behaviour in any case.

What had really caused the furor over Thompson's religion was the fact that he'd switched from one denomination to another. Laurier, who was born into a Catholic home, never faced the same kind of critical hostility. Because Thompson had *converted* to Catholicism in his twenties, he was somehow open to negative commentary. What is all the more ironic is that Thompson was never one to flaunt or promote his choice of faith. He always considered a man's religion to be a private matter.

Sadly, many Catholics and francophones criticized Thompson from the other side. A few of them felt that the new prime minister would end up kowtowing to the Orange Order. Israel Tarte, one of the leading Liberals from Quebec, accused Thompson of being "the instrument of fanatical Protestants and consequently our worst enemy." The impartial and fair-minded judge in Thompson must have fumed at the accusations that he would ever, based solely on religion, favour one side or the other in decisions. It seemed that the new prime minister could please neither side of the religious disagreements of the day.

The entire issue of religion exasperated Thompson. He was equally perturbed with the comments of Catholics and Protestants. In January of 1893, he said that he felt the greatest problem facing Canada was the "religious susceptibilities" of its people.

The Toronto *Globe*, a paper that was required reading for Liberal Party members, perhaps best addressed the controversial attitude toward Thompson's religion. Its editorials may have helped in a small way to mollify both sides. "It would be a poor tribute to the liberality and intelligence of the Canadian people if it were laid down that a Roman Catholic may not equally with a Protestant aspire to the highest office ... and any attempt to arouse sectarian prejudice over his appointment will not make for the dignity of Canadian politics or the welfare of the country."

As Thompson moved into the prime minister's office, he named a Cabinet that he hoped would streamline the functioning of the Privy Council. For instance, he created a new Ministry of Solicitor General to ease the load on the justice minister. The Department of Customs now became the Department of Trade and Commerce. Mackenzie Bowell, a man long familiar with trade issues was named as the new minister. Although not inspiring, Bowell was a slugger, a man with a reputation for working long hours and seeing projects through to completion. (Wallace, rather than having his own ministry, would have to answer to Bowell.) Many of Abbott's appointees remained in place: Foster at Finance, Caron as Postmaster-General, Charles Hibbert Tupper at Marine and Fisheries, and John Haggart at Railways and Canals.

All did not go smoothly. The Tory ranks were not overflowing with men of talent. The party had nominated and elected a slate of men who were comfortable, complacent, and owed their seats in the Commons to having ridden the coattails of John A. Macdonald.

Thompson felt that the previous minister of agriculture, John Carling, should retire. Carling had held the key riding of London, Ontario for many years and was popular with his constituents. He was not popular in the Conservative caucus, however. He reputedly had no friends in Ottawa. A rich man who was overly sensitive to any sort of criticism, he would prove difficult to exclude from the Cabinet. Thompson was forced to handle the man with kid gloves, using all the tact that he could muster. Thompson wrote to a friend calling his decision about Carling "this horrible responsibility."

Carling was incensed at the prospect of being publicly embarrassed if stripped of such an important role. Even when offered a seat in the Senate, he responded with notable fury. He'd already been a senator briefly in 1891 but had resigned to run once more in the election of that year, winning the seat in London for the Tories. He'd also been offered the lieutenant governorship of Ontario, but Abbott had changed his mind about that, feeling that the Conservatives could not risk losing the western Ontario London riding.

After Thompson's suggestion that instead of joining the Cabinet he could, instead, move to the Senate, Carling hurriedly took the train back to London and fired up his supporters in southwestern Ontario, relating the tale of his humiliation. A delegation set out for Ottawa within days, where they pleaded their case before the new prime minister. In fact, Carling made such a fuss that the governor general had to intercede on Thompson's behalf. A knighthood was promised by Lord Stanley and the London brewer-turned-politician was finally named to Cabinet but as a minister without portfolio. Carling held a grudge against Thompson for having been "disgraced and maligned."

Carling and Wallace were not the only thorns in Thompson's side. All political leaders have to deal with individuals who might share party affiliation but have opinions that deviate from the official platform. Jealousy and ambition make relationships uncomfortable at times. For Thompson, it was a lawyer from Barrie, Ontario, named Dalton McCarthy who proved to be his greatest problem.

McCarthy had been first elected to Ottawa in 1878. A renowned court-room lawyer — he'd defended Emily Stowe in her landmark 1879 abortion trial — he was highly regarded for his legal mind.[9] He was quick to form a bond with Sir John A. Macdonald, acting as the prime minister's advisor on constitutional issues. Macdonald, however, may have been reticent to promote McCarthy too much, as the Simcoe North MP was a virulent Orangeman, much opposed to French and Catholic rights across the country at a time when the Conservatives relied on the support of exactly those voters. When Thompson arrived in Ottawa in 1885, he supplanted McCarthy as the leading legal mind in the government. This was a significant cause of resentment for McCarthy.

The two men, at first, worked co-operatively on government business, but as the years went by, they drifted further and further apart. On issues such as the North-West Rebellion and the Jesuit Estates dispute, Thompson was a politician who advocated for fairness on the issues of race, religion, and language. McCarthy chose a different path. McCarthy spoke in a more divisive tone, asking his Ontario audiences to consider — repudiate even — what he saw as French Canadian bias in federal politics. Thompson defended the rights of the Roman Catholic religion; McCarthy attacked the Catholic Church and its influence in Quebec. The Ontario MP's rhetoric became increasingly menacing. He associated himself with a group called the Protestant Protective Association. He became less and less diplomatic in what became bombastic speeches. In 1889 he gave one particularly odious address at Stayner, Ontario, where he openly stated, "now is the time when the ballot box will decide this great question before the people, and if that does not supply the remedy in this generation, bayonets will supply it in the next."

Thompson threw himself into the role of prime minister with unstinting energy. He set an example that few could match. It had been that way when he worked as a counsellor in Halifax, then as a member of the legislature, then as a judge. He was known to toil into the early hours of morning after the other parliamentarians and bureaucrats had long gone home. Well after midnight, he would still be sorting through papers, writing memos, authorizing agenda, and looking into the minutiae of any number of topics. A brief carriage ride would take him home through the gaslit streets of Ottawa to his house on Metcalfe Street. After a brief night's sleep, he returned to Parliament Hill before many people had returned to their tasks in the morning.

At a time when women did not yet have the franchise, Thompson showed foresight as well as genuine concern that the vote eventually be given to the female half of the country's population. At a midwinter speech in Toronto, he offered an opinion about women being granted the vote. "The Conservative Party believes that the influence of women in the politics of the country is always for good. I think, therefore, that there is a probability of the franchise being extended to women on the same property qualifications as men." It was an enlightened policy in so many ways, but as with many noble proposals put forward by sitting politicians, it came to nothing during his lifetime. Women did not get to vote in federal elections until the First World War and even later for women in Quebec — 1940.[10]

The tenor of the times pushed religious and language issues to the forefront of both provincial and federal politics. Controversy over separate schools for Protestants and Catholics was nothing new. George Brown had railed against a separate Catholic system in what became Ontario. The same matter had arisen in other jurisdictions as well. None figured as prominently as in Manitoba, a province that had become the problem child for the Tory governments of Macdonald, Abbott, and now Thompson.

Manitoba had become a province in 1870 at a time when French-speaking Roman Catholics were about equal in number to the Protestants. The Métis, who held to the language and religion of their French ancestors, were on equal footing with the predominantly Scottish Protestants who'd migrated to the prairie region. Manitobans had been guaranteed state-supported separate schools. But, as the postage-stamp-shaped province grew in physical size and population, the English-speaking Protestants became the majority. A movement in the late 1880s called for an end to provincial funding for the separate school system. In 1890 Premier Thomas

Greenway's Liberal government passed the Public Schools Act. It removed the funding of denominational schools and, instead, established one system of non-sectarian schools funded by provincial tax dollars. At the same time, the legislature passed a law that made English the only official language of the province. The two acts caused great consternation, not only in the province but nationally. Both pieces of legislation contravened not only the intent but also the specific provisions of the Manitoba Act of 1870, the very law that had created the province. In that legislation, both the French and Catholics had been assured of rights and privileges which Greenway was now taking away.

Two high-profile lawsuits followed.

It first fell to Thompson, while he was justice minister in 1891, to review and assess the government's options concerning the Manitoba Schools Question. Ever the judge, Thompson spent a great deal of time assessing the legalities of provincial legislation regarding education, a provincial responsibility under the British North America Act. His conclusion, presented in a report to the House of Commons, was to declare that it would be wiser to have the courts decide the issue rather than have the federal government intercede.

The appeals following the first lawsuit went all the way to the Supreme Court of Canada. It declared that the 1890 Act conflicted with section 22 of the 1870 Manitoba Act. The court ruled in October of 1891 that the Greenway act was *ultra vires*, just as Thompson had suspected.[11]

But at that time, the Judicial Committee of the Privy Council in Britain was the highest court in the British Empire with power to overrule the Supreme Court of Canada. The City of Winnipeg appealed to the Privy Council. That "tribunal of last resort" overturned the decision of the Canadian Supreme Court. From across the sea, the London lawmakers analyzed the 1870 Manitoba Act and concluded that it had not guaranteed funding for denominational schools. It had guaranteed religious groups the right to establish their own schools, but it had not stipulated that they must fund them without public tax money.

The Manitoba Schools Question led to even deeper division within the Tory caucus. Dalton McCarthy, along with his fellow Orange Order members, openly advocated for the anti-French, anti-Catholic side, while Thompson called for tolerance and justice. McCarthy, rather than tone down his language or hide his prejudice, broke with his colleagues. When Thompson formed his Cabinet in the winter of 1892, McCarthy was notably absent from it. He was bitter that he had not been included — it even seemed to irk him that he had not even been consulted in the Cabinet's formation. It was a final straw and drove McCarthy out of the Tory Party.

McCarthy aired his complaints in a public speech of January 27, 1893. He stated, "It is not so much a question of policy that has driven me out of the ranks. It is the first time since I have been in public life that I have been ignored in the formation of a new Government. If I cannot be taken into the confidence of the councils of my party, it is time to assert my independence." McCarthy continued to complain publicly, spending the better part of that year speaking at different venues in Ontario, airing his grievances and further distancing himself from his former Tory colleagues.

The Manitoba Schools issue dragged on without resolution. In early 1894, Thompson, Mackenzie Bowell, and J.A. Chapleau sat as a subcommittee of Cabinet to hear the arguments put forward by the City of Winnipeg. The men listened to a delegation from the city's lawyer. They then invited the Government of Manitoba to argue its case. Greenway refused. The provincial government considered the issue settled, not open to discussion.

The second suit launched in 1894 — *Brophy v. the Attorney General of Manitoba* — arose from the Tories' desire to settle the matter in a way that did not ignore the British Privy Council's decision. The federal government sent the issue back to the Canadian Supreme Court as a "reference question," asking about the constitutionality of legislation. Once again, the matter was turned over to the Judicial Committee of the Privy Council in London and once again that "court" overturned the Canadian Supreme Court's decision.

The contentious battle went on for years. It took up a great deal of time in both houses of Parliament, required the considerable attention of five prime ministers, and caused internal strife in both the Liberal and Tory parties. It would ultimately take a compromise between Premier Greenway and Wilfrid Laurier, when he eventually became prime minister, to finally resolve the situation. But the fallout from the controversy affected every premier from Macdonald to Laurier.

The legislation and the actions of the courts had long-term implications. With French no longer an official language, its usage in the province of Manitoba declined noticeably. The French population of the country, especially in Quebec, felt marginalized if not mistreated. The issue was a major reason for the growth of French Canadian nationalism.

On the international front, Thompson took office at a time when the relationship between Canada and the United States was at a low point. The country was in the midst of what is now called an economic downturn. Protectionism in the United States dominated the talks between the North American neighbours. The Liberal Opposition believed in stronger ties with the Americans and less dependency on Britain. More and more Canadians, especially those employed in manufacturing, seemed to see the merits of the Liberal policy.

Akin to his mentor, John A. Macdonald, Thompson held strong opinions regarding the Americans. Both men distrusted the American attitude toward Canada and were opposed to many of its actions. Both suspected the motives of American politicians. While anxious to be cooperative with the United States, the prime minister felt that Canada should stand firm in any negotiations. Over the years, he'd had first-hand experience in negotiations during the Bering Sea dispute and in the offshore fisheries disputes. He knew that the Americans were strong-willed in any kind of international bargaining, so in turn, he felt it necessary that Canadian diplomats be equally resolute. American protectionism was not in Canada's best interest, no matter how sweet a deal reciprocity appeared to be. When it came to the matter of a trade pact, it was obvious that the American goal was to open markets in Canada for the output of their factories and businesses. Thompson was determined that Canada's burgeoning industries be protected. He also maintained that the current transatlantic trade with Britain should not be undermined by any legislated treaty with America.

Both Abbott and Thompson had similar intentions when they came into office: they both wished to continue the policy that the Conservatives had developed during the party's years under Macdonald. The so-called National

Policy had kept the party in power. That policy saw them elected one last time under Sir John A. as recently as 1891. Its promotion of protective tariffs had kept the country economically viable. The building of the transcontinental railway could be viewed as having successfully completed one of its three key principles. The third tenet of the National Policy was promoting immigration. More specifically, the Conservatives wanted to foster immigration to the western parts of Canada. That remained a work in progress.

Thompson began speaking at rallies and gatherings around Ontario shortly after taking office. Many in the audience had never seen nor heard the country's leader before. His first speeches as prime minister took place in January of 1893. One was at a Board of Trade dinner; the second was a more public event before a crowd of over three thousand people at a hall rented by the Young Men's Liberal-Conservative Association. He strutted confidently to the dais at the Toronto Auditorium to give a rousing speech that set the tone for where he saw the country going. Filled with confidence, Thompson stirred the partisan crowd with his lofty talk. As a Canadian nationalist, he wrestled, as did many in his audience, with pressing for too much independence as a nation. He could not help himself from espousing the benefits of the British Empire connection. Thompson speculated that perhaps Canada could become more independent from England once her population reached something close to *fifty* million people!

A short tour of Ontario to shore up support for his government was something that seemed important to Thompson. It was crucial that he make himself a more visible, authentic figure. As his train made frequent stops in cities such as Belleville and Berlin (Kitchener,) the prime minister repeated his message to audiences. At Stratford, an estimated crowd of ten thousand people packed the local skating rink to hear their new leader. Similarly, the town of Walkerton was overwhelmed when Thompson's train made its stop there.

His listeners were treated to Thompson's measured delivery. His speeches were, of course, partisan in nature. He spoke to great applause of the achievements of Macdonald and the Conservatives' National Policy over the years. His talk promoted the benefits of the imperial connection. Canada, he said, was a ship that carried the British flag. He talked about the terrible economic crash that had hit the United States, then he tied that to the reciprocity policies of the Liberal Party. He related how the Canadian economy was being relatively well-managed, its banks secure, its industries growing, and its farms continuing to produce and deliver. He waded into the debate over the Manitoba Schools Question, bravely facing the issue of religious bias openly.

The tour was seen as a great success for the prime minister. At the banquets, train stations, and community halls, crowds cheered enthusiastically. His message was delivered in terms that the voters of Ontario could understand. At a time when "getting the message out" was difficult, he managed to bring his policies to the people quite effectively.

The prime minister returned to Ottawa by train. He settled into his office where he wrote and dictated plans for the upcoming session of Parliament, which was set to open on January 26. The expectations of the new premier were high. Even the Opposition expressed high regard for the young man from Halifax. Wilfrid Laurier, the Liberal leader rose in the House of Commons on the January 30 to graciously praise Thompson: "There has been no public man in Canada at any time whose advancement has been so rapid. He came into this House at a comparatively recent date, preceded by a high reputation for ability, which he had earned in his own Province, which led everybody, friends and opponents alike to expect a great deal from him, and that expectation has been realized since he entered this House."

In March, leaving Foster in charge of proceedings in the House, the prime minister boarded a steamer headed across the Atlantic. He was about to take part in an international tribunal aimed at settling once and for all the dispute between Canada and the United States over seal hunting in the Bering Sea. The relationship with England remained one of Mother Country and quasi-independent state. On every international issue, British officials watched over Canada's envoys or included them in talks as part of the Empire's delegation, often more out of courtesy than respect. As he took over the job of prime minister, Thompson had already experienced first-hand the lack of deference Canada faced when dealing one-to-one with its southern neighbour. He'd also witnessed the paternalistic attitude that was shown by diplomats from Britain.

At the meetings held in Paris, Thompson was one of the two British judges. There were two representatives from the United States and three Europeans with the chair being a French judge. (Interestingly, no Russian delegates attended the meeting nor did the Russians seem to figure in any of the dispute despite their proximity to the contentious region.) No one could argue with including the Canadian prime minister as one of the judges. It was in large part a show of respect others had for Thompson's legal background. The discussions, according to Thompson's own notes, involved much attention to international legal precedence.

While the days were filled with tedious legal arguments, the evenings were a different matter. The French hosts lavished the men with every luxury and entertainment possible. A number of receptions built a camaraderie among the judges, which fostered cooperation in achieving a successful outcome. Thompson, with his epicurean tastes in fine dining was in his element. Annie was able to attend a few of the receptions, but she and daughter Frankie, their child with major health issues, spent most of their time on a pilgrimage to Lourdes Cathedral, in the vain hope that the girl could find some relief.

In the end, the arbitration favoured Britain's — and therefore Canada's — arguments. The Americans were told to pay indemnities to the Canadian sealers whose boats or cargoes had been seized. Licenses were required of the hunters. Nets and firearms were prohibited. A hunting season was set, and specific areas were designated to be off-limits. Within a few years, the two nations were comfortable with sharing the ample resources of the area.

The proceedings of the tribunal kept the prime minister away from Canada until August. He was greeted warmly at Quebec City upon his arrival. True to character, though, Thompson demurred to C.H. Tupper, his minister of fisheries, who'd in fact been the official Canadian representative at the talks, Thompson having played the role of independent arbiter. The prime minister stood back and allowed the crowds in Quebec and Montreal to cheer Tupper. Such was C.H.'s contribution that he was granted a knighthood shortly after his return to Ottawa. Laurier would later, contrary to his January praise, accuse Thompson of "brag and bluster" about the Paris accord.

Within days of his return from the Paris talks, Thompson had the honour of greeting the new governor general, Lord Aberdeen, upon his arrival at Quebec City. The prime minister had met Lord and Lady Aberdeen in 1891 during a trip the couple made to Canada. Lady Aberdeen had been greatly impressed by Thompson's manner and a deep friendship began between the vice-regal couple and the Thompsons. In a biography that was hastily written within a year of Thompson's death, it was Lord Aberdeen who wrote the flowery preface to the book.

There is some confusion about how well set Thompson was financially at this point in his life. The family seemed to lead a rather comfortable existence, but on the other hand Thompson claimed to have little money. In early 1894, they rented a home at 276 Somerset Street in the Sandy Hill section of Ottawa. Apparently, they had to rent because they could not afford the asking sale price of eleven thousand dollars. As well, after his death, Annie is said to have needed to hold fundraising events to pay for Thompson's funeral. However, Thompson's wife took a solo vacation in England. Such a trip in the 1890s was not something that the average person could afford. It was only the well-to-do elite who could afford transatlantic excursions. Sending their boys to private school in England and a daughter to an exclusive academy in France was a priority for the Thompsons but an extravagance affordable for only few people in Canada at the time.

At home, the couple often hosted dinners for as many as twenty or thirty people, usually politicians and their wives. Their social calendar was so packed that Annie described her evenings as "a whirlwind." The couple did have two servants to help, but it seems that their help wasn't sufficient to meet the family's needs, and so Annie did all the cooking for those elaborate dinners. Overall, the family fortunes were not as bleak as some were led to believe.

Of course, such social activities occupied only a tiny fraction of the prime minister's time. Thompson immersed himself in day-to-day parliamentary work. Thompson's belief in the vital importance of Canada's connection to England coloured many of his decisions as he attempted to move forward, governing the country. Thompson felt that Canada benefitted as part of the larger British Empire. The protection afforded by what was then the world's largest empire gave him some solace in light of what he saw as American expansionism. He urged people to consider that Canada should favour British products and imports, especially vis-à-vis American trade. Not only did he favour preferred trade with Great Britain, Thompson believed that it was in Canada's best interests to develop stronger ties to the other colonies in the British Empire. His promotion of CPR steamship traffic between Vancouver and Sydney, Australia followed from this. It was a Tory policy that resonated with a large percentage of the populace. The idea dominated the national economic debates during that last decade of the nineteenth century.

As he promoted keeping a strong British connection, the prime minister kept an eye on the giant neighbour to the south, whose aggressive approach to annexing territories in the Pacific was alarming. During one speech he made in Toronto, Thompson said, "Every man who is a Canadian at heart feels that this country ought to be a nation, will be a nation, and, please God, we shall help to make it a nation; but ... we do not desire that it shall be a separate nation, but that it will be a nation in itself, forming a bulwark to the British Empire, whose traditions we admire, whose protection we enjoy, and who has given to this country the fullest degree the right and the power of self-government." The Mother Country's protection was a theme that often came up in Thompson's thoughts. His experience in dealing with the United States during the Bering Sea dispute was, in his mind, proof that as an independent nation, without Britain's backing, Canada would have been bullied in any negotiations. The prime minister acknowledged that a country of five million stood little chance of holding its own in dealing with a nation whose population was close to sixty million.

As if to announce the Canadian pro-Empire thinking, Ottawa played host to an imperial conference in June of 1894. Discussions with English representatives and diplomats from the other countries in the Empire — Australia, New Zealand, South Africa, India — was meant to promote a network of trade relationships around the globe, especially in what was then called "the East." A noble undertaking, it did little to improve the economic fortunes of the participants but did much to build cohesion within the wider Empire. Mackenzie Bowell led Canada in the talks; Sir Sandford Fleming,[12] with his keen interest in transcontinental cable communication, was also part of that delegation. Thompson greeted the international participants by quoting Lady Aberdeen. "You are as welcome as sunshine."

Throughout his tenure, Thompson had reason to address several of the other concerns of the day. Two of the major debates taking place not just in Canada but across North America involved the issues of temperance and universal suffrage.

During the nineteenth century, alcohol had taken a terrible toll especially in the poorer sections of the nation's cities. The abuses and suffering caused by over indulgence had become a serious problem. Many of the country's religious leaders had taken up a call to ban liquor or at the very least limit its availability. Temperance groups became increasingly vocal in their calls for government action.

The prime minister could not avoid speaking on the matter. "If prohibition can be adopted and enforced in this country, I am in sympathy with that movement," he stated during a speech in September of 1893. Yet he deftly avoided committing to changing the laws regarding the sale or consumption of liquor. He met with temperance delegations and heard their arguments, but then he did what politicians so often do: he handed the concern off for others to decide. A royal commission was set up to study the matter; the courts were asked to study the matter; the provinces were asked to study the matter. He knew, as did others across the country, that booze was a big business and votes would be won or lost whichever way the government acted.

Thompson addressed the burgeoning issue of women's suffrage when speaking at Tara, Ontario, in 1894. "We look forward to it as one of the aims which are to be accomplished in the public life of Canada," he said. "I think, therefore, that there is a probability of the franchise being extended to women on the same property qualifications as men." The issue was contentious at that time, so his stance was as brave as it was radical.

In August of 1894, Thompson and his family took what was an all-too-seldom occurrence. They went to Muskoka for a holiday. But even relaxing at a lakeside resort near Port Carling, Ontario, the prime minister could not avoid the call of politics. Mid-vacation, he left cottage country to travel south to Toronto.

He attended a couple of events there — the inspection of construction work on Toronto Island and the opening of the Toronto Industrial Exhibition. With every speech he made, he referenced the youthful growth of Canada as a commercial nation. Pointedly, he continued to speak about the imperial connection. He reiterated how Canada needed to not only preserve but also promote ties to Britain. The speeches were met with enthusiastic cheers from crowds who were in complete agreement with that policy.

Although Parliament was still enjoying its summer recess, the prime minister kept busy travelling the country that late summer and early fall. He went to his home province to be part of a ceremony honouring one hundred and twenty-five miners who'd been tragically killed in an accident at Springhill, Nova Scotia.

Then it was back to Toronto, where on October 13, he dedicated a statue of Sir John A. Macdonald at Queen's Park, the province's legislative assembly. An estimated crowd of nearly forty thousand people gathered on the front lawn of the legislature. Troops and bands marched; school children waved tiny Union Jacks; dignitaries from all levels of government spoke; even the sculptor was given a few moments at the podium. (As mentioned in the previous chapter, Thompson took this opportunity to praise Sir John Abbott during this speech.)

It turned out to be Thompson's final public speaking appearance. His comments were brief in comparison to those of several of the other politicians. Thompson once again spoke of how it was in Canada's best interests to remain under the protective wing of Britain, an independent country very much part of a larger union. He reiterated that this was what Macdonald had both stated and practised during his time as the country's long-serving prime minister.

Thompson concluded, "May the statue speak of one who was great because he loved Canada much, and loved and served his Empire well."

The prime minister returned to Ottawa by train. He began to plan for a trip abroad. Word had come from England that Sir John was to be made a member of the Imperial Privy Council. He was to be invested in a special ceremony at Windsor Castle with none other than Queen Victoria herself presiding. Thompson planned to also journey on to Paris, where his daughter Helena was to start her studies at a private girls' school. It was the general opinion around the Thompson home that the time away from Ottawa would give the prime minister a bit of respite from his hectic schedule. The previous session of Parliament had been a particularly long and busy one.

As mentioned, Thompson was a "stout" man. He was also dangerously unhealthy. By 1894 he was more than fifty pounds overweight. The frenetic pace that he set as an active politician coupled with little in the way of exercise was not a healthy combination. He usually walked from his home to the Parliament Buildings in downtown Ottawa but otherwise engaged in no other form of physical exercise.

Even prior to his Muskoka holiday, he'd been plagued by several indicators of what we now would recognize as severe heart disease. There was no medication to treat his angina, heart palpitations, or the occasional pains in his left arm, but his doctors in Ottawa recognized the symptoms of heart disease and related kidney complications. Their recommendation was that he take time off work and spend the winter in "some warm country." Not much else could be done for a heart patient at the time. Thompson's response to his physicians was honest and characteristic of the man. He told them that their course of action would be so stressful and cause him so much worry that the cure would be worse than the disease. The doctors — and their patient — arrived at a compromise solution. The prime minister agreed that he would cut down on official business while away in Europe.

When advised that he should exercise more, the prime minister told a friend, "Exercise! Why the days are not long enough for all the work I have to do. About all the exercise I can get is the walk from my house up to the Hill and back again. I go up Elgin one morning and the next morning, to circumvent Henry Wentworth Monk, I go up Metcalfe Street."[13]

Was Thompson aware of the seriousness of his health situation? Although he kept his health issues largely to himself, he seemed to have had a premonition that he shared with Lady Aberdeen. In a letter to her on October 27, he mentioned the burdens of work. He concluded with the statement, "There is an end to the burdens which the greatest energy and the strongest constitution can bear. I did not think this a few months ago, but I found it out before the last Session was over and I see it now. Sometimes the warning to stop and rest comes very suddenly and sternly."

On October 30, the prime minister said a final goodbye to Annie, who was not going, as the couple felt they could not afford another overseas trip, and boarded a train for New York City. His travelling companions included daughter Helena and Senator William Eli Sanford, who was accompanying his daughter to the same Paris school. The little group arrived in London on November 7. Because he'd continued to feel the effects of his heart condition, Thompson consulted with a prominent London physician, Sir Russell Reynolds, who concurred with his Canadian colleagues, recommending the same treatment: rest in a warm climate.

The prime minister took the advice to some degree. The four Canadians set out for a tour of France and Italy. It turned out to be a rather hectic one. They visited Nice, Monaco, Genoa, Rome, Milan, Florence, and Venice before travelling back to Paris, where the young ladies settled into their boarding school. Several times during the trip Thompson suffered from shortness of breath. With the three-week tour concluded and Helena in her new quarters, Thompson spent a sleepless night travelling overnight from

Paris to London so that he could keep an early morning appointment in London with Lord Ripon, the British secretary of state for the colonies.

At some point during his visit to England, Thompson planned to meet with former prime minister of Britain William Gladstone. The old man was dying of cancer at the time and living out his final days at Hawarden Castle, his home in Wales. Although a Liberal and a man who was choosy about his visitors, he had consented to meet the young Canadian prime minister, at the recommendation of Lord and Lady Aberdeen. Unfortunately, the meeting never took place.

On December 11 John attended a meeting of the Royal Colonial Institute. An independent, non-government group, it met to discuss issues surrounding the British Empire. Their substantial archive dealt with imperial military matters, global exploration, and laws that governed Britain's overseas possessions. Distinguished British or Commonwealth figures chaired the meetings and gave speeches, which were in turn published as essays for members to read.

Canada's high commissioner to Britain, Sir Charles Tupper, was the chair of the particular meeting that Thompson attended. Modest as ever, the prime minister of Canada sat near the back of the meeting hall. His presence did not go unrecognized, however. Sir Charles called him forward to bring greetings from Canada. Thompson rose and came to the front of the room where he gave a cursory greeting and a message from the Empire's largest member state. He spoke of the success of the recent Imperial conference in Ottawa and his hopes for trade with other member countries of the far-flung Empire. Out of breath, it was apparent to all in attendance that the prime minister was not well.[14]

The next day, he was driven to Windsor Castle outside the city of London proper. According to Tupper, he was in good spirits, looking forward to his dinner with the queen. Thompson complained of feeling unwell when he arrived, but nothing was going to interfere with the honour he was about to receive. As arranged, at 1:30 p.m. the queen formally invited Sir John Sparrow Thompson to become a member of her Majesty's Privy Council. He signed his name to the official roll and then was ushered out of the room.

Accompanied by Lord Breadalbane, John made his way to what was called the "luncheon room." Thompson took his designated seat at the table. He suddenly fell over, obviously having fainted. Breadalbane and a servant took him to a window and, after a shot of brandy, the prime minister appeared to recover. Clearly embarrassed, he said to Breadalbane, "It seems so weak and foolish to faint like this." After a few moments rest, the two men returned to the luncheon room and sat down to eat. Thompson mentioned, ever so casually, that he'd also had some chest pain. He then suddenly keeled over into the lap of the queen's physician, Dr. Reid.

He was dead at fifty of a massive heart attack.

Queen Victoria, moved by the death of a man who had died too young, as had her beloved Prince Albert, took charge in the following hours. Under her orders, Thompson's body was placed in a coffin and moved to a room in the Clarence Tower.

The queen then cabled Mrs. Thompson.

"It is impossible for me to say how deeply grieved I am at the terrible occurrence which took place here today, and how very truly I sympathize with you in your deep affliction."

When notified that the late prime minister was a Roman Catholic, she ordered a requiem Mass. She insisted that the members of the royal family attend. The body was then taken to the Marble Hall, where it lay in state. The next morning, Victoria herself placed a memorial wreath on the casket. A sombre parade followed the hearse to the local train station for the trip to the gothic Roman Catholic Church of St. James in Spanish Place, in the Marylebone district of central London. Lord Tennyson, Cecil Rhodes, and Charles Tupper all paid their respects. The body lay in state for several days prior to a state funeral. Then, following a twenty-one-gun salute, the funeral train carried the late prime minister's casket past silent crowds and military officers. Queen Victoria granted the rare honour of having the body sent back to Canada aboard a British man-of-war, the *Blenheim*. The warship was painted black as a sign of mourning. Thompson's daughter and Senator Sanford accompanied the body. As the *Blenheim* set sail, Nelson's famous flagship, *Victory* — permanently moored at Portsmouth — discharged its guns as a salute to the late Canadian leader.

Lord and Lady Aberdeen arranged to be in Halifax to receive the casket bearing their friend when the *Blenheim* arrived on New Year's Day. The actual funeral was scheduled for three days later. Annie Thompson and her children had asked that there not be great black coverings, especially on the funeral carriage that took Thompson's body through the Halifax streets, but the decorating had been done by the time they arrived in the Nova Scotia capital. The entire city seemed to be cloaked in mourning black.

The funeral rituals were elaborately staged. Bishop Cameron from Antigonish conducted the requiem Mass at St. Mary's Cathedral. The cortege was comprised of not only the family members but also representatives from the government, the police, and the military. Five lieutenant governors marched, as did an entire row of bishops and archbishops. They passed packed crowds of black-clad Haligonians, each one there to pay respects, many with tears in their eyes. The burial took place at Holy Cross Cemetery in Halifax. The funeral itself was the subject of a book, and the transcript of the funeral service was widely published.

The entire nation was in shock at the sudden, unexpected death of the relatively young and vital prime minister. Newspapers across the country — Conservative, Liberal, independent — were unambiguous in their praise of Thompson. Former governors general, British nobles, Canadian universities and clubs sent their condolence messages to either Mrs. Thompson or to associates, such as Charles Tupper, expressing sorrow at the death of the prime minister. Even bitter rivals such as Sir Richard Cartwright and Oliver Mowat had noble, dignified comments to make.

The praise was effusive without exception. Lady Aberdeen wrote a eulogy that was published in New York's *Outlook* magazine. She mentioned that Thompson's calm, impassive exterior masked a "volcanic" passion. She also praised his "scrupulous honesty and incorruptibility."

At the time of his death, Thompson was far from being a rich man. For someone who'd been a successful lawyer and then a respected judge, he left his family with little in the way of financial security. His generous nature had been partly responsible. A great deal of money was spent on Frankie's health care. His estate totalled slightly less than ten thousand dollars. When the details became known, several family friends began a campaign to raise funds for Annie Thompson and her children. Donald Smith wired five thousand dollars from England. Many of the Cabinet members gave five hundred dollars each. Even Liberal rival Richard Cartwright gave one hundred dollars. With public donations, eventually the amount given to Annie exceeded twenty-five thousand dollars.

Thompson's unfortunate legacy is that he died too young, never fulfilling the promise that he had brought to the nation's highest office. There were no doubts about his honesty, as he was never touched by any scandal or even rumour of wrongdoing. His intellect was unequalled by anyone within the Conservative Party. Outside of the party, only Blake and Laurier could be considered his match. His skill as an orator, despite his self-deprecation, was also unmatched by most of his rivals or members of his own party. His devotion as a family man was unquestioned. In a profession where too often the egoists and grifters jostled for attention, he stood well apart from the crowd. A thoroughly decent, moral, and dedicated man, he was a template for the ideal minister of the Crown and indeed, as prime minister of the country.

He was prime minister for precisely two years and one week.

Chapter Four

◇

Sir Mackenzie Bowell:
The Accidental Prime Minister

THE WHITE-HAIRED BUT SPRIGHTLY MAN with the carefully coiffed beard to match his hair sat in his office at the Department of Trade and Commerce the morning of December 12, 1894. He and Finance Minister George Foster were chatting about that day's agenda for the House of Commons. When an ashen-faced aide barged into his office holding a telegram, Bowell had no inkling of what had happened hours before in London, England. The cable was shocking. Reading the telegram, his face went nearly as white as his snowy beard.

"11:36 a.m., Dec.12, 1894. Reported from Windsor Castle that Sir John Thompson expired after meeting of privy council...."

At first, Bowell refused to believe it.

"It is mere newspaper rumour," he said flatly to Foster.

The previous year, there had been a false report about Thompson's demise while he'd been in Paris. Rumour and pure fabrication often sold newspapers. No one knew better than the crotchety owner of the local Belleville daily. Surely, he thought, this was what was happening once again.

Within half an hour, however, an official from the CPR in Montreal confirmed the sad news. Charles Tupper had sent a message to validate the story. Bowell laid the telegrams on his desk and began to cry. The two men had been more than simply colleagues. Bowell had visited the prime minister at his Muskoka retreat the previous summer.

The sudden, unexpected death of Sir John Sparrow Thompson meant that Canada was to see yet another prime minister assume the post as a result of a death in office. First Macdonald, now Thompson. Even the man between them, J.J. Abbott, had left office with a terminal diagnosis. Whoever was selected would be the fourth man to hold the title in the space of three and a half years, heir to a job that seemed ominously fatal.

Although Bowell would never have wanted to admit it, whatever unifying force that Thompson had brought to the Conservative government ranks suddenly vaporized with his untimely end.

Almost instantly, the party divided itself once more into bickering cliques made up of men who were separated by their positions on the issues of the day — religion, language, reciprocity, the imperial connection. A few of the politicians had personal ambition that motivated their actions, but as had been the case three years earlier when Macdonald died suddenly, there was no obvious person to grasp the reins of power.

Bowell himself had limited ambitions as a politician. Yes, he wanted the recognition and perks that came with being an important man in Ottawa, but he did not pine for the job as Canada's leader. He knew his limitations and had never harboured ambition to be more than a well-respected Cabinet minister. But in the end, the party, more out of necessity than any kind of enthusiasm, fell in line behind the man who was leader of the government in the Senate, Sir Mackenzie Bowell.

Thompson of course had not looked ahead to who'd follow him as leader. Being a young man and new to the position at the head of the government, he had no inkling that his life was about to end suddenly and so soon.

Unlike today, where conventions of the party members select the next party leader, the choice of who would lead the government fell to the governor general, a political appointee of the Colonial Office in London. Canada's governor general, the astute Lord Aberdeen, had been a personal friend of

Thompson. He knew that there would be no consensus among squabbling Conservatives as to who should lead the party. Aberdeen chose quickly to avoid the kind of chaos that had occurred upon the death of Macdonald in 1891. In his opinion, Bowell seemed most qualified to lead. He had been a Cabinet minister since 1878; he was the government leader in the Senate; he had served as "acting prime minister" in several of Thompson's absences from the country. He was known for his quiet, workmanlike efficiency more than for any dynamic leadership style, but perhaps skillful if uninspiring guidance was what the party and the country needed at that point. It helped that the late nineteenth century was a time when considerable respect was shown for the elderly because of the alleged wisdom that came with long experience.

In the eyes of the governor general, Bowell's rivals for the top position were mostly unacceptable. John Haggart, the minister of railways and canals, was thought to be too lazy to take on the job. Lady Aberdeen labelled him "a Bohemian," although it is unclear what that description meant exactly at the time. George Eulas Foster, the bespectacled minister of finance, would likely have been able to handle the position, but he was highly voluble and quick to anger — characteristics that did not suit the prime minister's chair, especially during a sudden crisis. (Yet that was a characteristic of Mackenzie Bowell as well.) In addition, Foster's questionable marriage to a divorced former landlady from Chicago was deemed scandalous in Victorian Ottawa. (Lady Macdonald refused to see Mrs. Foster when she called upon the prime minister's wife. The poor woman was also snubbed when she called upon the governor general's wife at Rideau Hall.) Charles Hibbert Tupper was capable, but many saw him as too inflexible and strong-willed to manage the personalities within the Tory Party. None of the other Cabinet ministers had either the qualifications or ability to take on the job.

Charles Tupper Sr. had, in the past, been seriously considered for the position of prime minister following the demise of Macdonald and the resignation of Abbott. With the death of Thompson, his name again came up in discussions of who would succeed Thompson. He had impeccable qualifications, a larger-than-life personality, and a political following; however, none of those things seemed to convince the governor general. Neither Lord nor Lady Aberdeen cared for Tupper as a person. John Thompson himself may have sowed doubts about the old Father of Confederation with his jibes about both Tuppers acting only out of self-interest most of the time. In any event, the old doctor was perfectly content, it seemed, with his position as high commissioner in London.

So, Bowell it was.

Sir Mackenzie Bowell was sworn in as prime minister of Canada on December 21, 1894, six days short of his seventy-first birthday. It had been a long, slow climb to the top of the political ladder. Bowell was, like John Abbott, a man reluctant to take on the role. He was not suited for it; he did not seek it. Also counting against him was the fact that he was a senator, physically removed from the House of Commons; further, he lacked widespread support from within his party ranks. Despite all these things, Bowell was eventually selected to hold the premier's position. In the end, it did not turn out well for either the man himself or for the Conservative Party.

Mackenzie Bowell was born in Rickinghall, England, on December 27, 1823, but moved with his family to Canada in 1833. The eight-week trip across the Atlantic was memorable for the ten-year-old. He always recalled the journey across the cold north Atlantic with fondness. It was the beginning of a new adventure in a new land.

The Bowell family had relatives in the Bay of Quinte area, so they ended up settling in the village of Belleville, Ontario. John Bowell, Mackenzie's father, was a cabinet maker and his son learned the trade at a young age. During the day, he was supposed to go to school but he was often truant in order to work alongside his father.

As a teenager, although still working with his father in the evenings, he became a printer's devil at the Belleville *Intelligencer* newspaper. Ranked lower than an apprentice, he spent his days mixing ink or fetching type for the apprentices in the print shop. It was the beginning of a lifetime spent in the newspaper business. The young man learned the ropes quickly and mastered each stage of the printing process. Not only did he revel in the technical aspects of the job, but Mackenzie also harboured ambition to write for the paper as well. As an eager would-be journalist, Bowell ingratiated himself with the paper's publisher, George Benjamin. In the end, he became the publisher's right-hand man. The older man became a mentor to Bowell, not only professionally, tutoring him in all aspects of the newspaper trade, but also on a personal basis as well. A prominent Conservative in the Belleville region as well as a fervent Orangeman, Benjamin likely influenced many of the attitudes that young Mackenzie came to espouse.

At eighteen, Bowell enrolled in Sydney Normal School, a teacher-training college in Hastings, Ontario. He graduated in 1841, but never taught school for a living. It seems unlikely that he pursued that line of work with any enthusiasm. Teachers at that time were paid pathetically, lived a Spartan lifestyle, and tended to drift from rural community to rural community. The newspaper and printing businesses, on the other hand, offered stable and steady employment in the towns of Canada West.

Bowell maintained his close ties to George Benjamin and the *Intelligencer* newspaper. Somehow, he managed to save enough money to buy a share of the town paper, becoming Benjamin's partner in 1848. The twenty-four-year-old Bowell may have been able to become a partner because Benjamin seemed to have a finger in so many pies. The older man was a notary public and the village clerk for Belleville between 1836 and 1847. He held many other positions as well: clerk of Thurlow Township; clerk of the Belleville Board of Police; a councillor and reeve of Hungerford Township. Many of these appointments were political in nature, and Benjamin became a powerful man in the region, seemingly entitled to the privileges he enjoyed. He likely needed an energetic, capable hand at the tiller of his newspaper. Mackenzie Bowell fit that bill.

Bowell met Harriet Louisa Moore in 1842. By the standards of the day, he courted her for a lengthy period. Before they wed, he worked to save money for their home and also for the chance to buy into a business he could call his own. They finally married in late 1847. The couple would eventually have nine children — four sons and five daughters.

Mackenzie and Louisa's brother went into business together in 1848 when they purchased the *Intelligencer's* print shop, an adjunct to the actual newspaper. Technically speaking, they became the newspaper's publishers. The two men did not see eye to eye, however. They would get into furious and violent arguments with each other. It was at that time that Bowell earned a reputation as a hot-headed boss who would rant and rail at employees (and co-owners it seems). Eventually, after the two had engaged in many a heated argument, Bowell bought out his brother-in-law.

A deeply conservative young man, Bowell took over the editorship of the paper that same year, maintaining the same pro-Tory tone in its articles and editorials. By the mid-fifties, Bowell was able to buy the paper outright from Benjamin. He retained ownership of the paper right up to his death in 1917. His opinions were heard, and with a weekly public voice, his pro-Conservative bias was influential.

In 1859 he was one of the founders of the Canadian Press Association. (He became president of the group in 1865.) Among newspaper editors and publishers in Canada West, he became a leading figure. Bowell was respected for his understanding of all aspects of newspaper work— typesetting, printing, writing, and publishing.

With the newspaper as a personal platform to express his political, religious, and moral views, Bowell gained a reputation with the public in Belleville and then beyond. He had a sincere interest in public life and began to plan on using his position as the town's newspaper publisher to influence the life of Canada West. Like his mentor, George Benjamin, he began to put his energy into activities beyond the newspaper. He sat on the school board as a trustee. He served on the board of the local agriculture association and participated as a member of the arts board in Belleville. Bowell sat on boards of directors for several area companies. In 1865 he was instrumental in establishing a board of trade in Belleville.

He was a devoutly religious man. He became a Methodist who rarely, even late in life, would miss a Sunday church service. Like a lot of people in his denomination at the time, he wanted nothing to do with Catholics. In the middle of the century, if a man was a devoted Protestant and a man with political interest, he joined the Orange Order; this is what Bowell did in 1842. By 1860 he was the president of the local branch. He took on a major role in helping to organize the celebration when the Prince of Wales — the future Edward VII — visited Canada that year. Even though the prince shunned any public recognition from the Orange Order,[1] Bowell was recognized for the organizational skill he brought to the occasion.

Although Bowell was active in the fraternity throughout his life, he did not always give vocal support for its anti-Catholic sentiment, especially if he felt a different stance might advance his political ambition. He misjudged the public feelings, in 1863, when running for the local seat in the colonial legislature. He refused to oppose legislation that would allow Catholic school boards in Canada West. Orangemen in his district recoiled, campaigned against him, and helped to defeat him at the polls. Yet that incident did not stop him from rising to the top of the Order. In 1870 he was elected as the grand master of British North America, a position he held until 1878. At the group's 1876 convention in Londonderry, Northern Ireland, he was elected president of the Order's Triennial Council. Bowell remained an Orangeman all his days.

He and John Abbott — although they'd likely not met by the 1850s — shared an interest in the militia. Both men were key military organizers in their respective communities. It was an unsettled time. The rebellions of 1837 were still fresh in the minds of those old enough to have experienced them. With the growing unrest among the states south of the border, there always seemed to be a threat, though it was sometimes imagined, that the Americans would move north to take over British North America. A strong militia, prepared to repel the invaders, was something both men advocated. In 1857 Bowell set about organizing the First Volunteer Militia Rifle Company in Belleville. He served as an ensign in the company from 1858 to 1865. He was forever proud of the photograph that was taken of him in his militia uniform in 1864, chest puffed up, clutching a sheathed sword, his beard full and black. During the American Civil War and during the

Fenian raids that took place in the mid-1860s, Bowell saw active duty as a militiaman. Between 1867 and 1872, he was a lieutenant colonel with the 49th Regiment "Hastings Rifles." (In 1892 Prime Minister Abbott would name him minister of militia and defence. Bowell gleefully accepted the role he felt he was born to administer.)

Newspapermen in the nineteenth century made clear their political views. George Brown, William Lyon Mackenzie, and Joseph Howe had all pushed their partisan opinions by means of their printing presses. Papers were invariably of one political stripe or the other, highly partisan in both reporting and on the editorial pages. Filed stories were often biased to the extent that there was little truth in what had been reported. (One could argue it was a time of hyper-partisan politics and fake news!) Bowell's paper was no exception. His right-wing Tory preferences were openly displayed in the paper each week. He was unapologetic of his anti-Catholic, anti-French views. His low opinion of Liberals made its way into news items and editorials. When Bowell made the *Intelligencer* into a daily in 1867, it simply gave him a daily rather than weekly pulpit to express conservative — and Conservative — opinions.

It was no surprise that Bowell would eventually throw his hat into the political ring as a Tory candidate.

In the 1863 election for the legislature of Canada West, Bowell ran to replace none other than his former boss George Benjamin. As mentioned above, he was defeated because he had taken a stance that was contrary to what the Orange Order wanted, but that did not deter his interest in the political arena. When the very first Canadian federal election took place in 1867, he won the seat for Hastings North. He held it for the next twenty-five years until his appointment to the Senate in 1892.

Bowell initially sat as a backbencher in the House of Commons. From there he was able to see the political wizardry of Sir John A. Macdonald. The new MP watched the Conservative leader as he charmed, cajoled, and manipulated people. Bowell also bore witness to the near downfall of the prime minister when the Pacific Scandal broke in 1873. The member from North Hastings did not figure in the questionable payoffs from Sir Hugh Allan nor did he have much to say in the back-and-forth debates that eventually led to the Tories losing the 1874 election.

The next year, when Alexander Mackenzie's Liberals were in power and they proposed legislation to lease the new Pembina branch line of the CPR to Donald Smith, the Conservatives were outraged. Smith had split from the Conservative Party over the railway affair. His vote to censure the government in a motion regarding the Pacific Scandal had led to the fall of the government and the election of the Liberals to office. Although elected as a Conservative, Smith declared publicly that he could not support a government "shadowed by suspicion." The former Tory became a pariah with his former colleagues.

Now it was the turn of the Conservatives to accuse the government of scandalous behaviour. It was Bowell who rose in the Commons to denounce the Pembina line decision. He declared that the House was witnessing "the extraordinary spectacle of the champion of this proposed lease using his power and influence as a very humble and obedient supporter of the Government to secure to himself and his partners in this transaction the advantage of a lease." Smith refused to give in or admit fault, despite spirited attacks from both Bowell and Macdonald. The accusations never gained much traction and eventually the matter became forgotten. It was, as all the participants well knew, a time when patronage and graft were politically acceptable, despite the feigned outrage heard in Parliament. Bowell's contributions to the debate earned him the respect of Sir John A.

His standing in the party was further enhanced as a result of his actions relating to Louis Riel. The Métis leader had been elected as the member of Parliament from Provencher in the February 1874 election[2] and had made his way to Ottawa. He managed to sign in as an MP, but that was as far as he got. There was, at that time, an outstanding warrant for his arrest on murder charges related to the killing of Thomas Scott. Deciding it best to avoid Parliament Hill, he hid, allegedly in a convent across the river from Ottawa in Hull.

In Ontario, the Orange Order considered Riel nothing less than a murderer. As head of the provisional government in 1870, he had overseen the courtmartial and subsequent execution of Thomas Scott. Bowell, as the grand master of the British North America branch of the Orange Order, was expected to further condemn Riel. As the political representative from Hastings, it was also his duty, as the powerful Orangemen saw it, to lead the charge against the Métis leader since Thomas Scott hailed from that constituency. Bowell stood in the House of Commons to introduce a motion expelling Riel from the Commons. The April vote in the Commons on Bowell's motion split along the lines one would expect. Anglo-Protestants supported the motion; French and Catholics voted against. Riel wisely chose not to pursue any kind of action other than to quietly return to the West. Bowell's actions raised his own profile among Ontario Tories who were, in turn, overly influenced by their Orange supporters.

Mackenzie Bowell's parliamentary actions demonstrated the kind of support that Sir John relished. To Macdonald's way of thinking, such behaviour merited a promotion. When the Conservatives were re-elected to office in 1878, Bowell was appointed minister of customs, joining the likes of Charles Tupper, Leonard Tilley, and Hector Langevin at the Cabinet table. Macdonald was never particularly close to Bowell, but he saw that the newspaperman from Belleville had a loyal following among the more right-wing supporters of his party. The Cabinet appointment was a move motivated by the need to keep the Orange Order and its formidable influence supporting the Tory cause.

Bowell's Cabinet job was a crucially important one, as it involved managing the money that came in from customs duties, the government's chief source of revenue at that time. In the days before income tax and other general taxes on personal wealth, it was those customs duties that allowed the federal government to maintain its departments, the civil service, and the expenses associated with Ottawa power brokerage. It was a ministry with tremendous responsibility. It gave him status at the Cabinet table.

Macdonald's party had been elected on their new National Policy. One of the key planks to that policy was the implementation of new tariff rules. The Customs ministry was one where rates were constantly changing, where a large bureaucracy needed constant oversight. The ports — Halifax, Quebec, Montreal, Vancouver — and all points of entry along the American border demanded close attention. As minister in charge, Bowell had to put up with myriad requests from both importers and exporters. He kept busy poring over the fiscal details coming in from ports all over the country. An ability to understand the nuances of all the financial aspects involved was a prerequisite for the minister. Glued to his desk, swamped with paperwork, he dealt with the small details that were often invisible to the public.

Bowell believed that all ports, from Halifax to Victoria, needed to have common rates on the same goods. Until then, it had been up to local officials to put value to products coming from the United States for instance. The new minister created a board of customs appraisers who were tasked with assessing goods on an equal basis — fair market price in the country of origin. As the minister in charge, Bowell faced some push-back from unscrupulous characters in the port cities of the Dominion, but he held fast to his belief in fairness. In the end, his reforms made the system work efficiently, ensuring even higher and more consistent revenue for Ottawa.

Bowell was frequently denigrated by others, who claimed that he lacked the intelligence of people like John Thompson. His frequent silences at the Cabinet table and in the House of Commons were interpreted as indicative of a lack of mental acuity by those who held little esteem for the man. Those with a more generous attitude considered his silences to be the product of thoughtfulness. It depended on whom one asked.

Just like John Thompson in the Justice portfolio, Bowell worked through the late 1880s as an administrator who scrupulously oversaw his ministry with an eye on doing things properly and above board. He was organized and hard-working. He ran his ministry much as he ran his business: with astute organization, the ability to delegate responsibility, and an honesty that went a long way with those he encountered. The fact that he lost his temper from time to time — Bowell was known to shout at men who either disagreed with him or who opposed his orders — may have coloured others' opinions of him, but his longevity in office and his rise to the very top showed the capabilities of the man.

Macdonald had confidence in Bowell. He could see that the former newspaperman, despite his run-ins with underlings, knew how to run a department well. He saw that Bowell's work ethic was unquestionable and that he understood the complexities of a very labyrinthine bureaucracy. He had to be well informed and constantly up-to-date. The prime minister kept the North Hastings MP as his minister of customs through several elections and Cabinet iterations.

Bowell was trustworthy; as well, he was utterly scrupulous in his adherence to the rules the government had laid out for his department. Even the prime minister had to virtually beg him to occasionally bend those rules. In one minor incident, Macdonald wrote to Bowell regarding an insignificant customs appointment. It was a simple example of the kind of patronage that Sir John had designed to keep his party in power.

Macdonald said, "If you can *possibly* do this for the Bishop do it. It is of very great importance just now to keep him not only friendly but *Earnest* in the cause."

Unhappy about the request, Bowell grudgingly acceded to the prime minister's wishes even though it went against his morals.

Not only did Bowell, at times, have to agree to support such acts of patronage, he was, at times, called on to publicly defend them. When questions were raised about the ethics of its patronage, it fell to minister Bowell to defend the government's system of favouritism. In 1887, during a debate over the questionable practices in granting civil service jobs, he stated plainly to the House of Commons, "You consult your friends when anything is to be done." The Liberals had a hard time coming up with an answer for that.

His speeches did not inspire, but they served. In the Commons, he was a lacklustre speaker without the rhetorical flourish of Macdonald, the grace of Thompson or Laurier, and without the animation of Charles Tupper. Workmanlike was the adjective that best described the future prime minister.

In 1884 Bowell's wife Harriett died. The death of a spouse, always a source of sadness and often depression, seemed to push Bowell to focus more of his energy on his parliamentary duties and bury himself in his work. It was in the wake of Harriett's death that Bowell built a reputation on Parliament Hill for his tireless work ethic. He was a man who kept his eye on the ball, saw that things started were completed, and managed carefully those under him. He was assiduous in the management of his department.

Every detail — customs rates, shipping schedules, letters from importers and agents — he kept at his fingertips. He mastered the mundane.

From Ottawa, Bowell managed to keep his eye on the *Intelligencer* in Belleville as well, even though he was no longer actively involved in the day-to-day operation of the paper. He kept up with the comings and goings in the Hastings-Prince Edward counties by exchanging letters with his editors and with Tory leaders in the Belleville and Trenton area. His viewpoint still found its way onto the *Intelligencer* pages. The career of the member for Hastings was followed with consistent praise and admiration in the syco-phantic local press.

In 1885, the second Métis rebellion dominated the political landscape. Bowell, though a dedicated Orangeman, did not figure as prominently in the House debates as did people like Thompson. Bowell's anti-Catholic bias, coupled with his admiration for the militia, made it easy for him to support the government's military action. He did so in a quiet way. The subsequent execution of Riel did not bother Bowell in the least. He felt the Métis leader had been dealt with in the manner he deserved, that he'd finally got what was coming to him.

Bowell's personal relationships with other politicians, especially Conservative colleagues, was rarely a warm one. He was a severe, religious man, kindly described by one biographer as "a Victorian gentleman." George Bowering, one of Canada's finest poets, humorists, and historians described him as a "bad tempered little egotist with fewer brains than he thought he had."[3] Yet he had a kind of appeal, one that was as puzzling as it was hard to describe. Behind closed doors he could be warm with friends, but he was often seen as aloof by others. His closest colleague in Cabinet was probably John Thompson, although the two had little in common. There was precious little warmth enclosed in the letters the two sent to each other.

John Thompson's opinion of Bowell was that he was "scrupulous, faithful, and hard-working but vain." Thompson also wrote in a letter to a friend that Bowell lacked parliamentary panache. Others commented on Bowell's lack of modesty, a charge that could hardly be proven or disproven.

If Bowell did not know how to cultivate friendships, he knew how to keep himself near the apex of the political pyramid. He obviously had the ability to demonstrate his capabilities to fellow members of the Orange Order or he would not have risen to the top of the Order. He convinced voters to return him to Parliament for twenty-five straight years through four elections. The fact that the prime minister kept Bowell in charge of the crucial customs ministry for over thirteen years serves as a testament to Macdonald's appreciation of Bowell's organizational talents.

By the last decade of the century, Bowell could look back on his time spent in Ottawa, administering his department, with a sense of pride. Two decades in the capital had turned his full, bushy beard from jet black to completely white. He looked the part of the aging minister in an equally aging Cabinet as the Tories went into the 1891 election one last time behind the leadership of John A. Macdonald. The voters in Hastings County re-elected their local newspaper publisher. Once again, the Old Chieftain appointed the steadfast Bowell to be his minister of customs.

Macdonald's death a short time after the 1891 election unleashed a flurry of activity. Bowell, although a long-time Cabinet minister, had little support when his name came up as a potential successor. As mentioned, the choice for a replacement came down to Thompson, Abbott, or Tupper, and it was Abbott who — reluctantly — took on the job.

One of the first things Abbott did was make sure that the Cabinet that Sir John A. had named stayed in place. There was no advantage to mixing things up. He called upon Bowell to continue his work at Customs. From June 16, 1891, until the following January, Bowell presided over the ministry he'd already managed for thirteen years. Abbott had also tapped him to look after Railways and Canals, a post considered so important that Macdonald had kept it for himself. It says a lot about the respect that the new prime minister had for Bowell's ability in that he entrusted him with what were two of the most important Cabinet positions in the government.

Then, in late January, in a bid to freshen the look of the government front bench, Abbott shuffled his Cabinet. Joseph-Adolphe Chapleau left his Secretary of State portfolio and took over Customs. James Patterson became secretary of state and registrar general. Joseph Caron, who'd been minister of militia and defence moved to the position of postmaster general. John Haggart, who'd run the Post Office, took over the coveted Department of Railways and Canals. That left Bowell with the job he may have wanted all along: minister of militia and defence. His lifelong interest in military matters was finally rewarded with a posting that suited the interests of its minister.

With Abbott's resignation in the late fall of 1892, Bowell found himself once more in a new situation. There was some feeling among Conservative insiders that the long-serving member from Belleville could take on the job. Thompson — self-effacing as usual — made a case for Bowell in conversation with Abbott, stating that the man was respected and that the party would gladly follow his lead. The gravely ill prime minister would not hear of it. He did not have faith that Bowell had either the skills or, more importantly, personality that the job demanded. So, it fell to Thompson to take on the task, more out of a sense of duty than any driving personal ambition.

One of the first changes Thompson made as he took office was naming Bowell a senator. On December 5, 1892, the newspaper owner from Belleville was named to the Red Chamber. There were figures in the Conservative Party who worried about Bowell's infamous temper and how well he could control it in the sleepy Senate chamber. The newly appointed senator did, however, manage to keep his ire well-hidden, even during the heated discussions that arose following the exposure of the Tory scandals and mismanagement that took place that year.

The sixty-nine-year-old would hold down several important posts in John Thompson's Cabinet. He took on the newly created role of minister of trade and commerce. It fell to Bowell to oversee two other parliamentary offices — Customs and Inland Revenue. Bowell's long-term work at Customs prepared him well for the new positions. Throughout his government career, he'd shown interest in trade issues, and he was probably the most knowledgeable man in the country when it came to any kind of legislation dealing with international commerce. His administrative skills lent themselves well to setting up what was essentially a new ministry.

Although Abbott retained the role of leader of the government in the Senate out of courtesy, Bowell was the *de facto* leader. Ill health and absence meant Abbott could not truly perform any work there. When Abbott died on October 30, 1893, Mackenzie Bowell was named officially to that position the very next day.

As a capable administrator, Bowell would not only oversee the creation of a critical new department, but he would answer to the Opposition forces in the Senate when it came to defending all government bills that came to the Upper House for consideration.

Thompson also entrusted Bowell to keep a tight rein over fellow Orangeman Clarke Wallace, the unpredictable Protestant extremist from Ontario who'd been selected as someone to counterbalance the Catholic prime minister. Everyone from the prime minister on down seemed to have someone looking over his shoulder. Curiously, it seems that Bowell, as a former head of the Orange Order, was not seen as the Protestant counterweight to Thompson's Catholicism. It may be that, since he did not utter impetuous or provocative anti-Catholic statements in public, Bowell was not considered to have the qualifications for that role. Most of the public would not have been aware of his religion or his high rank in the Orange Order.

Life was arguably easier for Bowell with his elevation to the Senate. No longer did he have to deal with the daily grind of the House of Commons, although Senate debates could be taxing as well. He was mostly freed from the constant pleas, complaints, and trivialities of constituents in the Belleville area. Those jobs fell to the person who replaced him as MP, Alexander Carscallen. On the other hand, the process of building a new ministry out of the former Customs portfolio meant a lot of hands-on work. Much of Bowell's time was taken up with managing that crucial department.

There had been on-going talks for several years about opening up new trade venues with the yet-to-be-united Australian colonies and with South Africa. The railway construction across the country had stimulated the entrepreneurs of the day to think in terms of steamship routes across the Pacific. Britain, of course, was quick to promote the possibility of commercial ties throughout the Empire. Thompson, as much of an imperialist as

Macdonald, was eager to forge new ties with other countries that fell under the aegis of Great Britain.

In September of 1893, the prime minister called upon Bowell to make what was still, in those days, an arduous trip across the Pacific to Sydney, where he would meet with Australian trade representatives to pave the way for new commerce between the countries (although "Australia" would not become a separate nation for another eight years). He was the perfect delegate for such a mission. No other Canadian, other than possibly Sir Charles Tupper, was as well-versed in international business affairs. Bowell was himself enthusiastic about the task.

Setting out from Ottawa with a small team of advisors and secretaries, Bowell travelled by train to Vancouver. He boarded a steamship there and set off across the Pacific for Sydney, New South Wales. On board ship for several weeks, the Canadians relaxed but also spent time working on arguments that they would present to the Australians regarding trading arrangements and favourable duties.

It was a time of turmoil in Australia. A long economic boom, fuelled mostly by the gold rush of the 1850s, had come to an end. The colonies Down Under were suffering through a full-blown depression. Several banks had collapsed, taking down businesses and bankrupting thousands of citizens. One third of Melbourne's working class was unemployed. By July of 1893, fifty-four of the sixty-four financial institutions that had been operating in 1891 had either shut down temporarily or were out of business. The hard times fuelled civil unrest. The former penal colony, never easy with its history of social divide, was wrestling with labour strife that had its roots in unfair practices that favoured the wealthy. Much like British North America in the 1860s, the colonies were struggling with a movement to unite under one government. A new trade relationship with Canada would seem to be beneficial to all and could be advantageous in the long run for both dominions.

Upon arrival in Sydney, Bowell was welcomed warmly by his Australian hosts. He was greeted, said Prime Minister Thompson in a speech to the Commons, "with the cordial hand of fellowship, as warm and generous as one colonist could extend to another." (Ever the man to promote the imperial connection, Thompson spoke about drawing together the fellow *colonists*. Even the prime minister in 1893 thought in terms of Canada still being a possession of England.)

The chance that new North American markets could help the effort to revive their stagnant economy meant that the Australians (and New Zealanders) were as hopeful as their Canadian visitors that deals could be made. Talks proceeded agreeably, but Bowell was on a tight timeline, as he could not spend too much time away from his responsibilities in Ottawa. When the delegates from Melbourne, Adelaide, Perth, Wellington, and Sydney could not concur amongst themselves, the discussions did not amount to much other than positive feelings that Canada and the South Pacific colonies could eventually iron something out.

Bowell returned to Ottawa in January, buoyed up with hope that his recent discussions would lead to new agreements. He came up with an innovative notion. Why not bring the disparate states together in a formal meeting, one sanctioned by the Home Office in London? Out of that thinking came a proposal for a conference of nations from the South Pacific, Canada, South Africa, and Britain. Such a summit of political and business leaders from the British Empire's many holdings would offer opportunities for Canada to find new markets. Massey-Harris, the Canadian farm implement company, was already selling equipment to New Zealand. Why not send such Canadian manufactured goods to Australia, Fiji, and British holdings in Africa? The Ottawa civil servants set to work to plan and stage the Colonial Conference that would eventually be held in Ottawa. Mackenzie Bowell was rightly seen as the catalyst who not only formulated the idea but eventually brought it all about.

The Colonial Conference opened in Ottawa on June 28, 1894. While at imperial conferences the representatives were premiers or prime ministers, the delegates at this conference were emissaries of the colonial governments. They included the governor of New South Wales, the former premier of South Australia, prominent business leaders and politicians from New Zealand, Tasmania, Queensland, and the Cape Colony. Noteworthy was the inclusion of Jan Hendrik Hofmeyr, the leader of the Dutch *Afrikaner* element in South Africa. Newfoundland, West Australia, Fiji, and the

Natal colony (now part of South Africa) were all invited to the conference but declined because of domestic priorities. A representative from the still-independent Hawaiian Islands joined the talks. The Earl of Jersey, who'd spent time in Australia as the governor of New South Wales, came as the representative for England. He had been given instructions to listen and report back to London but not to make any kind of commitments on behalf of the Mother Country.

The Canadian contingent was comprised of Mackenzie Bowell, Postmaster-General Adolphe-Philippe Caron, Finance Minister Foster, and the renowned Sir Sanford Fleming, a key figure in the building of the Canadian Pacific Railway but more significantly known as the inventor of worldwide standardized time zones.

Using the Senate chamber for its opening ceremonies, Canada's governor general Lord Aberdeen greeted the ambassadors warmly. Prime Minister Thompson then spoke to the international delegates, sharing his belief that Canada and the British holdings around the globe were strong when united under the flag of England. Thompson talked of movements — in Australia, New Zealand, and Cape Colony — to join in federations just as Canada had thirty years earlier. He acknowledged the challenge of trade deals, especially ones concerned with steamship lines and "telegraphs," since a trans-Pacific cable was one of the projects to be discussed. He finished his eloquent speech with a call for unity among England's far-flung possessions.

An elaborate banquet that night, hosted by the Canadians, was filled with the kind of bonhomie one would expect. The next day, the group got down to business in the offices of the Trade and Commerce Department. First of all, Mackenzie Bowell was elected as chair of the proceedings. Bowell's opening address was lengthy as he set out the agenda. The parties would resolve to form a "customs union" between Britain and the rest of the Empire; the parties would discuss closer trade ties among Canada, Australia, and South Africa; the government in London would be asked to remove any international treaties that hampered trade between the colonies; the parties involved would ask Britain's help in surveying and then establishing a cable connection between Canada and the Australian colonies; England would be asked to divert subsidies to facilitate a rapid transatlantic steamship line, the implication being that the money would go to a Canadian-British company and the line would likely run from Liverpool to Halifax, rather than New York or Boston.

It was a heavy to-do list, especially given the limited time that could be spent on earnest discussions. Bowell, as both Cabinet minister and chairperson, was kept active dashing from meeting to meeting. It was his shining moment in politics and in international diplomacy. The septuagenarian could have sat back and acted as an observer, letting younger colleagues carry the ball for Canada. Instead, the meetings energized the man his fellow Cabinet members called "Grandpa Bowell." (He definitely looked the part.) His comprehensive understanding of duties, customs rules, and other administrative details meant that he was needed at each and every step along the way. He was proud to give advice, show off his knowledge of intricacies he'd learned over the years, and to bask in the praise that came from international colleagues.

Progress was far from guaranteed. In fact, the Australians maintained that they had already entered into trade agreements with the United States that had amounted to about twenty million dollars per year. Delegates from Sydney, Adelaide, and Melbourne pointed out that the products Canada might wish to trade with them could already be obtained under established agreements with the United States. Agricultural implements, carriages, chemicals, iron, tobacco, wood, and paper were already being sent to Australia by the Americans. What could Canada offer that the United States could not? Canada's trade with Australia was a meagre half a million dollars per year. Paltry shiploads of goods were currently traversing the Pacific, but the Canadian delegates argued that now there would be the possibility of sending salmon, flax, and rough timber — just a few of the things Canada had to offer — south of the equator. In return, the North Americans were hungering for products such as lamb, wine, diamonds, and fruit. It seemed as though there were new possibilities and Bowell — along with the other Canadians — did their best to advertise what Canada could bring to the table.

The twelve-day conference ended with good feelings all around. Many of the resolutions were accepted by all the participants. The recommendation of preferential trade within the Empire was eventually rejected by the Australian states, as they saw such a move would undermine their own protective tariffs. The government in London looked favourably on all the resolutions except the one calling for an imperial customs union. Such a move, it felt, would place too many restrictions on Britain's trade with other nations in the world. Eventually, there was increased trade among the participants of the conference but never as much as Bowell and others envisioned.

Bowell emerged from the meetings with the respect of those international associates; more crucially, he had earned the respect and admiration of his own colleagues. He had chaired the conference with a welcoming, cordial tone. He led negotiations that benefitted Canadian business, cemented existing treaties, and at the same time prepared the groundwork for new accords. If there was a "star" of the conference, it was the Canadian minister of trade and commerce.

As an Ontario senator, Bowell was able to travel about the province, free to act less as an active politician and more as a dignified statesman. In September, he was part of the prime minister's party as they attended the Toronto Industrial Exhibition. At the ceremony dedicating a statue to John A. Macdonald in October, Bowell was called upon to give a tribute to the man he'd served with for many years.

Bowell was the senior member of the Cabinet in terms of service. He was also the oldest man in a Cabinet full of aging men. The "Grandpa Bowell" sobriquet was not necessarily always a complimentary one. However, as the senior Cabinet minister it fell to him to be the acting prime minister when Thompson was out of the country. In 1893, when Thompson travelled to Paris to act as an arbiter for the Bering Sea Tribunal, Bowell became acting prime minister.

The Cabinet could not be described as a cohesive one. Macdonald, Abbott, and Thompson all had to coddle a collection of what Thompson biographer P.B. Waite called "discordant elements, held together by loyalty, patronage, tradition and power."[4] The overwhelming source of that discord was the struggle over Protestant and Catholic issues. According to Waite, the only two men with the "requisite tact and sagacity" were Bowell and Auguste-Réal Angers, but both men were in the Senate, removed from the activity in the House of Commons.

While Thompson was away in Paris, a seemingly inconsequential squabble broke out among the Tory members of Parliament, but it was one that revealed the deep disunity in the federal party. Clarke Wallace, the Orangeman who'd been brought close to Thompson's inner circle to counteract the prime minister's ostensible Catholic preferences, committed one of his characteristic indiscretions. He gave a speech in Kingston, Ontario, where he stated that Protestants in Northern Ireland could expect help from Ontario in opposing Irish Catholic home rule. It was a tactless comment, one that fired up Protestants and Catholics on both sides of the House. A motion of censure put forward by the Liberals pitted the Irish Catholics in the Conservative Party against their Protestant colleagues. In-fighting among the Tories included threats to side with the Liberals during the censure vote in the Commons. Bowell, showing a lack of a firm hand — or was it indifference about an issue brought up by a prominent Orangeman? — took little part in the heated internal debate, leaving it to Foster and Angers to rally the troops during a caucus meeting. The Conservatives survived the vote, but the conflict was an omen of things to come. Meanwhile, the Liberals sat back and watched the Tories squabbling and fighting among themselves. The entire episode had an ominous air to it. Bowell had not acted decisively, and that character trait was what would inevitably end his premiership.

"All's well, hallelujah!" Bowell said, somewhat naively, in a transatlantic cable message to Thompson after Parliament was prorogued on April 4. It wasn't all well, of course. Even from Europe, Thompson had his ear to the ground in Ottawa. It was only his skillful hold over the party that kept the Conservatives united and on-track. His overwhelming determination, and his energy combined to keep the squabbling MPs in line. His cables from the continent and letters to key party members made his opinions and wishes known. He tolerated no division, at least none for the public to see. Thompson wrote a flurry of cables back to Canada, issuing orders and directing the government from afar. His caucus members snapped back into place, quietly toeing the party line as a united front. Not all political leaders had that kind of control. It was a talent that Bowell lacked.

An intensifying concern in the last decades of the nineteenth century was the matter of prohibition. Alcoholism and alcohol-related social problems were seemingly out of control. Drunkenness was a terrible social ill that affected all strata of society. The crowded conditions in the poorer sections of Canadian cities were especially susceptible to abuses related to alcohol. The rise of temperance groups, with their incessant calls for banning liquor sales, badgered politicians of all stripes.

Oliver Mowat, the long-serving premier of Ontario, supported the idea of limiting or even banning liquor production, import, and sales. Mowat, who'd been a thorn in John A.'s side for decades,[5] proved to be equally at odds with Macdonald's successors. Mowat brought up the issue of prohibition with Bowell during Thompson's absence in Paris. It may have been a ploy on Mowat's part, thinking he could get an answer from the acting prime minister before Thompson returned from Europe. Did the provinces have the right to prohibit the sale of liquor? The acting prime minister could not commit in any way, no matter how he felt about the issue. Wisely, Bowell did not give the Ontario leader any kind of definitive answer, but Liberals like Mowat could see that anyone in the Tory ranks other than Thompson could be leaned upon.

Thompson returned from Paris and settled things down among his quarreling caucus members. But he did not by any means cure what ailed the Conservative Party. Still, the winter of 1893–94 was relatively calm in Parliament, with the Thompson government working efficiently. The prime minister toured Ontario, trying to shore up support. Many of his speeches (unfavourably compared to the dull Edward Blake in the periodical *Saturday Night*) centred on tariff reform. Minister Bowell was a source of knowledge on those matters and gave the prime minister plenty of advice during the tour.

For both men, avid imperialists and supporters of all things British, alarm bells were raised about American influence during the fall of 1893. Theodore Roosevelt, Henry Cabot Lodge, Andrew Carnegie, and John Jacob Astor had formed what they called the National Continental Union

League, a cabal of the richest men in America whose goal was the fomenting of an independence movement in Canada. They saw that as the first step toward annexation of the entire continent. Bowell was as alarmed as Thompson at such naked ambition on the part of those powerful and famous Americans. In Canada, a branch of the league included notables such as Amédée Papineau (son of Louis-Joseph) and former Quebec premier Honoré Mercier. Even prominent Liberal MP Israel Tarte was said to belong to the group. That the expansionist ambitions of the United States should spill over into Canada worried the minister of trade and commerce. All eyes in Ottawa needed to be sharply attuned to any action from either branch of the league. Thompson warned Bowell and the rest of the caucus to increase Conservative membership lists to combat the threat. He also urged the Tories to speak to the press on the issue.

Bowell was once again the acting prime minister when Thompson travelled to London for his investiture into Her Majesty's Privy Council in December 1894. With the Tory leader overseas and the Christmas season rapidly approaching, things were relatively quiet on Parliament Hill. Bowell did not need to rush any pending legislation through the Senate, so he was able to spend most of his time in his office sifting through papers that concerned his ministries, conferring with caucus members, and attending to committee reports. A sense of calm had settled over most of Ottawa, a sleepy backwater town at the best of times.

The general feeling in the capital was that the prime minister had been working hard (as usual) but did not appear to have any kind of serious health issues. Angina and heart disease were little understood at the time.

The fatal heart attack on December 12 was incredibly shocking.

The first telegram was vehemently denied. It had to be a misunderstanding or an example of the yellow journalism so popular in that day and age.

George Eulas Foster, the minister of finance was with Bowell in his office when a breathless assistant came in with another telegram confirming the tragic news. The two men looked forlornly at the second telegram.

"Poor Lady Thompson," Bowell said. "Who can we get to take the news to her?"

Foster said, "It is your duty, Mr. Bowell."

"My God, I cannot do that!" Bowell answered.

It took a few minutes but finally Foster persuaded Bowell that they would go together to break the news to Annie Thompson. Accompanied by Douglas Stewart, Thompson's secretary, they took a carriage to 276 Somerset Street. The three men hunched their shoulders to block the rain as they knocked on the door. As they stood on the doorstep, in the background church bells had already begun to toll in mourning for the late prime minister. Sadly, Annie had already received word of the tragedy. A newspaper reporter had telephoned the house. Bowell was spared the difficult task of breaking the news. When a servant admitted the trio, they were immediately aware that Mrs. Thompson already knew she was a widow. Her tears and look of anguish on her face made it obvious.

The sense of loss across the country was heart-wrenching. A young and dynamic leader had been taken well before his time, it seemed. Into that vacuum stepped an aged and tired leader who lacked the very skills needed at that moment.

Just as when Sir John A. Macdonald had died, there was no unanimous choice to succeed the prime minister. But nearly all eyes fell on Bowell, who was the senior Cabinet member and one who had filled the role of acting prime minister several times. And he did have other qualifications. Although never considered a leader in the sense of dynamically heading the party and the country, as a newspaperman and long-time politician he had an understanding of the myriad issues that dogged the country. He had demonstrated wisdom in his handling of certain government agenda items in the past. He had not let his Orange Order beliefs interfere with his political responsibilities. Despite his affiliation, he had an inherent sense of fairness, a decency that others could see. And being a prominent member of that brotherhood had its political advantages for the Tory Party in that less enlightened age.

Protocol deemed that the governor general, Lord Aberdeen, would approach the man best suited to form a government. Several of the ranking

THE LOST PRIME MINISTERS

Conservatives in the Cabinet might have been a better choice than Bowell intellectually, but they had other character traits that worked against them. As mentioned, Foster, the finance minister, was considered even more foul-tempered and cantankerous than Bowell. As recently as the previous April, Foster had stormed out of a Cabinet meeting in a fit of pique. Later in the day, he sent an apology of sorts via letter to the prime minister. Such antics were well-known in the small circle of politicians and bureaucrats in Ottawa.

C.H. Tupper was a very smart man but never a leader in the sense that his father was, although he arrogantly saw himself as more than capable. He was self-centred, obstinate, and never admitted to being wrong. Those were not skills needed or wanted in a prime minister. And, as one wag at the time put it, naming C.H. as prime minister would be "one Tupper too many" with one as premier and one as high commissioner in England.[6]

John Haggart had a questionable personal life. He was known as a womanizer and, although he oversaw an important portfolio in the government, Railways and Canals, some saw him as lazy. Lady Aberdeen did not like the man and that in turn coloured her husband's consideration of him for the leadership. A headstrong, opinionated woman, she had great influence over her diffident husband.

Although Bowell, the minister of trade and commerce, had no personal ambition to take over, the governor general was astute enough to see that the newspaperman from Belleville was probably the most preferable choice from a very limited roster. Just like Abbott, Bowell would fit the bill on a short-term basis.

Aberdeen summoned Bowell to a meeting on December 13, the day after Thompson died. When asked by the governor general to accept the position, Bowell initially refused. Perhaps he was more aware of his limitations than many have given him credit. Aberdeen suggested that he talk it over with his Cabinet colleagues. Instead, Bowell advised Aberdeen to search for someone "better qualified" who then should be tapped on the shoulder to lead the country.

That afternoon, Lord Aberdeen did his own consulting. He met with Senator Frank Smith, a prominent Catholic who sat in Cabinet but without portfolio. Smith, with years of experience, felt that Bowell was, given the limited choices, the most suitable man for the job. That evening, Bowell was summoned again to Rideau Hall where Aberdeen asked him once more to become the new prime minister.

Bowell sat pensive for a moment or two, considering both the honour and the incredible responsibility being presented to him. In his heart, he knew he was not prime minister material. He lacked the common touch that Macdonald owned in spades. And he did not have Sir John's intrinsic need to be popular, loved, and admired by the public. He did not share Abbott's calm demeanor. Bowell's renowned temper was a testament to that. Toning down his emotional responses to certain issues might prove to be a challenge. He could never match Thompson in raw brainpower. At a time when religious opinion mattered perhaps more than at any other point in Canadian history, he was biased, if only based on the ranking he held in the Orange Order.

Bowell wrestled with the offer at hand.

He had a number of useful qualities that he could bring to the office and an understanding of government few men could match. He knew how to administer his civil servants and underlings. Bowell was indisputably honest. He knew how to compromise. He was careful to allow opponents the opportunity to voice their opinions, but at the same time, he made sure that his own views were made clear. As with Thompson, he was unselfish as a member of his party. He believed in doing what was best for the Conservative Party, whatever that may be. That was a trait that earned him points among the Tory faithful. Furthermore, he knew the caucus well, having been a member of Parliament longer than any of them.

He likely had an understanding of the kind of man he was. Although he was a lifelong politician, he did not strive to stand above all others and lead his party as premier. That had never been his goal. He was not a great public speaker and knew it. He'd often let others handle the debates that were aimed at his ministry and his responsibilities. Thompson had at times answered on his behalf when the actions of the government, and his department in particular, were questioned in the House of Commons.

He was admittedly vain. In the manner of Sir John A. Macdonald, he dressed well. He took pride in his appearance. He was less magnanimous than a seasoned politician should have been. But both of those character-istics wouldn't affect a prime ministership to any great degree. Nearly all leaders were (and are) egoists.

Finally, after making the governor general wait in silence, Bowell stood, nodded to Aberdeen, and said that he would accept the role. The two men shook hands, as if to seal a deal. The narcissist in Bowell must have rejoiced; the realist must have had some doubts.

Thompson had died on December 12. Bowell was sworn into office by the governor general a little over a week later, on December 21, along with a Cabinet that was quite similar to that of his predecessor. The biggest chan-ges saw C.H. Tupper move into the Justice and Attorney General portfolios, a promotion for the pompous Nova Scotian. Replacing Tupper at Marine and Fisheries was John Costigan, a New Brunswick MP who'd first been elected to the Commons in 1867. At age sixty-nine, he was getting long-in-the-tooth to handle such a key ministry, although he'd had experience as Thompson's secretary of state and registrar general. William Bullock Ives took over Trade and Commerce, the ministry that Bowell had created. Most of the other ministers from Thompson's Cabinet stayed in their old depart-ments: Angers in at Agriculture, Foster in Finance, Thomas Mayne Daly in Indian Affairs, James Patterson at the Department of Militia and Defence. Mackenzie saw no need to shake things up at this point.

Along with the call to head the government, Bowell was knighted on New Year's Day, 1895, as a tribute to his long years in Parliament but more specifically for his role in organizing the Colonial Conference. Sir Mackenzie Bowell began his term in office with an eye toward governing the way that Sir John A. Macdonald had. Working under the Old Chieftain for many years, Bowell had watched the country's long-serving prime minister choreo-graph others. Bowell hoped to emulate his old boss, but he lacked several of Sir John A.'s character traits. Where Macdonald possessed "hail-fellow-well-met" congeniality, wit, and sly cynicism, Bowell was rather sombre, dull, and plodding in his style. He lacked the common touch that had carried

Sir John A. to such success. When he tried to mirror the style and approach of Macdonald, his efforts were not seen as demonstrating leadership and strength; rather, they were seen as pathetic and ineffectual imitation.

Almost immediately, the party began to implode. Outsiders could see it. Divisions that Macdonald, Abbott, and Thompson had been able to bridge within the caucus began to, instead, deepen under the less assertive and less charismatic Bowell. According to (supposed) neutral observers such as Lady Aberdeen, the Bowell government was characterized by indecision and weakness. The governor general's wife stated in a letter that Thompson had "managed to keep the incongruous racial and religious sections in his Cabinet together but now [in the Bowell Cabinet] all are working against one another." She went on to state her hope that Laurier would win the next election, since "they [the Liberals] seem to have a stronger set of men as leaders." It was definitely not a rousing vote of approval for the new leader of the country.

A major source of the discontent amidst the Tories was that constant albatross, the Manitoba Schools Question. The matter had plagued Macdonald, Abbott, and Thompson but came to bedevil Bowell the most since its resolution landed on his doorstep just at the moment he came to power.

The two legal appeals that had been launched to overturn the new act had plodded through the Canadian courts before eventually landing in the lap of the colonial overseers in London. The results of the Brophy case, the second court challenge opposing the Schools Act, was laid on Bowell's Cabinet table early in 1895. Britain's Privy Council, the final court of appeal in the Empire, had ruled that the federal government of Canada could intervene legally even though education had been established as a provincial jurisdiction. The operative word was *could*.

Bowell's ministers faced a dilemma. The first option was to accept the Greenway changes and let matters be. That would have meant abandoning the French-speaking Manitobans and those who wanted separate Catholic and Protestant schools. Taking such a course could result in a catastrophic loss of support among French and Catholic supporters. The second option — introducing federal legislation to restore separate schools or to re-institute bilingualism in the province — would alienate the majority of voters in Manitoba, i.e., the Protestant, English-speaking population. Like-minded people in Ontario would also be opposed. Furthermore, such a move was likely to be unpopular with the country's provincial assemblies, as no province wished to see direct orders coming from Ottawa telling the legislatures what to do or what not to do.

Each alternative offended sizeable portions of the population. The influential Orange Order wanted one solution; the Catholic-French population of Quebec something totally different. There were also those within the law profession who disputed the 1890 laws for their questionable legality.

Because of that quandary, the caucus split along racial and religious lines. Bowell, whose selection as prime minister was at least in part because of his relationship with the Orange Order, found himself trying to find a balance. Men with strong anti-Catholic, anti-French prejudices, such as Wallace and John Fisher Wood, neither of whom were in the actual Cabinet but held significant jobs in government, had no qualms about supporting laws that would result in Catholics or French-speaking people in the West losing basic civil rights. The Quebecers in Cabinet — Caron, Ouimet, Angers, Ives — wanted Ottawa to act on behalf of the ethnic and religious minorities in Manitoba.

Instead of taking a stand and leading, Bowell obfuscated. He delayed any decision. He waffled. More importantly, he did not direct his Cabinet or his members of Parliament to follow a common path.

At first, Bowell seemed to support a re-establishment of separate schools in Manitoba. He truly believed that the provisions of the British North America Act — Canada's constitution — should be honoured and that the Manitoba Act of 1870 was something that should not be altered. He further believed that a compromise could eventually be worked out between Ottawa and the Manitoba legislature. Macdonald had been a great dealmaker, and Bowell hoped that he could imitate Sir John A. Unfortunately, Bowell lacked that delicate skill. He was consistently haunted by the fear of losing support from Protestants of Ontario and Manitoba. On the other hand, he also dreaded losing the Catholics in Quebec and in Manitoba. He could not please everyone, no matter what decision was made. A strong leader would have chosen one side or the other and then, by force of personality or some other means, convinced his immediate followers to go down that road with him.

Instead of taking a position, he tried to do what Macdonald, Thompson, and to a lesser extent Abbott had done: put things off, let others investigate potential solutions and take a "wait-and-see" position. It didn't work this time. He had none of Macdonald's charisma, none of Abbott's serenity, nor enough of Thompson's wisdom to carry off such a strategy.

Lord Aberdeen, in private correspondence, felt that Bowell never made himself fully aware enough of any issues, choosing instead to feign knowledge. Like a student who hadn't done his homework, Bowell tried to fake his way through the problem. The governor general found the new prime minister "slippery" and felt he was not to be trusted.

Despite the premier's hesitation and inaction, there were federal politicians who stepped up bringing their limited skills and influence to bear on the Schools Question. Thomas Mayne Daly, the Manitoba MP who was the minister of the interior and superintendent-general of Indian Affairs probably knew the region best, having been Brandon's first mayor. He'd also travelled extensively throughout the western region of the country. Admirably, he defended minority rights. Early in 1895, during the debate in the House of Commons, he called for tolerance for the Catholic minority in his province, for Catholics in Ontario and for Protestants in Quebec. As the Cabinet voice for Manitoba, his word should have carried considerable weight. It did not unfortunately, partly because Bowell did not support his statements by backing him either in caucus, in Parliament or with the press.

In February, under the direction of Justice Minister C.H. Tupper, legislation was drawn up intending to restore the Catholic schools in Manitoba. An Order-in-Council issued in late March 1895 declared that Manitoba had to restore separate school privileges to the province's Catholics. It argued that they had the right to share proportionately in the educational grants. It was intimated that if this was not done, Ottawa would come up with remedial legislation that might in the long run limit many powers of the Manitoba legislature.

Premier Greenaway and his attorney general, Clifford Sifton, made it clearly known that if Ottawa passed such legislation, they would simply refuse to obey. They argued on behalf of the provincial government that remedial legislation offered no better guarantee of efficiency, which had been their argument for changing the laws in the first place. The province claimed the Catholic schools were inefficient; many of the citizens were illiterate because of that incompetence; and that the province simply could not afford to provide separate systems given their limited financial resources.

Ottawa responded by saying that if nothing was settled by 1896, remedial action was destined to follow.

As the federal Cabinet considered how best to handle the Schools issue, they had other things to consider as well. The government's mandate was nearing an end. The country would be going to the polls no later than May of 1896.

In an attempt to avoid having the Schools question become an election issue, Bowell decided to table Tupper's proposed legislation and add an additional parliamentary session, extending the government's term a few more months. Old Tomorrow would have approved. But by seemingly favouring the minority rights in Manitoba and then tabling the solution, Bowell was waffling. More critically, his unwillingness to move on the matter seemed to indicate that he did not fully support his minister's efforts.

Tupper was outraged that all his work to craft the new legislation had been rejected. He saw the Cabinet's hesitancy — meaning Bowell's hesitancy — to enact his Order-in-Council as a personal repudiation. Indignantly, he tendered his resignation from the Cabinet on March 21. In answer to his angry Cabinet minister, Bowell offered a rather limp but poetic response. He wrote to Tupper: "[T]o appeal to the country when the heather was afire would be inexcusable."

Tupper replied to the prime minister in a letter dated March 25. "The beginning of the blaze is a more auspicious period than the middle.... You cannot, I fear, keep Parliament together long enough to see the end of this fire."

To lose so important a Cabinet member as Tupper would be a serious blow to the Tories. Bowell, in a move to save face as well hold onto one of the few bright lights in his Cabinet, called on three men who could appeal to Tupper's better nature. It took personal intervention by the governor general, Senator Drummond (a prominent and influential political figure), and Donald Smith to convince C.H. to come back to the Cabinet table. The trio met with the younger Tupper and reiterated the promise that if nothing could be worked out at the provincial level, then Ottawa would enact his remedial action in 1896.

Bowell now appeared to be backing the plan that Tupper had formulated. Licking his wounds but nursing a considerable grudge, the younger Tupper came back to the Cabinet table. However, the damage had been done and it was irreparable. Most of the Cabinet sided with the justice minister, although most kept their thoughts private. They felt that the prime minister had not supported Tupper and had not taken the firm stand that they could have all stood behind. An opportunity to show solidarity had been missed. Bowell's dithering cost him the respect and support of his Cabinet, and their feelings were increasingly shared by the rank and file of the Conservative caucus. Bowell's refusal to act decisively doomed his premiership.

The Tories bumbled on through 1895, accomplishing very little. The government seemed unable to achieve anything of real worth, and to make matters worse, the party was becoming less and less cohesive. For the most part, all these problems could be traced to one man: the prime minister. Bowell, as a senator, was not part of any debates in the House of Commons. He was not a part of the fellowship that the MPs shared in either the Commons, nor was he included in the private conversations held in nearby offices or taverns. A cool and remote individual at the best of times, he further alienated party members by not meeting with key individuals and developing a united front. Whispers and accusations, grumbling and discontent festered in those rooms. Bowell also did not have many strong allies to argue on his behalf.

On July 8, Finance Minister Foster announced that the government would not be passing remedial legislation before the next session of Parliament. That very day Senator Auguste-Réal Angers submitted his resignation in protest, citing his government's inaction. Two other prominent Quebec Tories, Adolphe-Phillippe Caron and Joseph Ouimet, followed suit, although they were hastily coaxed by more practical-minded members of the party to withdraw their resignations. Angers stubbornly refused to withdraw his resignation. Bowell continued his hands-off approach, refusing to discuss the matter with his fellow senator.

Public support for the government also crumbled in the face of its refusal to act in support of the French-Catholic minority in Manitoba. Two by-elections were held in Quebec following the government's decision; both resulted in resounding Tory losses.

By the end of the year, the Conservative Party was in total disarray. Nathaniel Clarke Wallace, the controller of customs, resigned from his position on December 14, 1895, citing his own government's policy — or lack thereof. Wallace — the staunch Orangeman (he was still grand master of the Orange Lodge) — had been brought to the Cabinet table to appease the Orange Order of Ontario. Through most of 1895, those very same Orangemen put persistent pressure on Wallace to resign, claiming that the Conservatives, in proposing remedial legislation, were taking a pro-Catholic stance. For several months, Wallace had been able to resist quitting, arguing to his supporters that his presence as a strong loyal Protestant was needed in the inner circle of the government. But staying on the government bench did not prevent him from stating his opinions. At various speaking engagements over the summer and fall, including during two by-elections in Ontario, Wallace criticized the idea of any kind of remedial action. In fact, he campaigned on behalf of anti-remedial candidates. Finally, by December, Wallace could take no more sitting on the fence, so he resigned from office. He also left the Conservative Party, knowingly taking a swath of the Ontario Orange vote with him.

Bowell did nothing to censure his maverick caucus member. His own association with the Orange Order was likely responsible, in part, for his failure to fight back against Wallace, but his lack of action can mostly be attributed to his characteristic inability to take a stand. Had he been more assertive and decisive — and frankly, less cowardly — the eventual outcome of all these resignations might have been quite different.

The opening of Parliament came on January 2, 1896, for what turned out to be the final session of the Conservative's tragic, unusual mandate.

It was plain to see that the governing party was in shambles. Conservative members refused to speak to each other. The secretive whispers that took place behind the backs of hands provided clear evidence that Tories were pitted against Tories. Laurier and his party sat smugly across the floor of the House of Commons, grinning at the open hostility on display. Within twenty-four hours of the Throne speech, the house of cards that Bowell sat atop came tumbling down.

The entire caucus was on the brink of open revolt. A not-so-secret cabal had been plotting within the Conservative Cabinet. Few of the ministers had confidence in their leader any longer. Seven members of the Cabinet — nearly half the Privy Council — met in secret to decide on a way forward. They felt that pressure needed to be brought to bear on the prime minister to force his resignation. The way to achieve that was to resign *en masse* from their positions as an open protest of Bowell's leadership. Finance Minister George Foster led the rebellion; joining him was Walter Montague — the Manitoba MP had succeeded Angers as agriculture minister — who could no longer bear the pressure from his home province. John Fisher Wood, the controller of customs, also resigned. He had been a subordinate when Bowell was customs minister. In that role, he, more than the others, had likely witnessed Bowell's fiery temper and monumental ego up close. That may have affected his decision. Justice minister C.H. Tupper's resentment had simmered, and he openly fumed at the prime minister's inertia, so his quitting the Cabinet — for the second time in less than a year — was not surprising. John Haggart, the minister of railways and canals, a key portfolio in the government, was openly disparaging of the prime minister, stating that Bowell, "from day to day, from time to time, like a sick girl hanging on to life, had refused to resign." Trade and Commerce Minister William Bullock Ives submitted his resignation, with similar sentiment. They all demanded that Bowell quit immediately. What was unclear was who they thought should be named as his replacement.

Bowell, quick of temper at the best of times, was irate. Calling the resigning Cabinet ministers a "nest of traitors," Bowell stormed out of the Parliament Buildings and raced to Rideau Hall to meet with Lord Aberdeen. The prime minister, nearly speechless with indignation, declared that he too was resigning, knowing that he had failed as a leader to keep a disparate group of men in line. Later historians have labelled Bowell "paranoid," but that is hardly true. There was no imagined mistrust or feeling that others were against him. It was very real and obvious.

In a typical display of narcissism, desperate to maintain his reputation, Bowell misled the governor general. Instead of letting Aberdeen know that the men no longer had confidence in him as a leader, he told the viceroy that that the ministers had resigned over the issue of remediation. The truth of the matter was much different. There was much more behind their decision to quit. They thoroughly disliked Bowell, and they especially disliked his manner of running the government. But the prime minister simply could not accept that he was a failure. Narcissists rarely if ever admit their defeats. So, he hid it from Aberdeen. The governor general may have suspected that there was more at play than Bowell was admitting, but he was not made aware of the exact nature of the ministers' mutiny.

Showing patience and calm deliberation, Aberdeen refused to accept the resignation of his prime minister immediately. He understood the quandary Bowell was facing with regard to the question of remedial action. He knew that the issue inspired strong emotions and thought it best to avoid making a decision that might worsen the situation. A composed, thoughtful man, the governor general felt it was his duty to keep the ship of state as calmly afloat as possible. The resignation of half a Cabinet was an unprecedented and serious political crisis, one the country did not need. To also lose the prime minister would be disastrous. The government had faced enough disruption over the past four years. The earl's hope was that he could manage to put a lid on this rebellion, keep things as serene as possible, for at least a few more months until an election was called.

The resignation of the prime minister would be catastrophic if the true reason for it was made public. A minor factor affecting the governor general's refusal to accept Bowell's resignation, and one that might even be seen as petty, was Aberdeen's strong distaste for the man likely to replace Bowell: Charles Tupper. Both Aberdeen and his wife strongly disliked Tupper. A few of the upper-crust Brits found the Nova Scotian doctor to be brash, self-serving, and lacking the graces they expected from someone serving as the Canadian high commissioner to England. For one thing, prim and proper Lady Aberdeen likely frowned upon the old physician's flirtatious nature.

With an election looming, Aberdeen argued that changes were likely anyhow. He spoke quietly to calm down the outraged Bowell, who paced about the drawing room of Government House.[7] The earl was trying to convince him that this was not a time to be hasty, nor could Parliament function without a prime minister and nearly half the Cabinet. He asked Bowell to patch things up if possible and bring the seven rebels back to the council table.

Thomas Mayne Daly, a Bowell loyalist in the Cabinet, recommended much the same thing to his friend and leader: bring the seven men who had resigned back into the fold. He wrote Bowell a letter in which he stated that he hoped the prime minister could find it in himself to forgive the "traitors." But he was realistic and direct in his letter. Daly flatly admitted to Bowell that if he could not form a government, the governor general would soon find someone else who could.

Bowell took four days to make an attempt. It went against his stubborn nature. He felt he'd been wronged and insulted. Considering the prime minister's attitude toward Foster and his co-conspirators, any effort to smooth the waters was at best half-hearted.

Bowell then tried a different tack. He felt that if he could pick a new group of seven ministers from the MPs in his caucus, then that problem would be solved for the time being. What he did not realize, though, was that the so-called traitors had done their legwork prior to their mass resignation. They had warned off all potential replacements, telling fellow Tory MPs that they should not answer the call from Bowell should they be asked to head up one of the vacant ministries. As a result, the prime minister was unable to replace the ministers who had resigned. Most of the caucus was decidedly behind the rebels. No other MPs stepped forward into any Cabinet role that Bowell offered.

The presence of Sir Charles Tupper in Ottawa made the situation all the more unstable. The so-called traitors had not formally sought his intervention and leadership that winter. When the prime minister summoned the high commissioner for his advice in early December, neither Bowell nor any of the Cabinet "bolters" had any sense of the drama and crisis that was to come.

There is no doubt that Tupper's son, C.H., at some point raised the possibility of Sir Charles taking over with both his father and with the conspirators. In a letter sent the previous autumn, C.H. had proposed giving up his own seat in the Commons for his father in order that the older man could enter the Cabinet and then take over as the head of the government.

The possibility that he might succeed Bowell was certainly on Sir Charles's mind, although he could not actively make that happen from his far-off perch in London. In a letter to Charlie dated November 25, 1895, Sir Charles admitted that he could not return to Canada without being "asked by B." [Bowell.] Then he speculated about some peculiar possibilities. "If B. wished to come here [as high commissioner] I might take his place in the Senate. The idea of taking your place for Pictou is preposterous. Nothing would induce me to go into the government if you left the Cabinet." The two Tuppers, ever in pursuit of bettering "Tupperdom," were considering some of the possible scenarios that would see Sir Charles take over the country's premiership.

Tupper's presence at the very moment the Cabinet imploded seemed serendipitous. But was it? He had been summoned back to Canada by Bowell. The prime minister and the high commissioner had kept up a continuous correspondence regarding the progress Tupper was making in his lobbying for the Pacific cable proposition and a fast Atlantic steamship service, an endeavour that would see a closer and faster link between Halifax and England. Shortly before Christmas in 1895, realizing that the government needed to consider changes in the areas of immigration and transportation, the prime minister had called Tupper back to Ottawa, knowing that he could provide invaluable information.

"Regarding fast line, come out to consult. Get all information possible." Bowell had wired Tupper on December 2, 1895. Tupper was on the first available steamer and arrived back in Ottawa the week before Christmas.

To the rebels in the Cabinet, it seemed that the high commissioner had arrived like a white knight to provide a solution to a disturbing problem.

Early on the morning of January 8, having failed in his efforts to reconstitute a Cabinet, Bowell submitted his formal resignation from office. The governor general took the letter to his office but did not act upon the matter immediately. He had other options to consider.

That afternoon, an aide-de-camp from the governor general rapped on the door of room 24 of the Senate offices with a message for Auguste-Réal Angers. The French Canadian senator, who had left the Cabinet the previous August, was considered a wise, sober elder member of the Conservative Party, even if he no longer sat at the Privy Council table. Aberdeen wanted his advice on what to do about Bowell's resignation. Angers hailed a cab and made the short trip to Rideau Hall, where he sat down with the governor general to discuss options. Anger's advice was that Bowell's resignation be refused, on the grounds that the House had not yet voted on the Speech from the Throne. It was a flimsy excuse, but it worked. That evening, Aberdeen informed Bowell that he was refusing to let the prime minister step down.

That same day — perhaps through a lowly messenger, servant, or parliamentary page — several of the rebel ministers learned that Bowell had misled the governor general when explaining why the seven men had quit. The "bolters," by means of a spokesman, emphatically told Aberdeen that they were not anti-remedialists. They also let it be known that they'd be willing to follow Sir Charles Tupper as leader. Aberdeen listened to their version of the story but took no immediate action that night. His feeling that Bowell was slippery had been confirmed, but now he was faced with appointing a man he strongly disliked as prime minister.

The next day, news appeared in the Ottawa papers that Aberdeen's aide, the same man that had summoned Angers, had been spotted meeting with Wilfrid Laurier, the Opposition leader. C.H. Tupper and Foster took the news badly, thinking that the governor general might be planning to call upon the Liberals to form a government. The very idea shocked the Conservatives to the core. Could Aberdeen seriously be considering asking Laurier to become prime minister? C.H. Tupper said, "We all turned in like sheep into the fold, at the very rumour." On January 15, all the so-called traitors returned to the Cabinet, except C.H. He stayed out of the mix pending his father's ascension to the premiership.

What most people did not know was that there had been a secret meeting held between the prime minister and Sir Charles in Ottawa. With his self-confidence utterly eroded, the prime minister was ready to turn things over to Tupper. The Cabinet members, at least those who knew of the behind-the-scenes dealings, were now more than willing to throw their support to the old Nova Scotia physician.

It was a humiliated Bowell who called on Tupper. (C.H. knew of the meeting, as it took place in his front parlour. However, he did not attend.) Accompanying Bowell was Senator Frank Smith, one of the few loyalists that the prime minister could count on. Bowell knew the game was over. The trio of old politicians hammered out a most unusual arrangement. Bowell would see to it that a reliable Tory gave up his seat so that Tupper could run in a by-election. He offered to then name Sir Charles as leader in the House until Parliament dissolved. At that point, he would resign his post, and Tupper would take over as leader of the party and as prime minister.

(Bowell had made it known that he would have preferred to turn things over to Donald Smith, the MP from Manitoba who had been a key figure in building the CPR.[8] But the Cabinet revolt and the presence of Charles Tupper at such an opportune time had scuttled that plan. At any rate, Smith refused the offer.)

Bowell spoke openly to Sir Charles. "I have no quarrel with your son," he said. "I've always found him frank and candid."

Charles nodded silently, knowing that C.H. detested Bowell but had kept it mostly hidden from the man. Charles and Mackenzie, on the other hand, had always been on good terms with each other.

The prime minister went further, even offering to name Charlie as the successor to his father as high commissioner in London. Bowell, Tupper, and Smith then discussed a few other details. The Cabinet ministers were to be re-instated in their posts. Sir Charles would be sworn in as secretary of state. As soon as the last session of the House ended, Bowell's resignation as prime minister would become official, but he would remain as leader of the government in the Senate. Tupper would officially become prime minister at that point.

It was all rather civilized, carried out with calm negotiation despite the fiery temperaments of both Bowell and Tupper. Then again, there was no reason for them to lose their tempers. The two men had little in the way of antagonism between them. They were old comrades-in-arms, and there had never been any quarrels or bad blood to colour their relationship. Both were determined to do what was necessary — or what they believed was necessary — for the party as well as for the country.

A chastened Bowell had finally acknowledged that his time as leader was at an end. He once again visited the governor general and told Aberdeen the details of what he had worked out with Tupper and Smith. He intended to stay as prime minister until the last session of Parliament expired on April 26. He would then turn over his office to Tupper. Aberdeen accepted.

It was a humbling end to a short and tumultuous ride.

Bowell's final act before leaving office on April 26 was to name Donald Smith as high commissioner to Britain. The next day, his official resignation was greeted with little fanfare and not much in the way of sadness among the Conservatives in Ottawa. (The Liberals didn't care much for the man either.) Dr. Charles Tupper, the seventy-five-year-old Father of Confederation from Nova Scotia, was sworn into office four days later. Canada had what turned out to be its fifth prime minister in five years.

The press seized upon the end of Bowell's term to criticize the governor general — and his domineering wife — for what was labelled interference in the partisan politics of the day. Lord and Lady Aberdeen had been in favour of Bowell being named Thompson's successor. Aberdeen had tried to keep Bowell in office despite the "advice" of several ministers. Now, it was the governor general's turn to be criticized for yet another change in the leadership of the Conservative Party.

Bowell did not slink away to lick his wounds in Belleville. As a senator, he was appointed for life.[9] He showed no intention of giving up that position, despite the rejection he'd experienced at the hands of his own party. Showing remarkable compassion, Tupper kept Bowell on as government leader in the Senate and a member of the Cabinet. Although he fumed at those he had to deal with and disliked many Conservatives that he passed daily in the halls of the Parliament Buildings, he continued to do what was asked of him.

He spoke in Senate debates for the next two decades, usually staying loyal to the Tory Party line. He did make a remark in his later years that he was so disgusted with party politics that he planned to vote according to his principles, but those principles always seemed to be aligned with his conservative views and the policies of the Conservative party. He was never comfortable with the label of rebel or maverick.

Almost immediately after resigning from the prime minister's position, he returned to his hometown of Belleville. With some flourish, he resumed active control over the Belleville *Intelligencer*, a job he had given up with his promotion to Cabinet in 1878. He continued to make regular visits from his home in Ottawa to his newspaper office in Belleville even past the age of ninety. The roles of newspaper publisher and senator kept him active and vigorous through the election of Laurier's Liberals, the Boer War, the arrival of a new century, the death of Queen Victoria, and even the start of the Great War. He lived to see Robert Borden's Conservatives win the federal election of 1911.

In 1916, at the age of ninety-three he took the train west to visit his son in Vancouver and made an even more arduous trek north to visit the Yukon territory. Not an easy trip even today, he had to put up with numerous hardships that would have taxed the endurance of much younger people.

Bowell died in Belleville on December 10, 1917. He was ninety-four years old. Sadly, at his funeral there were no elected representatives present — none serving at the time nor any who had served with Bowell. It spoke of his lack of personal connections that, after fifty years as a member of Parliament, as a Cabinet minister, as a senator, and as prime minister, he did not warrant official government recognition. Although never a pariah to his fellow Tories, there was an obvious lack of affection for the man who was prime minister for a year and a half.

Bowell, like every man, had his strengths and weaknesses. He was a tireless worker who ran his business and his political offices with efficiency. He began his political career as a rabid Orangeman but he eventually tempered his views to the point that the Toronto *Globe* acknowledged that it was Bowell who made the Orange Order more tolerable to Catholics. He was both vain and fussy, but his honesty was never questioned. That was a notable thing in an era of flagrant political deceit. Although not a great lawmaker or speaker, he endured the ups and downs of politics from Confederation all the way to the First World War. Administration seemed to be his talent. Political deftness was not.

Chapter Five

————————— ◈ —————————

Sir Charles Tupper:
"Finally … It's About Time
You Were Prime Minister!"

THE BRITISH WINTER OF 1895 was typically chilly and damp. Seated at his dark but functional office in Bexleyheath, a suburb of London, Sir Charles Tupper was a long way from his roots in rural Nova Scotia. As he sorted through a number of letters and memos, he reflected on his long years of service to Canada. Life had been good for the country doctor from Amherst. He was a relatively famous man, known for his accomplishments across the sea in Canada. He loved England and all the finer things that came with living in what was then the world's largest and most progressive city. He regularly met with nobility, diplomats from all over the world, royals, and even from time to time with Queen Victoria herself. He thoroughly loved the job of high commissioner. He had given up, for the most part, the rigours of electoral politics for the different, though not necessarily easier life as Canada's representative in London. He still argued. He still discussed the matters of the day. He still spent long hours ironing out deals. All those activities satisfied the old politician in him. Yet the job of high commissioner was different from being a member of Parliament. The political actors were much the same, but the stage was more grand, more worldly. And all that suited the Nova Scotia doctor known as The Bulldog.

The square-jawed Tupper, with his full head of wavy hair and prominent sideburns, looked the part of the successful doctor and politician. His prominent belly, usually tucked into a tight vest, betrayed his fondness for the sumptuous meals and brandy on offer in the finer homes of upper-crust London. Although he walked through life with a permanent scowl on his face, he was not an unhappy man. All in all, it had been a good life for someone who started from humble beginnings in a small town near the Bay of Fundy.

He'd been Nova Scotia's premier; became a founding Father of Confederation; over many years had persuaded his province to stay in that very federation; had worked in Ottawa as a Cabinet minister for years; had personally advised several prime ministers; and now was more than comfortable acting as Canada's ambassador to Britain, living and working in the heart of the Empire. He enjoyed the entry into London high society that his lofty position afforded. He felt at home among the diplomats and aristocracy who came to the British capital to mix, do business, and feel good about their place in the world.

Canada was never far from his thoughts, though. And he kept his ear to the ground, well aware of the vicissitudes of Ottawa politics. C.H. kept him abreast of events as they unfolded, as did party colleagues from across Canada. Thanks to one of the marvels of the age, the transatlantic cable that spanned the five-thousand-kilometre distance between Canada and England, he was able to be in touch almost instantly.

Charles Napier Tupper was born in Amherst, Nova Scotia on July 2, 1821. His father was a pastor of the local Baptist church and his mother, not unexpectedly, was described as a pious, devout woman. Tupper grew up on a small farm in the northwest corner of the province, a stone's throw to both the Bay of Fundy to the southwest and the Northumberland Strait to the north, so one might have expected Tupper to become a shipbuilder or that he would have some connection to the sea. Farming or the ministry were among the other limited career choices for him.

Tupper's parents, however, were ambitious for the success of their children and were zealous in the education of their sons (Charles had a brother, two sisters, and eventually six half-sisters and brothers). Charles Sr. tutored the young Charles and his brother Nathan at home while at the same time sending them to local grammar schools. In 1837 the sixteen-year-old Charles was sent to the Horton Academy in Wolfville, the forerunner of Acadia University. Tupper studied Latin, Greek, science, and became a proficient reader, if not speaker, of French. Upon graduation, he taught school in New Brunswick for two years before deciding that that was not the career path he wished to take. Moving to Windsor, Nova Scotia, he began to study medicine with a family doctor there. That profession piqued his interest, so he decided to take up the study of medicine formally. At that time, the only medical school in Canada was at McGill University in Montreal; the most reputable one in the British Empire, though, was the one in Edinburgh. Tupper took a risk. He borrowed money, boarded a ship in Halifax, and enrolled at the prestigious Scottish school. He graduated with his MD degree in August of 1843.

Scotland provided the young Canadian with an education beyond the walls of the college campus. In university, Tupper acquired a taste for fine Scotch, good theatre, and the company of attractive women. He developed a persona that was at the same time sophisticated and down-to-earth. He was not a shy man and touted his own strengths if given the opportunity.

Although he could boast of his intellect and his social skills, Tupper was not an especially attractive figure physically. Shorter than average in height, he tended to be slightly overweight, even as a young man. He had a full head of dark hair and exceedingly bushy sideburns, a fashion he adhered to even into his seventies when he eventually became prime minister. Contemporaries throughout his life noted that he tended to be stern, his face rarely breaking into a smile unless it was to show his scorn for an opponent's gaffe. Yet despite that seriousness, he could turn on charm when opportunity called for it.

The newly minted physician returned to Canada in late 1843 and set up a practice in his hometown. In addition to being the local doctor, he also owned the local pharmacy. As a physician, he bragged that he never refused a sick call. He travelled about the countryside on horseback, paying house calls to farm families. He dealt with not only illness and disease but also with farm accidents and mishaps. He was known to stay up all night nursing ill patients. A devoted doctor he may have been, but it seems that his methods of treatment were not always in keeping with accepted medical practice. One apocryphal anecdote told of Tupper spending an entire night beside the sick wife of a political rival, giving her half-hourly doses of champagne.

As a doctor and a surgeon, he chalked up a noteworthy number of successes. According to research done in 1932 by medical historian John D. Comrie, Tupper performed 116 obstetric operations by the time he was twenty-two years old.[1] While still a young man, Tupper achieved renown as a doctor in the colony of Nova Scotia.

Practising medicine was not as lucrative in Tupper's time as it eventually became. Patients often paid with services; some even paid with farm produce. The doctor himself, though, made a point of paying his own debts on time. That was something he did throughout his life. According to his secretaries, he also developed early on a habit of never making appointments that he feared he could not honour.

Tupper enjoyed the company of women. He was a flirt, a man who knew how to charm women quite easily. One nickname he earned as a young man was "the ram of Cumberland County." That sobriquet stuck with him for most of his life and may have coloured some people's attitudes toward him. He reputedly broke off at least two engagements before he eventually met, courted, and married Frances Morse, the granddaughter of a prominent founder of the town of Amherst. Fellow Father of Confederation Edward Whelan described her as being a "very fine and handsome woman." Charles and Frances were married in 1846 and eventually had six children. The couple remained married for sixty-six years. Although he himself had been brought up a Baptist, Frances and the children were all baptized Anglicans. Those kinds of things mattered in nineteenth-century society.

Throughout Charles's political life, Frances Tupper acted as his most trusted advisor. Just as Annie Thompson and — to a lesser degree — Agnes Macdonald counselled their husbands, Frances often had the final word when Dr. Tupper asked for advice. She was an intelligent woman. Although she mostly stayed in the background, her strong opinions influenced her husband's actions.

Frances may have participated in her husband's political decisions from the background, but she enjoyed the social aspects of political life. When Charles was appointed high commissioner in the 1880s, she appreciated the high life in London too, spending weekends with the likes of Lord and Lady Carnarvon at Highclere Castle or with the Cunards, the Canadian-born shipping magnates.

Tupper did not enter active political life until 1855. That year, the leader of the Conservative Party in Nova Scotia, James William Johnston, recruited the young physician to run against the best-known politician in the province, Joseph Howe. There was, it seemed, little likelihood that the upstart doctor could defeat the legendary Howe.

Howe with his irrepressible newspaper, *The Nova Scotian*, had been influential in bringing responsible government to the colony in the 1840s. Howe was a famous — or should that be infamous? — individual in Nova Scotia. He was the subject of charges in a libel trial in 1835, of which he was quickly acquitted. The duel that he fought with the judge's son following the court case added to Howe's colourful reputation. (The other duelist missed, and Howe fired his shot into the air.) He'd been part of the first "responsible" government formed in the British Empire in 1848 and had held the important position of provincial secretary. He resigned as an MLA in 1853 to become Nova Scotia's first commissioner of railways, a position that was secure and paid more than the pittance given to legislative members. Yet Howe could not keep his attention away from elected politics in the colony. After all, he was the man most responsible for achieving responsible government in Nova Scotia and politics was in his blood. So, he decided to once again throw his hat into the ring.

As the 1855 election approached, however, Howe was not able to focus his energies on winning back his seat. As well as fulfilling his duties as commissioner of railways, he was also deeply involved in recruiting Americans to assist Britain in the Crimean War.[2] It is unsurprising, given the fact that he was being pulled in several directions, that Howe did not give the Cumberland election the attention he should have. In truth, he and his advisors believed that he did not have to put in much of an effort since he was up against a newcomer who had yet to make a political reputation of any sort in his own riding, let alone the colony. To many people's surprise, Howe lost the election, although the following year he was able to return to the legislature when he was acclaimed in the seat formerly held by the retired provincial secretary L.M. Wilkins.

Tupper and Howe, who held distinctly different views on the way forward for their province, became rivals. During the 1855 campaign, Howe labelled Tupper "the wicked wasp of Cumberland," a pointed reference to Tupper's cutting tone of speech. The young doctor was boisterous and was described more than once as a "blowhard," but he was sincere in his convictions. Tupper pulled no punches during his fiery addresses to the voters. They liked that about him. He had a remarkable memory and could snatch facts seemingly out of thin air, throwing them at an opponent. His arguments were, perhaps, too facile at times, and what he said would often haunt him in the following days. Goldwin Smith, the renowned British historian and writer once said of Tupper that he was a man of "extraordinary force and a thunderer of the platform, although the staple of his oratory was purely exaggeration with a large measure of rather vulgar invective." That assessment held true from his earliest campaign to his last.

Following the election, Howe declared in a rather self-serving way but one that acknowledged the abilities of his opponent, "I have been defeated by the future leader of the Conservative Party."

In the legislature, Tupper quickly displayed his political talents. The Tories had lost the election, but the Opposition bench gave Tupper ample opportunities to attack the policies of the Liberal government. He revelled in the rough-and-tumble arguments of the legislature. He brought to the Conservative Party an energy and passion that drew attention to both himself and the issues he championed. At a caucus meeting in 1856, he laid out a radical direction for his party to follow. He suggested — and this was revolutionary in its day — that the Conservatives consider actively appealing to the Roman Catholic population of the province. Such were his powers of persuasion that several Catholic Liberals crossed the floor to join Tupper and his Tories. The Liberals were thus reduced to a minority government, defeated in the legislature and subsequently defeated in the colony's 1857 election.

Tupper was named provincial secretary in Premier Johnston's new Tory government. The job was multi-faceted. Tupper was essentially the treasurer of the colony, managing the finances of a region that had scattered communities linked by only a few roads. The other essential part of the job was to act as liaison between the government in Halifax and the Colonial Office in London. That involved being the government representative at many ceremonial occasions, meeting with dignitaries from England and the other colonies, as well as maintaining regular communication with the lieutenant governor. Tupper used his time in office to establish a number of long-lasting connections. Even the illustrious Howe eventually fell under his spell.

In his first speech as provincial secretary, Tupper announced the new government's ambitious plan for railway construction. He began talks with counterparts in New Brunswick about building an intercolonial railway. In 1858 he took the bold step of travelling to England to secure London's backing for the venture. Nothing came of the discussions since, it seemed, the British were "too much engaged with their own immediate interests." The imperial rejection in some ways coloured many of Tupper's attitudes in future dealings with the Mother Country, although he was always a monarchist and great admirer of all things British.

Secretary Tupper touted the colony's ample mining resources as something that had the potential to enrich the provincial coffers, if only they could get those resources to market elsewhere. Nova Scotia's mines produced great quantities of coal, gold, iron, gypsum, and salt, but all those riches were virtually worthless unless they could reach British Empire or American markets. Tupper convinced the premier to abolish a mining monopoly that had existed for years, opening the way for fresh investment and exploitation of the assets. To Tupper, it was essential that Nova Scotia promote what he called their "inexhaustible mines."

In the Nova Scotia election held in May of 1859, Tupper barely held onto his seat. The same was true of the rest of the Conservative Party caucus. The day after the results were in, the Tories held the slimmest of margins and formed only a minority government. Early in 1860, the party lost a confidence vote in the legislature. Premier Johnston asked for dissolution, but the lieutenant governor, Lord Mulgrave, instead called on the Liberals to form a government. Tupper was outraged at Mulgrave's decision. He claimed that five of the Liberals who were elected should have been disqualified. The irascible doctor petitioned the Colonial Office for Mulgrave's recall but to no avail. Tupper then turned his vitriol on the Liberals and his old rival Joseph Howe, who'd become premier in late 1860, and for the next three years hectored the governing Liberals on policies such as restricting the voting franchise. In speeches in the legislature and around the colony, Tupper was able to give voice to his criticism of the Liberals. He was offered another venue too: writing editorials for the Halifax *British Colonist*, a highly partisan Tory newspaper.

His political duties kept him away from his constituency of Cumberland for long stretches. As he took on more responsibilities, he wisely decided to give up his medical practice in Amherst, transferring it to his brother Nathan, who had also become a physician. Charles made Halifax his new base out of political practicality. He set up a new medical practice in the capital, where he kept seeing patients despite his political duties. Such was his reputation — and ambition — that he was named chief medical officer of the city of Halifax. In 1863 he was elected as the first president of the Medical Society of Nova Scotia. Tupper never gave up practising medicine. Even when he eventually moved to Ottawa, he kept his black medical bag under his desk in the House of Commons. He made as much money from doctoring as he did as a politician.

In a time when religion played such a crucial role in determining political decisions, Charles was thoroughly unbiased in his opinions. He grew up in a Baptist household but never professed any strong religious views. Later in life, he was known to attend Anglican services because his wife was a member of that church. He never formally became affiliated with any religious denomination, however. As a man of science, he was likely an atheist (or possibly agnostic) but taking such a stance would have been political poison at the time. He once commented that when it came to religious matters, he "indulged in no speculations and harboured no doubts."

Tupper's lack of interest in religion was mirrored by a lack of interest in alcohol. The nineteenth century was one where alcohol abuse ran deeply through all strata of society. Macdonald was a public drunk. Thomas D'Arcy McGee descended into such a state of alcoholism that had he not been assassinated in 1868, he would likely have died early from his severe drinking problems. Macdonald once told McGee that "this ministry cannot afford to carry two drunks. You will have to stop." Tupper on the other hand was never seen to be drunk or affected by liquor. He socially imbibed but only to the extent of having a solitary drink out of courtesy.

In 1863, the Conservatives returned to office with a huge majority, winning forty of the fifty-five seats in the colony. They were elected on two key platform issues: the reform of education and the expansion of railway building. The voters of Nova Scotia were very much in favour of both. Tupper was the chief architect of the party platform, so he devoted much of his energy over the next few years to ensuring its success. He eventually shepherded through the legislature the Free School Act, establishing state-funded common schools. At the same time, he called upon people such as Sandford Fleming to extend the reach of Nova Scotia's railway system. Government surveys and tentative lines were planned, although most of the work was never undertaken.

In the wake of the election, Tupper initially returned to his duties as provincial secretary. It was only for a short term, however, as Premier

Johnston accepted a call to the Nova Scotia bench to become a judge in May of 1864. Tupper, as predicted years earlier by Joseph Howe, became party leader and premier of the vibrant coastal colony.

Almost immediately, Tupper became a central figure in what would be his defining legacy: a Father of Confederation. For years, the colonies of British North America tossed around the idea of colonial union. The Canadas, Newfoundland, Prince Edward Island, New Brunswick, and Nova Scotia all had reason to merge into one entity, but each of them also seemed to have issues with union. Defence, intercolonial trade, and sharing the building of rail lines were key influences in favour of union. Avoiding annexation by the United States was probably the overriding concern of the proponents of Confederation. On the other hand, control of customs duties, the threat of higher taxes, and the potential for military conscription were some of the reasons put forward to oppose the proposal. A big concern among the "anti-confederates" was the loss of power to a central, federal government — especially one more than a thousand kilometres away in central Canada. Colonial delegations had debated the issue as early as the 1850s, although there had been advocates in favour of the plan even years before that.

Tupper himself had initially been one of those opposed to the proposal. In that regard, he was on the same page as Joseph Howe. Yet by 1860 he had completely altered his views and had become one of the colonies' loudest proponents of the plan. In many speeches around the Maritimes, Tupper spoke of the commercial advantages, particularly for resource rich Nova Scotia. In a lecture he delivered in Saint John, New Brunswick, in 1860, he reflected on the state of British North America. Tupper argued that the small, sparsely populated colonies of British North America could "never hope to occupy a position of influence or importance except in connection with their larger sister Canada [Ontario and Quebec.]" His futile attempt, in 1858, to get financial backing in England likely opened his eyes to the lack of concern that Britain had for the affairs of her British North American colonies. "A British America, stretching from Atlantic to Pacific," Tupper said, "would in a few years exhibit to the world a great and powerful organization, with British Institutions, British sympathies, and British feelings, bound indissolubly to the throne of England." John A. Macdonald could not have said it better.

Tupper, in the same way as his fellow premier Macdonald in the Canadas, looked at the civil war raging south of the border and worried about American threats to annex Canada. A genuine concern ran through all of the British colonies that a victorious North could easily mobilize its existing army and march north to conquer Britain's disparate, weakly defended colonies. The fear was not unfounded. The American policy of *manifest destiny* was popular in the United States. Presidents James Monroe, Andrew Jackson and James Polk had all touted the idea that America should encompass the entire continent under one government. Many Americans sided with their leaders (although, fortunately, both Abraham Lincoln and Ulysses S. Grant opposed the idea).

Premier Tupper pushed a resolution through the Nova Scotia legislature in March of 1864 proposing a formal conference to discuss Maritime union. This, he believed, was at least a step toward further merger with the Canadas. The governments of the other Maritime colonies agreed to meet in Charlottetown in September with Tupper and New Brunswick premier Leonard Tilley as co-chairs.

The political leaders in the Canadas learned of the conference and decided to more or less "crash the party." Governor General Monck asked that the Canadian politicians be granted time to address the meeting. Tilley and Tupper both agreed to allow the delegation. John A. Macdonald, Georges-Étienne Cartier, George Brown, D'Arcy McGee, and Alexander T. Galt made the trip to Charlottetown, setting out from Quebec City on August 29.[3] Tupper warmly welcomed the men (and some of their wives) from the Canadas. It suited his own ambition and plans. He cleared the original Maritime union agenda so that Macdonald and Brown could make a pitch to their colonial counterparts.

Each politician brought his own bias to the plan. Macdonald believed that uniting the colonies would save them from American expansionism, a great fear that wove its way all through his long public life. He dazzled the Maritimers with his knowledge of British history and clear and convincing critique of the American system. He condemned what he saw as its weak

THE LOST PRIME MINISTERS

central government in Washington. Cartier felt that Canada East's French population needed the Maritime votes in order to balance with Canada West's booming English population. Brown hoped that a full union might end what he saw as French domination over the affairs of government. He also believed that a federal union would finally solve the political stalemate that had plagued the Canadas for several years. Galt, the Canadian inspector-general, had thought-out the details of a possible union and had very clear ideas about the division of powers. He was also an expert on banking and trade protocols. As for Tupper, he foresaw Nova Scotia's fortunes improving with an intercolonial railway and intercolonial trade to open markets for his province's myriad resources.

The bottles of champagne that were brought ashore to be consumed after the formal meetings may have helped to convince the Maritime leaders to listen.

Macdonald, Cartier, Brown et al. were persuasive enough in their presentations that everyone agreed to meet again a little over a month later in Quebec City for another conference. There, they worked out details to plan a way forward for bringing the colonies together in a federal system, one that respected individual colonial — now provincial — differences. In many ways, the folks from Canada East and Canada West were preaching to the choir since a majority of the men attending the Charlottetown conference — Tupper, Tilley, George Coles of Prince Edward Island — were enthusiastic about the idea and had been touting such a plan for years.

No one was more enthusiastic about the scheme than Tupper. He and Macdonald hit it off immediately, beginning a close friendship that lasted for decades. The two men were similar in some fashion. Both had oversized egos. Both were energetic, able to work long hours on matters that they cared about. Both had steel-trap minds and photographic memories. Both men loved to have a good time. Tupper could never hope to keep up with Macdonald's prolific drinking, but his enjoyment of parties became something that brought him some notice — especially if women were invited to participate.

At the Quebec Conference, Tupper led the Nova Scotia delegation.[4] As details were ironed out, he became convinced that this would be an easy sell to his fellow Nova Scotians. While he had certain principles to which he held, he also demonstrated an ability to compromise. During the initial discussions, he supported the idea of a legislative union — a single legislature would serve the united colonies. When Cartier and Hector-Louis Langevin opposed that, fearing for the French minority, Tupper was able to be convinced to back their alternative plan: a federal union with a strong central government and legislatures for each of the individual provinces.

It was Tupper who took the lead in developing the idea of regional representation in the form of a Senate. Like all the other colonies, he could see that unless there was some form of equal regional representation, giant Canada West would dominate and control every issue. An upper chamber of Parliament with equal representation for each region would allow the smaller, less populated parts of the country to have an equal say on legislation. That provided a counterbalance to the huge majority from Canada West.

He held firm in a belief that the provinces should retain control over their individual natural resources. The one discussion that proved to be difficult to sell to his constituents was Tupper's backing of the plan to let the federal government control customs, the chief source of revenue for each of the legislatures. In exchange, he held out for a per capita subsidy for each Nova Scotian. Opponents of Confederation in his home province jumped on this compromise as being a poor deal for Nova Scotia. It was.

The delegates to the Quebec conference drafted what they called the 72 Resolutions, a comprehensive outline of how the union would function. It laid out many of the plans that eventually became the *British North America Act*. But first, the men had to sell the idea in their home colonies.

Tupper returned home with high expectations. He figured that his fellow Nova Scotians would see the logic of the items in the 72 Resolutions. Although he had the backing of both London and Nova Scotia's Opposition leader, Adams George Archibald,[5] it was not an easy sell to the average fisherman, farmer, or merchant in Nova Scotia. Politics in the province changed almost immediately. Instead of Conservative versus Liberal, it became confederate versus anti-confederate.

Bad news arrived in September of 1865 when Leonard Tilley, the pro-Confederation premier in neighbouring New Brunswick, was defeated in his colony's election, one that was basically a plebiscite on Confederation.

In his own colony, Tupper was facing vocal opposition to the idea from the likes of influential newspaperman and sometime politician Joseph Howe. Tupper could see that going to the polls over the issue might be a disaster.

Instead, Tupper managed to keep his government intact and, with a wiliness worthy of John A. Macdonald, promised changes to the 72 Resolutions so that the deal was a better one for Nova Scotia. On April 18, 1866, he nursed a motion through the legislature to accept the terms of union. He then boarded a ship for England where he, Archibald, Macdonald, and many of the other representatives from the colonies planned to hold yet another conference to hammer together the actual act creating Canada. After the politicians of British North America had done the heavy lifting, it was up to the Colonial Office in London to rubberstamp the plan. While waiting for the other delegates to arrive, Tupper penned many letters in the British press expounding the virtues of Confederation. He was more or less forced to publish his opinions so as to counteract an anti-Confederation pamphlet campaign written by Howe, who was in London to argue against the proposed union.

The London conference of December 1866 made a number of changes to the earlier resolutions. In one important edit, the delegates agreed to give the federal government the power to take remedial action to protect separate schools. This would prove to be a revision with very significant consequences. Twenty-five years down the road, the existence of this power would cause a vexing problem for future prime ministers. Tupper also agreed to allow the federal government to take responsibility for the coastal fisheries, a policy that did not sit well with Nova Scotia fishermen.

With the conference concluded, the enthusiastic premier sailed home to Halifax early in 1867. He began to implement many of the changes that needed to be made in his colony prior to Confederation. He reduced the size of the legislature and the executive council, since many of the tasks previously handled at the colonial level now fell under the responsibilities of the federal government in Ottawa. He prepared a list of prominent Nova Scotians suitable to serve the new province as its senators. Thomas Archibald was prominent on that list, as were fellow Fathers of Confederation Robert Dickey and John Ritchie.

Significantly, an act was passed that prevented anyone from holding a seat in the provincial legislature and the federal House of Commons simultaneously. Knowing that he was likely to be named to the federal Cabinet, Tupper shuffled his papers and turned over the premiership to Hiram Blanchard. In the first Canadian federal election that summer,[6] Tupper was elected for Cumberland but was the only pro-Confederation candidate to win in all the province. Eighteen of the nineteen Nova Scotia constituencies voted for the anti-confederate forces of Joseph Howe. It was going to be a hard sell.

Undaunted, Tupper arrived in Ottawa in June 1867 ready to take up a major portfolio in Macdonald's first federal Cabinet. Macdonald consulted with both Tupper and Tilley about who should be named privy councillors from their provinces. In fact, he basically left the decision up to the two former premiers. Tilley took on the Customs portfolio. A snag developed, though, as it often did (and does) in the actual naming of the ministers. Setting the precedent for every prime minister who followed, Macdonald had to take into account the religious affiliation of his choices, allow for proportional representation from the regions, and consider things like the particular interests or talents of a potential member. In the end, Tupper — along with Thomas D'Arcy McGee — did not make the final cut, but it was a tribute to the Nova Scotia doctor's persona that he advised Macdonald to select an Irish Catholic, Edward Kenny, to take one of the Nova Scotia seats. The other Cabinet position went to newly minted Senator Adams Archibald, who was a Protestant and very much pro-Confederation but also a member of the Liberal Party. That was an astute move, as it had the potential to change the opinions of some Nova Scotian Liberals. Graciously, Tupper accepted that he, one of the key men in putting together the new country, was not named to the Privy Council table where the important decisions were made. It was a big sacrifice and a blow to his ego, but Charles saw the wisdom in the choices that had been made. He swallowed his pride and took his seat as a mere member of Parliament.[7]

Through all the intensity and tumult of pulling together British North America, Tupper kept his fingers in other pies. He was still a medical doctor, very concerned with improving the health and welfare of Nova Scotians.

Somehow, he found the time to organize, with other doctors in the colonies, the Canadian Medical Association. Perhaps not so remarkably, he was elected as its founding president. During the 1860s, Tupper was also the moving force behind establishing a medical school at Dalhousie University in Halifax.

Tupper and his old rival Joseph Howe butted heads early in the first Parliament but within a year, things changed dramatically. Howe went to England to push for a repeal of the portions of the British North America Act that had affected Nova Scotia's entry into the federal union. Macdonald could choose no better a representative than Dr. Tupper to sail to London to counteract anything Howe might say. In the British capital, the two Nova Scotians got together to discuss what Tupper called "better terms." So effective was Tupper that the country doctor talked the urban newspaperman into not only accepting Confederation but into accepting a seat at the Cabinet table. Howe was a very bright man, and despite the fact he had a bloc of other Nova Scotia MPs to back up his opinions, he saw that Confederation was a *fait accompli*. Might as well make the best of things. Running in the Hants County by-election of 1868, Howe campaigned on the issue of "better terms" for Nova Scotia. Tupper, as incongruous as it may have been given the animosity that had existed between the two a year previously, campaigned on his old rival's behalf and the two men stood side by side against what was still a strong anti-confederate faction. Howe prevailed, entered Cabinet, and served as secretary of state for the provinces, an influential office from which to obtain those better terms he sought so dearly.

Dramatic events filled Tupper's days. A year later, when the Métis rebellion in Manitoba began, Tupper's daughter Emma went to the Red River region with her husband, an army officer, who made the journey west with William McDougall, the newly appointed lieutenant governor of Rupert's Land (the name given to the land, transferred from the Hudson's Bay Company to Canada, that now comprises northern Ontario and Quebec and all the land between Ontario and British Columbia). Tupper was understandably alarmed when he heard of the Métis uprising, fearing for the safety of his daughter and son-in-law. Word came to Nova Scotia that McDougall's party had been stopped and some of their possessions seized. Several of the Canadian contingent, including Tupper's son-in-law and daughter, were being held under house arrest. Although he was 3,500 kilometres away in Halifax, Dr. Tupper decided to go west to rescue her.

The trip was a taxing one, partially because the route was so circuitous. From Halifax, he took a ship south to New York City and then by train to Ottawa, where he consulted briefly with Macdonald. He then boarded another train that took him west to Toronto, Detroit, and on to Chicago. He then pushed northwest to the end of the rail line at St. Cloud, Minnesota. He hired a stagecoach to take him directly north to Fort Abercrombie, North Dakota. The next part of the trek was by sleigh through the early winter snow to Pembina, the last American town before crossing the border into Manitoba. Nights were spent sleeping under buffalo robes in the snowy, December chill.

The situation at the Red River settlement was tense. Armed men patrolled the streets. Tupper arranged to meet with Riel promptly. Charles arrived at Fort Garry to find Riel seated at the head of a table, surrounded by "wild looking fellows."

Riel rose from his seat in the council chamber, walked toward Tupper and shook his hand.

"What business brings you here sir?" asked Riel.

"I am Dr. Tupper from Halifax, an independent member of Parliament. I am here to take my daughter back home."

Tupper then explained that the wagon, horse, and baggage belonging to his son-in-law had been seized and that he wanted to take them back.

Riel said, "If you will return with the man who brought you here and remain at his house until four o'clock tomorrow, I will undertake to say that all the things belonging to your daughter will be there."

Tupper said, "You are very kind, but as I am here, would it not be as well for me to go into the town and see the person who has these things in his possession?"

Riel said, "No, I think I can manage this matter better than you, and I only undertake to do so on the conditions stated."

Seeing that he could get no further with the Métis leader, Tupper said, "I dare say you are quite right, and I will accept your kind proposal."

The two shook hands once more and Tupper left the fort. A day later, the family was reunited. Good to his word, Riel saw to it that the Cameron wagon and all their belongings were returned intact.

According to Tupper's account of the meeting, there was no discussion of the rebellion or the grievances of the Métis. The brief interview was strictly about Emma. Tupper's undercover intelligence about the state of affairs in Red River came not from Riel, but, rather, via discussions with Father Richot, a Catholic priest who had his hand on the pulse of the rebellion, sitting as he did at the Métis council table. In the end, Tupper returned to Ottawa with a much-relieved young couple and a few minor snatches of information to pass on to the prime minister. The trip took six weeks but demonstrated a father's protective nature. The long trek accomplished little else. (It did show Louis Riel's kindness and honour.)

Tupper was finally named to the Cabinet in 1870. He became president of the Privy Council. He moved into a house at 274 Daly Avenue in Ottawa, a solid yellow-brick home where he and Frances lived for the next four years. It was during those years that his reputation as a philandering doctor took root. Tupper almost daily made a "surprise" visit to Madame Desbarats, the wife of the Queen's Printer, before heading to his parliamentary office. The Desbarats lived at 213 Chapel Street, which was in fact the opposite direction from the Parliament Buildings. Neighbours sardonically joked that Tupper watered her flowers so much that they feared the garden might drown. A euphemism for an affair? We will likely never know.

Although they were brief, his early years in Ottawa as a Cabinet minister were productive. The Conservative government fell, thanks to Macdonald's questionable dealings with railway tycoon Hugh Allan. Tupper, along with the majority of Tories at the time, were innocents in the Pacific Scandal, since most of the intrigue was kept secret.[8] At any rate, Tupper refused to believe that the matter was all that reprehensible. In defence of his friend

Macdonald, he called the whole fiasco "the Pacific Slander." Tupper, out of loyalty to leader and party, became the party's chief defender in Parliament but to no avail.

In the disastrous 1874 election that followed the fall of the Tories, Alexander Mackenzie's Liberals won power. Tupper was one of only two Conservatives elected in all Nova Scotia. He sat for four years in the Opposition benches alongside Macdonald. Glaring across the aisle at Alexander Mackenzie and the Liberals, Tupper rose almost daily to take the Grits to task on some subject or other. Their mishandling of the economy; their dithering with the railways, particularly the transcontinental line; their predilection for free trade and individual enterprise; their shoddy treatment of the new province of British Columbia. All these things were fodder for Tupper in his attacks against Mackenzie's government. The doctor's blustery speaking style was a constant irritant to the Liberal government. Few in Parliament could match Charles for his memory and command of minute details. One wag noted that Macdonald steered the ship of state but that it was Tupper who provided the wind.

That being said, in a time when verbose public men and speeches could go one literally for hours, Tupper was relatively straightforward in parliamentary debates. That is not to say that his tirades against the government were brief or that he was he always courteous. Tupper, a member of the Opposition in Parliament, naturally delivered speeches that were critical of the government. He was accused of having a reputation for "parliamentary blather," but there was never any doubt as to where he stood on an issue. He stridently attacked the Liberals for pretty much everything they did. He had not changed from his time in Nova Scotia. He still detested Liberals.

Tupper was not alone in thinking that the Liberal government of the mid-1870s was not up to scratch. Alexander Mackenzie himself was not happy with the Cabinet he'd named, and too many of those brought into the Privy Council were simply not up to their responsibilities. The party was terribly lacking in cohesion, with many in the party openly wishing that former Ontario premier Edward Blake take over the leadership. (Blake himself confronted Mackenzie at one point, saying that he should take over as leader since he had more support and ability than Mackenzie did. The dour Scot stubbornly declined.) Tupper took advantage of the disarray in the Grit ranks. He needled and scoffed at the efforts of men such as Félix Geoffrion, a French Canadian brought into Cabinet by Mackenzie but one who proved utterly inept at the jobs he was given.

As the Conservative Party tried to recover power in the mid-1870s, they came up with the political strategy that came to be known as the National Policy. It was Dr. Tupper who took credit for coming up with the name and many of the proposals. Whether or not that is true cannot be verified, but there is no doubt that he was in on many of the major discussions at the highest of levels. Macdonald trusted his Nova Scotian colleague. As mentioned before, the major planks of the National Policy included high tariffs to protect Canada's burgeoning manufacturing and resources sectors, the building of a transcontinental railway, and fostering immigration to the West to fill what was seen as virtually empty space between Ontario and British Columbia before the Americans could move in. (Of course, the land was not "empty." It was inhabited by a a number of First Nations, groups that had lived on the lands for thousands of years.) Tupper wholeheartedly believed in all these positions.

The country went to the polls in 1878 after four years of Liberal rule. Macdonald and the Conservatives returned to power with a resounding majority. It was a remarkable comeback for Sir John A. The Conservatives elected twice as many MPs as the Liberals. In Nova Scotia, the Tories won sixteen of the twenty-one seats.

Tupper's reward for his part was to be named minister of public works, a position where one managed a lot of patronage appointments. As always, Tupper ran things with brusque efficiency. He was a hands-on minister, one who oversaw the work of his subordinates with an eagle eye. While he patiently listened to his aides, he preferred to follow his own opinions in managing affairs. He meticulously studied the details of issues before him. He could never be accused of being careless or slipshod. In the department, he was undoubtedly the boss.

It was Tupper who was responsible for the completion of the biggest public works project ever undertaken in the country: finishing the railway across the Prairies to British Columbia. He colourfully called it the "imperial highway across the continent of America completely on British soil." Interestingly, during the Opposition years, he'd advocated for private enterprise to fund the railway; now, as the newly appointed minister in charge, he favoured public funding of the CPR. His change of heart likely had something to do with his recognition of the fact that as a result of the economic recession, entrepreneurs and what we'd now call venture capitalists were less able (and willing) to commit the large amounts of capital needed for the project. Only the federal government could hope to finish the task efficiently. In the end, completion of the railway required funding from both of the two sources.

In 1879, seeing that Tupper's focus was predominantly taken up with organizing and financing the transcontinental line, Macdonald created a new government department and named Charles the minister of railways and canals. Part of his mandate in that position was to strategize the means of selling off public land in the West to pay for the railway. Tupper travelled to England that summer to meet with British prime minister Benjamin Disraeli, in hopes of convincing London to guarantee a bond sale, which then could be used to fund the massive construction project. The British government turned him down, but during his brief trip abroad, he did manage to buy up fifty thousand tons of steel rails at a bargain basement price.

Throughout 1880, the Premier of British Columbia, George Walkem, was threatening secession if the railway promises made to the province by the federal government were not fulfilled. In Ottawa, Liberal leader Edward Blake was demanding (during speeches that lasted as long as five hours) that the government stop all construction west of the Rockies. Macdonald admitted to the Cabinet that the plan to build something akin to the Union Pacific in the United States, i.e., a transcontinental line done all in one shot, was not really his plan. Macdonald foresaw a railway slowly creeping a few hundred miles at a time across the Prairies. Tupper vehemently disagreed with such a plan.

Tupper confronted Macdonald.

"Sir John, I think the time has come when we must take an advance step. I want to submit a proposition for building a through line from Nipissing in Ontario to the Pacific coast."

"That is a very large order," Macdonald replied. Then he added, "I shall be pleased to consider anything you have to submit."

The railway project proved to be a major challenge for the minister, requiring an extraordinary amount of his time and efforts. The chief engineer on the CPR was Sandford Fleming, Tupper's close friend from his Nova Scotia railway building days in the early sixties. As costs mounted and work lagged behind schedule, Fleming faced severe criticism. Tupper put pressure on Fleming to reduce costs. The easiest answer for the chief engineer was to cheapen the materials, something that would seriously degrade the quality of the actual rail lines. In May of 1880, under pressure from Macdonald, Tupper reluctantly relieved Fleming of his duties on the grounds that the chief engineer was unable to keep costs down. The dismissal of Fleming became a contentious issue between Macdonald and Tupper. The two had been very close up to that point, but that controversy opened a crack in what had been a solid friendship. Macdonald was adamant that Fleming be let go. Tupper was unwilling to do so; he only caved in when he saw that Sir John A. had the support of the rest of the Cabinet.

The firing of Fleming resulted in a temporary chill in the friendship of the two politicians. But the two men were so close in their political thinking and their ambitions for the country that any rift could not last for long. Their letters to each other remained cordial. In August of 1882, for example, while holidaying at Rivière-du-Loup, Macdonald wrote to Tupper when he heard that Sir Charles had fallen ill following the recent election. The diagnosis was "overtaxation" according to other doctors, probably what we would now call a nervous breakdown.

My Dear Tupper — I am sorry to learn of your continued indisposition.... By all means take a rest for a couple of months in Ireland or elsewhere. It is very probable that Council will want you to attend something in England.... I am enjoying myself here. The weather is charming and the air bracing. I work from 9 til 1:30 with my secretary and loaf the rest of the day but there is an interminable amount of work on my hands. Perhaps I may take a run down to Rimouski to see you on your way to England. Always most sincerely yours, John A. Macdonald

Tupper made the trip to Ireland with his wife and upon return to Canada, immediately jumped back into the old routines. He was off to the West, examining the CPR progress. At one point, he named a stop "Morse" (between Swift Current and Moose Jaw) in honour of his wife's maiden name.

Debate began in early December of 1880 over the contract with the CPR. "It is the most important question that has ever engaged the attention of this Parliament," Tupper said at the time.

It was the longest debate in the history of Canadian Parliament up to that time. Over one million words were uttered during the debate — more words than in the entire Bible. The Liberals, led by the ever-verbose Edward Blake, introduced dozens of amendments to the government bills related to the railways, some taking up page after page in *Hansard*. The members in the Commons were driven to a state of exhaustion.

At various points, as the arguments dragged on into late January of 1881, Macdonald, Tupper, Alexander Mackenzie, and John Henry Pope all became seriously ill and unable to attend certain sittings of the House. (Pope acted as Tupper's wingman on the railway issues and eventually succeeded Tupper as minister of railways.) The men sent letters back and forth inquiring about each other's health. Macdonald became so ill that his life was allegedly in peril. He suffered from exhaustion and abdominal cramps. At one point, his pulse was a very low forty-eight. In May he made the arduous trip to England to be assessed for what was suspected to be cancer. It was not. Tupper also "miraculously" recovered, being told that he'd survived "catarrh of the stomach." Doctors at the time used such phrases for illness and disease that they did not truly understand.

Thanks to Sir Charles's insistent lobbying and cajoling, the Tory government rescued the CPR from further financial crises in 1883 and again early in 1885. (By then, Tupper had abandoned Ottawa to take on the role of Canada's high commissioner to England.)

In December of 1883, Macdonald famously cabled Tupper in London with the brief message, "Pacific in trouble: you should be here."

From England came the terse reply, "Sailing on Thursday."

Tupper returned to Ottawa where he spent weeks defending the government's contract and the progress of the railway. Then, early in 1885,

George Stephen wrote in a panic to Macdonald that the CPR had no way to pay wages nor could work continue unless it was bailed out by the government. In Cabinet, at least one minister threatened to resign if more funds were given to the railway syndicate. Eventually, Tupper once more came to the side of Macdonald to defend the prime minister's plea for more money. Although no longer a minister at that time, he spoke with close colleagues and twisted arms so that they all fell back into line behind their leader. Money was found and the CPR resuscitated.

In the end, the deal negotiated by the two Fathers of Confederation resulted in the construction of an efficient railway that spanned the continent. It was completed on November 7 of 1885, when the last spike was driven (by Donald Smith of all people) at Craigellachie, B.C. Tupper could take pride in his role in helping to complete the engineering marvel. He'd staunchly defended the actions of the CPR backers. He had all along felt that the company that finished the railway should be allowed to benefit from the completed task. That way, the private company functioned more efficiently in completing the project than any government in far-away Ottawa. He stated at one point, "I have always supposed that the great object, in every country, and especially in a new country, was to draw as [many] capitalists into it as possible." Spoken as a true conservative.

Tupper accomplished other significant but less notable work during his time as minister of railways and canals. For instance, he lowered the freight rates on the Intercolonial Railway in eastern Canada as a means to increase traffic. He pushed through Parliament a number of subsidies for railways in Quebec and Ontario. Under his watch, the Welland Canal was widened and canals along the St. Lawrence River were deepened to accommodate larger ships.

What is especially remarkable about his accomplishments as a Cabinet minister is that a good portion of his work was done from far-away London. Tupper had a lifelong adoration of England and all things British. His education at Edinburgh had awakened him to the virtues of the British Isles.

When A.T. Galt, Canada's first high commissioner to England, ended his term in 1883, Tupper lobbied for the job. Initially, Macdonald refused to name the Halifax doctor to the post, mostly because he needed Tupper's Maritime influence at the Cabinet table. Sir Charles — he had been knighted in 1879 — was in his early sixties however and was looking for something to fulfill his need to serve yet be less taxing both physically and mentally. Finally, in 1883 Macdonald named Tupper as high commissioner. As it was an unpaid position, he retained his Cabinet portfolio and began to divide his time between London and Ottawa.

His duties as high commissioner were similar to that of an ambassador. Promoting British emigration to Canada was one responsibility but much of the role was ceremonial. The socializing with movers and shakers at the centre of the British Empire suited Tupper's personality. The high teas, debutante balls, and formalities of entertaining ambassadors and royalty were far from tedious for the sophisticated doctor from Amherst.

Tupper was always a man who spoke his mind and confidently wore his heart on his sleeve. His lack of tact was said to have rubbed some of the English aristocracy the wrong way. He saw his forthrightness as a virtue; some of them saw it in a rather different light, believing it indicative of a lack of discretion or worse. For instance, Tupper freely spoke about his estimation of British Liberal politicians, something that was considered tawdry and vulgar in high society.

Nevertheless, he warmed to the rituals, used his energy to promote Canada, and tended to make good impressions — with most people — wherever he went. London became his base, but he made numerous trips back to Nova Scotia and to Ottawa to look after government work that couldn't be done from the English capital. As one might expect, there was extensive criticism of Tupper holding two important positions and not fully committing to either one.

Tupper spent a good deal of his time as high commissioner securing loans, working on financing deals such as the one to market new CPR bonds with financial house Baring Brothers. These transactions went a long way in finding the money that the railway company needed to finish the line.

During a conversation with Macdonald, Tupper explained how he'd been well treated and respected at a conference concerned with intercontinental cables in Paris. Sir Charles attended as the Canadian representative. He said to Macdonald, "I may say to you that I feel some pride in the fact that Canada took her place in an International Conference and on an equal footing with all the other Powers."

Macdonald answered, "I congratulate you on the result of the Cable Conference, and have sent for your official report to prepare a nice little editorial for the *Mail* [a Conservative-leaning newspaper in Toronto.]"

Both men were pleased by the fact that Canada was being recognized as an independent nation, something the two politicians could gloat about considering their efforts and contributions.

Managing the two lofty government posts at the same time required him to zigzag across the Atlantic Ocean, something that eventually proved to be too much even for such an indefatigable figure as Tupper. Things came to a head in April of 1884 during a Cabinet meeting in Ottawa. Tupper insisted on having his way on a minor issue and threatened — in front of the rest of the Cabinet — to resign if he did not get his way. Macdonald lost his temper at the threat, especially because it was stated in front of the other ministers. Tupper stormed out of the Cabinet meeting room. Macdonald came around and apologized to his old friend, but the rift never fully healed. On May 28 that year, Tupper announced his resignation from Cabinet, opting to give the high commissioner post his full-time attention.

One of his first major accomplishments as high commissioner was to conduct trade talks with Spain. He did so on his own, without much in the way of assistance from colleagues back home in Ottawa or those in London. He acted as a liaison, connecting Canadian exporters with British importers. He played a key role in convincing Prime Minister Gladstone to exempt Canadian cattle from a British ban of North American beef. Tupper was able to impress upon the British government that Canadian cows were free of disease.

He travelled to several European countries to encourage immigration, extolling the virtues of the Canadian West in particular. He met with politicians and the crowned heads of Europe, invoking his charm to Canada's advantage. For example, it was well known that the German government (the Kaiser in particular) resented any Germans emigrating to North America. Sir Charles did his best to ease that resentment. He went to Berlin, called upon the Crown Princess and was received openly. As one biographer stated, Tupper had the "open sesame" to social and political gatherings in both Great Britain and the Continent. How far he got with the Kaiser in that particular case is unknown. German emigration to North America continued unabated, especially with the opening of the Canadian West.

In 1884 W.S. Fielding was elected as the Liberal premier of Nova Scotia on the platform of taking his province out of Confederation. It seemed that the anti-Confederation movement had never truly lost its grip on some people of that province. Macdonald was in a panic and several times throughout 1886 begged Tupper to return to Nova Scotia and fight that old battle once again. The embattled prime minister cabled the high commissioner early in autumn: "In Nova Scotia the outlook is bad, and the only hope of our holding our own there is your immediate return and vigorous action. It may be necessary that you should, even if only for a time, return to the Cabinet. M'Lelan, [sic] I know, would readily make way for you. Now, the responsibility on you is very great, for should any disaster arise because of your not coming out, the whole blame will be thrown upon you."

Tupper hesitated. The mantle of Nova Scotian leadership had been passed to John Thompson, the young judge who'd recently become the federal minister of justice. But Thompson's name did not carry the same weight as did Sir Charles's. Macdonald pleaded again a few weeks later, "I cannot too strongly urge upon you the absolute necessity of your coming out at once, and do not like to contemplate the evil consequences of your failing to do so."

Convinced by the panicky tone in Macdonald's telegrams that he was the only one who could save the day, Tupper cabled back that he was on his way. He quickly booked a Halifax-bound steamer and arrived back in the Nova Scotia capital early in January of 1887. On to Ottawa by train, he met with Macdonald. Good to his word, the prime minister shuffled his Cabinet. Archibald McLelan moved to the Office of the Postmaster General, allowing Tupper to enter the Privy Council as minister of finance. One condition that Sir Charles insisted upon before accepting the office was that he be allowed to hold on to the high commissioner posting in London. He simultaneously sat in the House of Commons as the member for Cumberland County, Nova Scotia.

In the 1887 federal election, Tupper had to once again battle the anti-Confederation forces that he had faced two decades earlier. That he was once more a sitting MP from Nova Scotia pretty much assured victory for his side. The Tories won fourteen of the province's twenty-one seats, and the issue of withdrawing from the federal union withered on the vine. As minister of finance, Tupper promoted protectionism for Canadian industrial products, most notably in the iron and steel sector. Canada's young industries were starting to flourish, and Sir Charles, ever one to believe in the role of government in the economy, felt that the factories of Ontario as well as the resource regions of Quebec and Nova Scotia, needed help to compete for markets in Europe and the United States. He intended to do all he could to promote and protect those sectors of the economy.

In 1887, a joint commission was established to deal with the ongoing fisheries dispute between Canada and the United States. As both high commissioner and the Canadian finance minister, Tupper pressured the government in London to defend Canada's position. Tupper fittingly was named one of the three British commissioners. As mentioned in the chapter on John Thompson, he took the lead in the talks, but he relied heavily upon Thompson for legal advice. The end result was the 1888 Treaty of Washington, a flawed document but one that temporarily solved the dispute thanks in a very large part to Tupper's leadership.

With those negotiations settled, Tupper felt his time in Ottawa was over. Macdonald, as was his way, tried to persuade his friend to stay. He even proposed to name him as his successor, but Tupper rejected the proposal. Tupper, knowing Sir John A. often made promises he couldn't keep, was unsure if he could believe the prime minister. Only a year before, Macdonald had promised Langevin that he would be named successor. He never carried through on that either. Thompson was also a dynamic presence in the Commons and had become the government's predominant spokesman. Tupper opted to return to London.

He kept a close eye on far-away Canada, though. He was in constant contact with not only Macdonald but also his colleagues in Halifax and Ottawa. His son, Charles Hibbert Tupper, had followed in his father's footsteps.[9] The younger Tupper entered the federal arena as an MP in 1882, representing Pictou County, Nova Scotia. He was named to Macdonald's Cabinet as minister of marine and fisheries in 1888. Very sure of himself and a self-promoter, he was thought by many to be as bumptious as Sir Charles. Father and son communicated regularly so that Tupper Sr. could be kept abreast of developments in not only Ottawa and Nova Scotia but also with the larger breadth of the national Tory Party.

Sir Charles's active participation in Canadian politics, even from so far away, was a bone of contention with the Liberals. That someone in the most important diplomatic posting Canada had to offer still participated actively in partisan politics rankled the likes of Blake and Laurier. But there were advantages to having a sitting Cabinet minister serving as the high commissioner. It gave clout to whatever Tupper proposed. It gave him an added status. He was not merely a political appointee but a sitting, elected member of the government of Canada. People on both sides of the Atlantic listened to such a figure.

Sometimes he overstepped his boundaries. Certain people found him overbearing and apt to interfere in matters that were beyond his concern. Lord Rosebury, the prime minister of England in 1894, accused Tupper of "gross indecorum" for his meddling in a Scottish by-election. A more blatant example of his exceeding his mandate happened in 1893. He arranged a trade agreement with France early that year that led to some controversy, mostly because Sir Charles exceeded his orders from above. Hoping to play the London and Paris counterparts against each other to get the treaty ratified quickly, he leaked false news items to the press. The Canadian prime minister at the time, John Thompson, was in Paris as judge in the tribunal dealing with the Bering Sea dispute. Upset by the high commissioner's actions, he found the entire matter a distraction to say the least. The prime minister and the Cabinet in Ottawa were confused by the terms and information that filtered back. Thompson stepped in to sort out matters and reassure all sides that the confusion was simply a matter of miscommunication. Tupper meekly travelled from London to Paris, where, hat in hand, he admitted his mistakes. The incident did nothing to endear him to his colleagues in Canada. Mackenzie Bowell, the acting leader of the government, cabled Thompson with the message that the Cabinet was unanimously opposed to what Tupper had done.

Likewise, Tupper shouldered the blame for the collapse of the Imperial Federation League. Tupper had been in on the initial meetings to establish the league as a political union of the Empire's colonies. Tupper was criticized because he'd spoken just months before against the notion of such a political unification within the Empire. In any event, both Lord Salisbury and his successor as prime minister of England, William Gladstone, dismissed the proposition out of hand.

Tupper often cloaked himself in the mantle of a crusader, someone above party politics, working on behalf of the common man. He was not a populist in the modern sense of the word, but he could read the mood of people and adjust his approach to convincing them that he spoke for them and was correct with his particular solution. It was a remarkable political talent and during the final election of Macdonald's life, the Old Chieftain called upon Tupper to return home to fight the election on behalf of the Conservatives.

Macdonald cabled him January 22, 1891. "Immediate dissolution almost certain. Your presence [could affect] election contest in Maritime Provinces essential to encourage our friends. Please come. Answer." Sir Charles's one-word cabled response was, "Yes."

As high commissioner, he should have stayed neutral in the political arena. That was simply not part of Tupper's makeup, however. His partisan feelings ran deep. He was quick to respond to Macdonald's request and set sail almost immediately. In a matter of days, he arrived in New York and promptly boarded a northbound train to Ottawa, ready to fight on behalf of — as it said on the Conservative campaign poster — the old policy, the old flag, and the old leader.

During the 1891 election, Tupper stumped about the Maritimes as a partisan politician. As high commissioner he readily admitted that it was "improper under ordinary circumstances ... to act as a partisan" in the election." Despite that admission, he gave speeches, glad-handed the public, and made his presence (and feelings) well known throughout his native province. He spoke on behalf of his party, touting the advantages that Conservative rule would bring to Canada. The proposed Liberal policy of reciprocity with the United States was so odious to Tupper's thinking that he could not resist fighting the concept with all the energy he could muster. Identical to Macdonald in this way of thinking, Tupper feared closer ties to the United States might eventually lead to annexation. The old bulldog could simply not abide any threat as he saw it to Canada's sovereignty nor to its connection with Britain.

The ever-ready Tupper arrived in Ottawa on February 6. After a brief meeting with the prime minister at Earnscliffe, Tupper boarded a train and set off for Kingston, Ontario, Sir John A.'s home constituency. There he addressed the nomination meeting for Macdonald, making excuses for the prime minister, explaining that he was too wrapped up in the affairs of state to attend. Macdonald was nominated with the largest majority he'd ever received in the riding.

Tupper returned to Ottawa where he sat down with Macdonald to plot the strategy for the election. It was the beginning of a whirlwind campaign. Tupper met with Donald Smith — newly reinstated with the Conservative Party — in Montreal to relay strategy and then travelled on to Amherst, Nova Scotia, where he spoke for an hour and a half. His hometown crowd adored him. Taking an overnight train, he arrived in Halifax by nine o'clock the following morning. A telegram from Macdonald awaited him: "If you can be spared want you up here. Should be here to attend meeting at Toronto on the 17th."

Tupper gave a scheduled address in the Nova Scotia capital and then hopped aboard a special train to the Ontario capital. He and Macdonald travelled to Hamilton on February 18. Since no hall could hold the number of people expected, two venues were rented with Sir John addressing one crowd while Tupper spoke at the other place. Then it was on to Strathroy and Windsor where both men spoke.

Such was the hectic schedule Tupper kept. Speeches at the time were often more than two hours in length. The pace had noticeably opposite effects on the two aging politicians. For Macdonald, the rigors of carrying his party on his broad shoulders was exhausting. Visibly tired, his voice lacked its traditional power. His energy sagged. His prolific memory failed him. He developed a midwinter cough and cold that made matters worse. In fact, Sir John A. was unable to complete the entire campaign.

Being back on the political trail seemed to invigorate the aging physician. He was in his element — energized, motivated, and ready to take the fight to the hustings. Although only seven years younger than the prime minister, Tupper seemed ageless by comparison. He used his bulldog style to full advantage, railing against Laurier and the hated Liberal policies. Whether it was in Quebec City, Springhill, Amherst, or Halifax, the hyperactive Tupper met with fellow Tories, plotted the best way forward, and delivered heartfelt, rousing, and lengthy speeches to adoring crowds. Tupper travelled over six thousand kilometers between different points in Canada during the campaign.

In the end, Macdonald and the Tories were returned to office with a majority of twenty-seven. They received 48.6 percent of the popular vote. Laurier was supported by 45.2 percent.

The results — with the Liberals actually gaining ten seats in the House of Commons — were a sign to the Conservatives that perhaps a trade agreement with the Americans was not all that terrible. Within a matter of days, Tupper accompanied George Foster and John Thompson to Washington where they met with British ambassador Julian Poncefote and U.S. Secretary of State James Blaine. The Canadians, despite their recent attacks on the proposal of reciprocity, wanted to negotiate a limited trade agreement that benefitted the country but also stole some of the Liberals' thunder. Macdonald's final word to the trio as they set off for the U.S. capital was, "Good luck to you."

Meanwhile, the Liberals began to make noise in Parliament about the conduct of Tupper in the recent election. In committee at first and then in the House of Commons, the Grits accused the high commissioner of unduly influencing the voters in ridings he visited. Laurier rose in the House and delivered a scathing attack on Tupper and the Conservatives, claiming that Sir Charles was "interfering in the recent elections and imputing treasonable and disloyal motives to a large proportion of the people of this Dominion." It was left to Tupper's son and to John Thompson to defend Sir Charles's actions. The Tory majority assured that any censoring proposals were voted down. Meanwhile, Tupper returned to his ambassadorial duties in London, so he was beyond the nitty gritty politics of the matter.

Late in May, as he was attending meetings in Vienna, Tupper received word that Sir John A. Macdonald was gravely ill. A private telegram from a friend asked if Sir Charles would accept the nomination for Kingston, Macdonald's long-standing constituency. Tupper responded tersely, "Thanks. Have no intention of re-entering Parliament."

C.H. cabled his father on June 4. "Sir John is dying. Rumour of cabal against you in favour of Thompson. I propose to resign if he is elected." Tupper Jr. was upset about what he saw as the party's ingratitude toward his father.

Sir Charles responded from Vienna, "In case of lamented death of Premier I hope you will give hearty support to Thompson. As I told you at Ottawa, nothing would induce me to accept the position."

In a longer letter to his son, Tupper expressed great satisfaction and personal relief that Thompson would succeed his old friend Macdonald. That did not happen of course, but Tupper believed he deserved to. Sir Charles related the story of how Macdonald had half-heartedly wanted to switch places with him. The letter also told how Thompson was Macdonald's choice as leader. Charles advised C.H. to stand by Thompson out of duty to the country.

When Macdonald finally succumbed on June 6, Tupper played little role in the wrangling over who should become the new prime minister. His correspondence with Macdonald and others during the previous few years had intimated that Sir Hector Langevin was likely the successor but that had changed. Langevin was already under investigation for scandalous behaviour, and even Macdonald saw in the months before his death that his title could no longer be passed to his French Canadian lieutenant. Tupper instead backed Thompson.

It was Abbott who was awarded the post, of course. He was followed in short order by Thompson and then Bowell. Each time a prime minister resigned — or died in the case of Thompson — Tupper's name arose instantly as one of the leading contenders for the premier's chair. He demurred, however, following Macdonald's death and Abbott's resignation. And at the time of Bowell's selection, Charles was so strongly disliked by the governor general, the man making the ultimate decision, that he was rejected.

The year of 1895 was a troublesome one for the Conservative government in Canada. Dr. Tupper, even from his faraway perch in Great Britain, was well aware of the turmoil brought about by the Manitoba provincial government's insensitive action. Charles knew of Prime Minister Mackenzie Bowell's lack of decisiveness. From his son he learned of the dissatisfaction that was brewing in the caucus and indeed, throughout the dominion. Tupper was upset that his son had felt obliged to resign briefly from Cabinet, although he admired the fact that C.H. had stood on principle.

Charles heard a number of pleas from former colleagues in the Conservative Party, such as Donald Smith, asking him to return to Canada to solve the dilemma that divided the party. But, until he was summoned back by the very man he would replace, he did not overtly interfere in the problems of the Conservative Party.

C.H. had been pushing for his father to take on the prime ministership since at least January of 1895. In January of 1895, C.H. wrote to his father with a very open, direct appeal to bring the old man back to Canada. "Everyone outside of our weak Cabinet demands you as leader, and in our Cabinet the best men want you as well. If you came out and wished to, you could be elected hand over hand in Antigonish! If you are ready for a strong fight for doing the minority in Manitoba justice … you could sweep Canada and be premier. The country yearns for you…. We want a leader bold and ready."

Tupper had a strong, forceful personality and had a solid reputation, built over years of prestigious service. It was generally accepted that he would be welcomed by a large percentage of the party faithful. He knew it;

the elected politicians of both parties knew it; even Mackenzie Bowell knew it. Tupper just was not sure that he wanted the challenge.

As outlined in the chapter about Mackenzie Bowell, Tupper was summoned back to Ottawa by the prime minister just as things came to a head with the January 1896 Cabinet revolt.

It is impossible for anyone looking rationally at the situation to think that the rebels in the Cabinet did not see the alternative to their dithering leader present and ready to take over. And since Sir Charles and C.H. had kept up a constant correspondence about the leadership problem and had even speculated on the scenarios that would see Sir Charles become premier, it seems implausible that Charlie, a leader of the rebellious group, would not have let his father in on the details of the Cabinet resignations.

Dr. Tupper must have known of the cabal, and he most likely approved of their actions. Although he had demurred often about returning to electoral politics, this opportunity was about to fall into his lap. It was not like the Macdonald years where Sir John would offer the position then back away and keep it to himself. This time, the possibility of becoming prime minister was very real and possible.

The seven ministers — Charlie Tupper, Foster, Haggart, Ives, Dickey, Montague, and Wood — tendered their resignations from Cabinet the same day that Sir Charles and Bowell were meeting to discuss the steamship service. The rebel ministers called on Tupper later that same day. Enigmatically, Sir Charles told them that he was in Ottawa at the behest of the prime minister and that he would offer no advice nor entertain any proposals from them unless Bowell sent for him.

Three days later, after an unsuccessful effort to cobble together a new Cabinet with replacements for the "nest of traitors," Bowell called upon Tupper. He offered to resign and hand over the government to Tupper. He made only one vindictive condition: that Tupper not include Foster or Haggart in his Cabinet. Sir Charles thought the stipulation was not in the best interest of the Cabinet or the party, stating that the hatchet needed to be buried and everyone involved should unite going forward. Bowell gave in.

None of this was unexpected for Tupper. He'd had correspondence from advisors such as farm implement manufacturer Hart Massey, who regretted that their "dear old friend, Mackenzie Bowell, who had done grand service for the country" could not hold the party and Cabinet together. Massey hoped that Tupper would accept the leadership. Foreseeing the Conservatives losing the impending election, J.A. Macdonnell, another Tory supporter, wrote to Sir Charles on January 3, "With you at the head of the government … we may be saved from destruction which otherwise will be as overwhelming as that which smote the Grits on the 17th of September, 1878."

A sense of peaceful transition settled over the Tory ranks in Ottawa during the winter of 1896. Bowell never forgave the men that he considered "bolters" but they managed to sit with him at the head of the Cabinet table and keep everything at least civil. Meetings must have been extraordinarily tense. But, with the prospect of Tupper taking over the reins, the Conservatives felt buoyed at their prospects in the upcoming election. There was a general confidence in the old doctor's ability to carry the fight to the Liberals. For many, it seemed that the old bulldog's day was finally at hand.

Six men came forward to offer him their seat in the Commons. He accepted the one held by David Mackeen, who'd held the riding of Cape Breton in Nova Scotia since 1887. (Mackeen was named a senator as a reward and eventually became the lieutenant governor of his province.) A lightning-fast by-election was set for February 4, 1896, and Tupper, never one to sit still for too long, set off by train for his home province. He spoke at a number of stops along the way between Ottawa and Halifax. He addressed the Montreal Board of Trade and Chamber of Commerce. Moncton, New Brunswick, received him with open arms, as did his hometown of nearby Amherst. He continued through Nova Scotia, speaking sometimes briefly and often at length in Springhill, Truro, Pictou, Grand Narrows, Boisdale, North Sydney, and Leitche's Creek.

A midwinter campaign was never an easy chore, and this one proved to be difficult at times. Snowstorms blocked roads and even the railways, but Tupper plodded on despite the harsh weather. At a scheduled stop in Sydney on January 23, he spoke for two hours to a crowd of fifteen hundred people. The next day, he addressed thirty-five hundred potential voters at Glace Bay. That speech lasted an hour and a half. Large crowds turned out at Cow Bay and Sydney Mines. On January 28, he delivered his nomination speech at Sydney to over nine hundred people. The miners, fishermen, and farmers plodded through the snow and bitter cold into the Temperance Hall, where they enthusiastically cheered Sir Charles. He truly was a political legend to many of them. Every time he got up in front of a crowd, Tupper could hold them in the palm of his hand for at least an hour, often for double or even triple that amount of time. The Nova Scotians on the island knew their new candidate well. The former premier and soon-to-be prime minister knew how to hold a crowd, how to address them on a near-personal level, and how to give them a vibrant rendering of his vision for the country.

Tupper stayed at Sydney Mines the night of the February 4 election. As expected, he won by a comfortable margin of 820 votes over a strong Liberal candidate, George Murray (who'd quit the provincial Liberal Cabinet to oppose Tupper in Cape Breton). In each speech along the long campaign trail, Tupper had delivered the same message, "The grand old man is all right, the grand old policy is all right, Cape Breton County is all right!"

Tupper spoke to his new constituents at Sydney that night and then boarded a train south to Halifax. But even then, with his own by-election over, he was campaigning for the coming federal contest. He spoke to large crowds at both Antigonish and at New Glasgow on his way south. At Halifax, a banquet was held in his honour. That event gave him an opportunity to review his long service to Nova Scotia, to Canada, and to the Empire. All his actions did not go unnoticed. The newspapermen who followed Sir Charles were impressed and commented on his alertness, his hard work, his stamina, and the zeal that he brought to the political hustings.

As he took on the role of prime minister, his financial situation had to be evaluated. Tupper was a man who liked to make money but was never as wealthy as the Opposition press liked to paint him. He was never a millionaire. He never used his positions in government to enrich his himself. During his time as high commissioner, Tupper was unable to supplement his government salary with any sort of sustained medical practice. Instead, he relied in a large part on the honoraria given to him by various companies on whose boards he was a member. At a time when the average Canadian earned less than one thousand dollars a year (or about five hundred British pounds), Tupper was making five hundred pounds as a director of the Bank of British Columbia, one hundred and seventy-five pounds a year as a director of General Mining Association, and two hundred pounds a year as chairman of the South African Cable Company. Although those positions had occupied very little of his time, they'd been lucrative. Now that he was an elected member of Parliament once again and the prime minister-in-waiting, he had to resign all those directorships. Coming back to Canada as a politician was, in fact, a costly, self-sacrificing move for Sir Charles.

On February 11, Tupper confidently walked into the House of Commons. He was introduced to the members present and confidently took his seat in the middle of the front row on the government side. The budget was being debated. Sir Charles felt elated to be back in the action, back to the give-and-take of parliamentary debate that he fondly remembered and at which he was so successful.

Cabinet meetings were held at a long table in the Privy Council corner office. A heavy, gaudy chandelier hung over the ministers as they seated themselves for meetings. The dark velvet wallpaper, bare wooden floor, and the cavernous ceiling gave the room an echoing sound that amplified what the ministers had to say. Bowell sat as chairman, but it was really Tupper who now led the party and faced the music outside of the Cabinet room. The rebellious ministers, happy to have shunted Bowell to the sidelines, sat obediently through the meetings, biding their time until Bowell's term was over.

The Manitoba Schools Question dominated the discussions. Never has religion — before or since — played such a key, divisive role in Canadian politics. Tupper, who knew full well that his job was to unite a splintered party, spoke with a wealth of experience on the issues at hand. He had been one of the original team that had drafted the British North America Act. It had guaranteed the rights of minorities. As neither a francophone nor a Catholic and with no ties to the Orange Order, he professed no hidden bias.

He asserted his beliefs in Cabinet, and when the remedial bill came for a second reading in the House of Commons, it was Tupper who rose in the House to move the measure.

In his clear, resonant voice, Sir Charles began with the charge that the kindness and tolerance professed by all Christian denominations was "in striking contrast with the war of race and religion" being waged by the two factions in the Schools issue. Why would anyone wish to deny the minority rights that had been sacrosanct since Confederation? The highest court in the Empire, he argued, demanded that the Dominion government remedy the situation in Manitoba. He called for all members to unite to support the legislation.

The Conservatives carried the vote 115 to 94 on March 20. The bill went back to committee for further discussion. Early in April, an unexpected message arrived from Premier Greenway of Manitoba, offering to negotiate a compromise. Donald Smith and two other government representatives were dispatched to Winnipeg to discuss a deal, but nothing came of the talks, much to the dismay of the federal government. Greenway was not as willing to negotiate as he'd led the prime minister to think.

The Liberals — plus a group of stubborn Protestants led by the now-independent Dalton McCarthy — managed what amounted to a filibuster. Tupper had no choice but to abandon all hopes of passing the existing remedial legislation before the next election.

Meanwhile, there were other concerns that needed attention. A railway company whose line was to connect the Bay of Fundy to the Gulf of St. Lawrence had asked for funding to complete construction. Money was found. Funding of the Fast Line service across the Atlantic was passed unanimously in the House. Increased funding for the militia was also approved, in light of the Canadian fear of American invasion that had been aroused once more as a result of American relations deteriorating with Britain. (The United States had sided with Venezuela over a land dispute with Britain in British Guyana.)

Parliament was prorogued on April 23. The governor general announced the next day that the House was dissolved. An election was set for June 23, 1896.

The January deal between Bowell and Tupper meant that with dissolution, Sir Charles was set to take on the mantle of leadership officially. With little ceremony, he was officially sworn in as Canada's sixth prime minister on May 1, 1896. A new Cabinet was named, with few notable changes from the Bowell council.

The change in Tory leadership was made a bit more palatable for the outgoing prime minister when Bowell and Donald Smith (the new high commissioner) immediately set sail for England to be delegates to the international cable conference. Sandford Fleming accompanied them. Having the crusty ex-prime minister out of the country as the premiership changed made things easier on Bowell's fragile ego.

Tupper remade the Cabinet, bringing back Angers and installing a couple of other French Canadians — Louis-Olivier Taillon and Alphonse Desjardins — on the promise that he would implement remedial legislation if he won the election.

Sir Charles found himself immediately back on the campaign trail, defending the old policies, fighting the religious prejudice that was wholly rampant in Ontario, struggling with smoothing things over with both Quebec and Manitoba, and trying to battle increasing public support for the Liberal policy of reciprocity with the United States. It was definitely an uphill slog.

The very afternoon he took office and announced his Cabinet, Prime Minister Tupper left by train for Montreal. He spent three days there meeting with party organizers and Quebec colleagues to go over the strategy to win in that province. He then set off for Winnipeg, with electioneering whistle stops at Mattawa and North Bay, and speeches in Port Arthur and Fort William. There he met with Tory workers for northern Ontario before proceeding the next day to Rat Portage (Kenora), where he met with the Board of Trade. Then it was on to Winnipeg. As his train pulled into the station, thousands of people stood along the tracks and inside the city's central station to cheer the prime minister. The old man still could draw a crowd.

He spent the next day meeting with party organizers, and in the evening spoke to a gathering of over four thousand people, appealing to the Protestants in the crowd to support the rights of the minority. Despite the makeup of the audience, he heard only a smattering of boos. After more consultation with his Western allies, he once again boarded the train and returned to Fort William and Prince Arthur. By May 13 he was back in Ottawa. During the following week, he spoke in Montreal, Quebec, Rivière-du-Loup, Rimouski, Campbellton, Amherst, Wallace, and Pictou. His energy never sagged, and despite the length of his speeches and because they had to be delivered without any amplification, it was remarkable that he still had a voice left by the time he reached North Sydney on Cape Breton Island.

He penned an interesting entry in his diary following a speech he gave from a steamer docked at Port Hood. Tupper accused his Liberal rival, McLellan, of bringing a gang of "roughs" from Margaree Harbour. Canadian elections were seemingly not as cleanly fought or as noble as some wished.

Tupper continued his electioneering trek, speaking at places such as Antigonish and Charlottetown before finally making it to Halifax on June 3. Back in Ontario the next week, he spoke at Ottawa, Brockville, Kingston, Trenton, Brighton, and Oshawa. At Bowmanville, he was greeted with not only a fancy reception but also a lengthy parade.

An overnight train took him to southwestern Ontario. The Conservatives bragged that three meetings at Exeter (to a crowd of six thousand), Strathroy, and Peterborough were without precedent for the number of supporters who turned out to see a politician. Each event included a parade, a meal, and an address from the prime minister. At Chatham, the crowd was an estimated ten thousand.

Despite the party rhetoric, Tupper was not met with the adulation at every meeting. Instead, he was heckled often and criticized endlessly in the press. At Massey Hall in Toronto, he spoke for over two hours but with considerable interruption from members of his own party. His message, notwithstanding the jeers, was that the right thing had to be done in relation to the minority rights of Catholic and French-Manitobans, even if it meant "the downfall of the Conservative Party." He rarely varied from that election theme, although he knew it did not sit at all well with the Protestant Orangemen. Rowdy Lodge members yelled from the crowd, "Manitoba," interrupting Sir Charles as he spoke.

His tour took him through the southern part of Ontario. At Niagara Falls, many had to be turned away at the door of the hall where he spoke. That became a common occurrence as the campaign wound down.

The election was predominantly fought in Ontario. Between June 9 and June 22, Sir Charles alone gave forty-two speeches, most of them lengthy and loud. The Conservatives were up against the highly organized tactics of the Orange Order, a group determined that the remedial action in Manitoba never take place.

The Liberals appealed to the farmers and new industrialists of the province with a reciprocity promise of new markets, profit, and financial prosperity — if they voted Liberal. Laurier had a charisma that transcended the reality that he was a francophone from Quebec. In comparison, the existing Tory government, even with renewed leadership, was tired, aging; it lacked the slate of potential Cabinet ministers the Liberals touted.

The Grits had a very strong slate of candidates. Laurier was much respected for his calm and articulate manner. William Stevens Fielding, the former premier of Nova Scotia was the finance minister in waiting; Clifford Sifton led a strong contingent of men from Manitoba; Sir Oliver Mowat, who for twenty-four years had been premier of Ontario, had been convinced to run for the Liberals; Israel Tarte was a leading voice in Quebec, as was Henri Bourassa; fiery debater Richard Cartwright was likewise seen as a voice to be reckoned with in Ontario. The Tory Cabinet could not match the Liberal potential. Unfortunately for the Conservatives, their leading candidates were seen to be yesterday's men, a tired group who'd chewed up several leaders since the death of Macdonald. None of the Cabinet, outside of Sir Charles Tupper, seized the imagination of the voters. Even the party's advertising seemed dated: "The Old Flag! The Old Guard!" Shades of the 1891 campaign.

Tupper proclaimed, "I stand by the principle of ample protection to Canadian manufacturing industries, and the extension of protection to Canada's greatest industry, agriculture, by obtaining for the Canadian farmer a preference in the markets of the United Kingdom."

It almost worked, as many of the farmers of the country supported such a policy. But in the end, the Liberals came to power.

There were many other considerations in the voting decisions of course. Laurier, a handsome and classy man, captured the hearts of many of his fellow francophones, turning some long-time Tory voters into Liberals. The residual resentment of the Conservative treatment of Riel had added to the Liberal vote in Quebec. The Orange Order, at the very apex of its influence on the politics of Ontario, motivated its members to turn on the party of Tupper, even though it meant voting for a French Canadian in the person of Wilfrid Laurier. That the one-time Tory and hard rightwing Orangeman Dalton McCarthy threw in with Laurier made that choice a bit more palatable. Reciprocity, the Liberal platform cornerstone, appealed to many merchants and newly transplanted workers in the factories across the Dominion. Its promise of prosperity after years of economic uncertainty turned the heads of many men. The close ties to Britain hadn't always worked out well for them. Perhaps a closer bond to the United States meant better days ahead. As in so many elections, the people were simply ready for change. Canada had only known two prime ministers in its first twenty-four years of existence. The Conservatives had ruled for all but four of the years between 1867 and 1896. Perhaps, as the men entered the polling booths, they felt that it was time for a change. Their wives and mothers may have hoped so as well and influenced those votes.

When the final results were tallied following the June 23 contest, the Tories were ahead in the popular vote by a measure of 430,874 for Tupper's party and 401,425 for the Grits under Laurier. The Liberals, though, had won one hundred and seventeen seats compared to eighty-six for the Conservatives (of which fifteen were still calling themselves Liberal-Conservatives). Laurier had carried forty-nine of the sixty-five constituencies in Quebec. That had been the determining element in the outcome.

The day after the election, from his office in the Ottawa Parliament buildings, Tupper assessed the numbers and spoke to members of the press. He admitted that he'd found his party demoralized when he arrived back in Canada the previous winter. He gave his opinion that mistakes had been made regarding the remedial legislation over the Manitoba Schools Question. Then, slipping into his typical mode of self-promotion, Tupper told the reporters that, "I have fought the fight with all the energy and ability I possess, and am able to say that no public man has ever received more overwhelming evidence of the regard, and I might say affection of the great Liberal-Conservative Party than I have during the past seven weeks while speaking and travelling incessantly." He went on to refute a rumour that he'd said disparaging things about Laurier's fitness to be prime minister on the grounds of him being both French and Catholic. He finished his address to the press by stating that it was time for the Conservatives to take on their duty as her Majesty's loyal and constitutional Opposition.

From London, Mackenzie Bowell cabled his replacement. "To say that I am surprised [at the election result] would be but a faint expression of my opinion.... I have not yet recovered from surprise and astonishment at the returns from Quebec.... On the whole, I do not envy the position which Laurier now holds." He hoped that Tupper was not worn out by his "arduous labours" during the campaign. There was no obvious bitterness toward the man who'd followed him in the leadership of the Tory Party.

Tupper had another reason for sadness in the days after the election. Leonard Tilley, his old friend and compatriot, his fellow Father of Confederation and one-time premier of New Brunswick passed away on June 25. The two men had shared many political struggles over the years.

Tupper was still the prime minister and had been going to his office daily, carrying on as if there had been no change in the government. He and a few close associates came up with a long list of patronage jobs that needed to be approved by the governor general.[10]

On July 2, Lord Aberdeen returned to the capital after a brief stay in Quebec City. Tupper called upon him at Government House with the list of appointments that he wished to be named prior to Laurier taking power. Much to Sir Charles's consternation, Aberdeen refused.

Macdonald in 1873 and Mackenzie in 1878 had been allowed to dole out patronage on the eve of leaving office. Tupper was flabbergasted. It was a genuine breach of protocol and practice for a governor general to refuse the wishes of a prime minister. Aberdeen also refused to endorse the Order-in-Council authorizing the government to sign a contract for the fast steam service.

One of the founding principles of responsible government was that the monarch, or their representative, take the advice of his or her elected representatives. Here was a governor general refusing to take the advice of ministers. There was much that could have been made of that refusal but after some indignant remarks to the press, Tupper conceded that he had no further recourse with Aberdeen. The country needed to move on. The Conservatives vowed to bring the issue to Parliament once the House began sitting again. Tupper's resignation as prime minister was accepted on July 8.

Laurier was sworn in as prime minister on July 11 and the House began sitting on July 20. The first matter brought up for debate was Tupper's accusation that the governor general had acted unconstitutionally in refusing to accept that last set of Tory appointments. The debate fizzled out rather quickly, as few members of House had the energy for a constitutional debate. The Liberals squelched any meaningful discussion, flatly announcing that the matter had already been settled. Neither the press nor the public had much interest in the matter. Nothing came of the Conservative protests and by summer's end, the issue was moot. Laurier quickly filled the patronage positions with loyal Liberals.

Sir Charles Tupper was the prime minister of Canada for only sixty-nine days. At age seventy-four, he was the oldest man to ever hold the position and the one who held the job for the shortest time. It is an odd fact that he never actually sat in the House of Commons to face the Opposition as prime minister. The irony in all this is that, although he was highly qualified for the job, the circumstances were such that he was not able to assume the leadership until he was an old man. After a lifetime in politics, he came into office near the end of a long, eventful career, one where he was second only to Sir John A. Macdonald as the most important politician in Canada.

Tupper and his wife celebrated their fiftieth wedding anniversary that summer. Lady Tupper had returned from London in poor health but was recovered enough to enjoy the festivities. Congratulations came from the various lieutenant governors, both Liberal and Conservative politicians, high-ranking contacts from the British Empire, and of course from supporters across the country. Mackenzie Bowell delivered a flowery and complimentary address from the Senate. Even that most Liberal of newspapers, the Toronto *Globe*, wrote a flattering piece that congratulated the pair on their accomplishments. Lord and Lady Aberdeen sent a small golden box as a gift.

Tupper kept active. He was unanimously selected as the leader of the party (and therefore of the Opposition) in the weeks after the election. It meant he continued to meet with Tory supporters, members, senators, and funders across the country. But he could not resist the pull of England and London society, in particular. Early in November, he and his wife boarded a steamer bound for Liverpool. During the visit to London, he addressed the British Empire Club. He was the guest of honour at a January 1897 banquet that marked his retirement as high commissioner. He saw to his grandson being enrolled in a private school and then sailed back to Canada.

The job ahead of him was to rebuild the Conservative brand across the country. His party had been deeply divided by the Manitoba Schools Question. Now it was time to heal the wounds in the party elite and woo back the voters who'd turned away from the Tories. A strong, energetic leader was needed. New men with new ideas had to be recruited to run for the party in every province.

Even though he was well into his seventies, Tupper still had nearly boundless energy. He still had the zeal that had driven him to many successes throughout his life. He continued his peripatetic visits to towns and villages all over the nation, drumming up support. In Parliament, he attacked the Liberals just as he'd done as a young doctor fresh to the Nova Scotia legislature in Halifax. He was especially angry about what he saw as Laurier's failure to protect the rights of the minority in Manitoba.[11]

Tupper's bulldog demeanour was actually well suited to the Opposition side of the House. He was good at debate; he had a clear mind that allowed him to cut to the meat of an argument; he was critical of fine points in measures that the Liberals tried to pass through Parliament. For instance, when Finance Minister Fielding brought forward a so-called preferential tariff for Britain, Tupper was the first to point out that the exact same measures applied to Belgium, Germany, and other nations in Europe. Sir Charles backed up his accusation with detailed reasons that had been put forward already from the Colonial Office in London. He kept the new Laurier government on their toes.

His contempt for Liberals showed itself later that year. During the summer, Tupper, his wife, and a granddaughter sailed from Montreal and arrived in London to find an invitation to attend a dinner with High Commissioner Donald Smith. The Lauriers were in London on the occasion of a conference of colonial premiers. Tupper refused to attend the dinner. Instead, he went to a reception of the British Empire League, followed by a party at Buckingham Palace. During his holiday in London, he and his wife attended numerous parties thrown by the elite of the British capital city.

As he'd done all his life, Sir Charles could not seem to sit still. He'd always lived at a frenetic pace, and now, although he was no longer prime minister nor high commissioner, his schedule was more hectic than ever. The Tuppers returned to Canada early in September. Leaving his wife in Ottawa, Sir Charles continued by train all the way to British Columbia. He'd recently accepted a directorship with a gold mining company, and the visit west was to check out the progress of the company's efforts. During his western excursion, he received a message from the head office of the New Gold Fields of British Columbia, summoning him to an important meeting in London. Once again, the old man set off — this time via New York City — for England. He spent a month there dealing with matters of the gold company and then returned to Canada. Immediately, he was on the road again, travelling to Winnipeg, where he and Sir John A. Macdonald's son, Hugh John Macdonald, courted the party faithful of Manitoba.

In January he was in Montreal, part of a group that set up a new French-language newspaper. In February, he was in his seat as Opposition leader in the House of Commons. In June, he was back in England once again to look after personal business interests. (After all, an MP's salary was not that great at the time, and he had given up medical practice.) Returning from Britain, he toured the Maritimes, touching down at a number of places in his Cape Breton riding and then met with Tory officials in Montreal. Parliament seemed to be low on his list of priorities because in late November he and his wife found themselves once more crossing the Atlantic. This time they travelled not only to England but went across the Channel to France and Italy. The ever-curious Tupper visited the ruins of Pompeii as well as Rome, Turin, and Pisa.

At seventy-nine, Tupper kept a pace that would have exhausted men one third his age. He seemed to race from town-to-town, meeting with party operatives, speaking at fairs or exhibitions, and touring the entire country. His train trips took him all through Ontario, back to Quebec, to Winnipeg, and even further west to Vancouver. As he was making his return trip to Ottawa, he addressed an enthusiastic crowd at Lethbridge (in what was then still the Northwest Territories). As there was no available train service north to Strathcona, he went by horse-drawn sleigh. Crossing the Saskatchewan River at about midnight, the sleigh capsized, and the old man was thrown onto the ice. He severely injured his knee but, being the trooper that he was, Tupper chose to grin and bear it. He completed the tour, arriving back in Ottawa hobbling from the train.

The pace of his life never seemed to slow down. Charles and his wife hosted a number of dinners for members of Parliament. In Ottawa, he attended official functions, such as a formal reception given by the new governor general, Lord Minto. On a visit to Toronto, he dined with former rival Oliver Mowat, recently named the lieutenant governor of Ontario.

The House resumed sitting on March 16, 1899. As was the custom, the Speech from the Throne was answered by the leader of Her Majesty's Loyal Opposition. Sir Charles rose with his patented stern look and spoke in his still powerful voice. For four and a half hours, he took the Laurier Liberal government to task for their policies, their errors, and their omissions. He touted the old National Policy achievements and commented on the recent Alaska boundary dispute. He brought up several other lesser policies where the Tories found fault with what the Liberals were doing.

That summer, Tupper, his wife, and several family members spent time in England once again. The Boer War was taking up much of the time for those in the Colonial Office, but Tupper was able to have his audiences, where he assured the British government of his party's support for sending Canadian troops to the conflict in South Africa. Upon his return to Ottawa, Sir Charles discussed the matter with Laurier. While they agreed on the principle of sending forces overseas, Laurier faced harsh opposition in Quebec. He acceded to sending a small force of volunteers. (Canada did not have a professional army at the time.) To Tupper's way of thinking, the Liberal response was inadequate.

Ever one to express keen interest in the British Empire, the war in South Africa became a touchstone for Tupper. He was invited to speak on the subject at Harvard University in Boston, where he outlined the policy that he would have pursued had he been in Laurier's shoes. But that was not his only interest. In the Commons, he pushed for parliamentary representation for Yukon Territory (as the region's population had exploded thanks to the recent Klondike gold strike). He advocated that Newfoundland should be invited to become part of Canada, forty-nine years before it actually happened.

The summer of 1900 found him once more — with Lady Tupper — in London, where he attended the queen's garden party at Buckingham Palace. He also spoke at a meeting of one of his favourite causes, the British Empire League. Then it was back to Canada. He paid a visit to his hometown of Amherst, where he took part in the nomination of C.H. Cahan as the Conservative candidate in the upcoming election. Coming down a flight of stairs from the room where the meeting was held, Sir Charles missed a step and fell, wrenching his knee badly. Although in considerable pain, he stoically carried on, speaking to the crowd for most of an hour. Those around him marvelled as his stoicism, stamina, and determination.

In politics, it is noteworthy when one finds extreme examples of honour and principle. The election of 1900 was set for November 7. Tupper had already told his supporters in Nova Scotia, and specifically on Cape Breton, that he was needed in Ontario to fight against the strong Liberal presence there. He left his own territory to men such as Robert Borden, a rising star in the Tory Party. Seeing that this might be a fatal political error, the backroom Conservatives tried to work out a deal with Alexander Johnston, his Liberal opponent in the constituency. If Johnston could be persuaded to accept a position with the Dominion Steel Works, that would allow Tupper to win by acclamation. On principle, Tupper refused to see the deal carried out. He was determined to fight to the very end and, win or lose, accept what the voters wanted. No easy ride for the old bulldog! At eighty years old, he was still determined to fight his own battle and return to the office of prime minister.

As it turned out, Tupper lost in his constituency in the November vote. He'd not devoted enough time to campaigning in his home riding and the Liberals had taken advantage of that. Needless to say, he was not happy with the result, as he felt he'd not only been outflanked but that the Grits had resorted to cheating. He wrote a rather vitriolic letter to the constituents of Cape Breton (from Vancouver) on November 15, a week after the election.

"I was as you are aware obliged from the outset to inform you that my duties in other parts of the Dominion would necessarily prevent me giving any attention to my own election, and I have to thank you all the more sincerely for the efforts which you have put forth to secure my return as one of your representatives in the Parliament of our country.

"Largely, as I am advised, by means of unfair voters' lists, many ignorant and partisan deputy returning officers, the illegal expenditure of public money during the campaign, not to mention many other unscrupulous acts on the part of the Government and its supporters, my colleague and I have been defeated.

"… Personally, my own defeat is to me not wholly unwelcome. I have worked and lived to see the unification of Her Majesty's possessions on this continent; Her people self-reliant, prosperous, and imbued with love of country and of Queen; and now, having reached my 80th year, I may fairly claim exemption from duties which have seriously taxed my strength for the past four years."

"The good people of Sydney have released me," was a line he delivered more than once as he announced his retirement.

Although he was apparently through with public life as a politician, he could not resist making some final speeches and addresses as he, his wife, and son Charlie travelled west to Vancouver. Getting off the train in places such as Winnipeg, he was greeted often as a conquering hero. Never accused of being short-winded, Tupper spoke for hours at a time to these post-election crowds, always to rousing cheers.

Unlike in the last years of Macdonald's rule, a viable successor to Tupper was waiting in the wings. However, true to recent Tory tradition, the man himself denied that fact. Robert Borden, a forty-seven-year-old lawyer and fellow Nova Scotian, had risen steadily in the party. His partnership in a law firm with Charlie Tupper had not hurt his possibility of advancement in the party by any means. The Conservatives, however, had finally learned how to pass the mantle of leadership. Sir Charles wrote a lengthy, glowing letter to Borden on February 28, 1901, asserting that the lawyer from Grand-Pré was "eminently qualified" to take on Tupper's role as Leader of the Opposition.

"I have not either the experience or the qualifications which would enable me to successfully lead the party. It would be an absurdity for the party and madness for me," said Borden.

C.H. Tupper, despite Borden's modest protest, introduced a motion in the Tory caucus to name the relative newcomer to politics as their next leader. The Tory senators met with the elected MPs and the parliamentary representatives of both houses unanimously elected Borden leader of the Conservative Party on February 6, 1901. There was a mite of nervous skepticism about how the inexperienced new leader would manage, but Borden had a calm manner that reassured nearly everyone. The welcome that Borden received was accompanied by a general feeling of sadness that the old leader was finally leaving Ottawa.

That Sir Charles Tupper was appreciated by his fellow party members was not surprising. The Tory papers of the day were congratulatory in their assessment of his accomplishments. What was somewhat surprising in that era of rampant yellow journalism was that some of the praise that came his way was from staunch Liberal newspapers. J.S. Willison, the long-time successor to George Brown as editor of the Toronto *Globe*, was effusive in his praise for Tupper and the old man's long career. "His history will give him a great place in the story of confederated Canada. With all his faults he was essentially a policy-maker and a constructive statesman. His work was done when the country needed builders, and it was done boldly and courageously."

The Tuppers decided to settle in England following Sir Charles's retirement. They opted for the London suburb of Bexleyheath, southeast of Charing Cross. The community was comfortably close to the action of central London but far enough away to be remote from the industry, shipping, and manic activity of the great capital. The couple named their home "The Mount" although Tupper often used the name "Broomwood" as the address near the top of his letters.

For Tupper, retirement did not end his travels or limit his social life. Indeed, the freedom from political duties allowed him to partake in what he'd always enjoyed — travel, parties, and social engagements. The gregarious old doctor was now free to visit friends that he'd made over his lengthy career on both sides of the Atlantic. In his eighties, he took up golf and played it frequently on courses near his home in London.

Honours poured his way, as was the nature of how famous men were treated. Queen's University at Kingston, Ontario, granted him an honourary doctor of law degree in part to thank him for his role in establishing a Chair of Political Economy there. His role in Confederation and his rise to the role of prime minister, brief as it was, were also reasons to salute Sir Charles.

Granddaughter Marie became the constant companion of Sir Charles and Lady Tupper. The trio went everywhere together. Tupper's journal recorded that the family made sixteen trips across the Atlantic between 1900 and 1908. They viewed the long funeral cortege of Queen Victoria from the home of a British MP.

He continued to work as a committee member on behalf of the British Empire League. As a former prime minister and having such an outgoing personality, he was often asked to speak at public functions and fund-raising dinners throughout England and across Canada.

A 1905 trip to Rome provided Tupper with an opportunity to show what would be known in the twenty-first century as being a "life-long learner." While in Italy, he and his granddaughter began taking Italian lessons. The eighty-four-year-old proved adept at the language, writing in his diary that after only a few weeks of study he could read the newspapers and carry on a simple conversation. He then gave proof that he was immersed in the language when he wrote that he was even "dreaming in Italian." On that same trip, Sir Charles accompanied his old friend Bishop Cameron to the Vatican, where the former prime minister was granted an audience with Pope Pius X. The pontiff blessed Tupper and was likely surprised when the newcomer to the Italian language responded, *"Io apprezzo altamente il grande onore di essere presentato a Vostra Santita."*[12]

Well into his eighties, Tupper kept his mind active. He corresponded with both Robert Borden and Wilfrid Laurier. He wrote lengthy, pointed letters to newspapers in both Canada and England when he felt the need to express an opinion on issues dear to his heart. During the heated debate in the Canadian Parliament about the so-called Naval Bill that dealt with helping to fund the Royal Navy, Tupper made known his opinion that he agreed with Conservative leader Robert Borden that Canada should build its own navy, a policy that not only signified the nation's independent status but at the same time, one could argue, could be used to support the defence of the Empire. In the end, the Canadian Parliament voted unanimously to do just that.

In November of 1907, Tupper was given the very special honour of being named to the British Privy Council. In a ceremony at Buckingham Palace, King Edward VII also promoted him to the rank of Knight Grand Cross of the Order of St. Michael and St. George, entitling him to write the initials GCMG after his name. The rare award went to those who held high office in the Empire or who rendered extraordinary service in a foreign country. Tupper qualified on both counts.

When George V succeeded his father as King in 1910, a large contingent of Canadian politicians arrived in London for the June coronation. A few days prior to that event, a different ceremony was held at the Westminster Palace Hotel. It was the venue, where forty-four years previously, the Fathers of Confederation had gathered to unite the British colonies in North America. Of those famous men, Sir Charles was the only Canadian "Father" who had survived. From the British politicians involved in the discussions in 1866–67, only Thomas Skinner was still alive. The two nation builders were honoured with speeches praising their accomplishment. Laurier and Lord Strathcona (Donald Smith, now promoted to a baron) as well as the premiers of Saskatchewan, Ontario, New Brunswick, and Alberta were part of the gathering, and each politician offered warm compliments. When Tupper was introduced, there was a great cheer from the crowd. Sir Wilfrid Laurier, who sat beside Sir Charles on the dais, spoke eloquently about Joseph Howe, George Brown, Tilley, Cartier, and Macdonald, but it was his long-time opponent, Tupper, that he praised the most that day. A commemorative plaque was unveiled to celebrate the achievements of 1867.

Sir Charles was pleased to be honoured in such a way, but the eighty-nine-year-old found himself exhausted after speaking at the reception. "My speaking days are done," he commented somewhat sadly.

That November, the United Empire Club wanted to pay tribute to the old man with a dinner in his honour. The Duke of Marlborough presided at the event. He related a personal anecdote. As a young boy in the 1870s, he'd been told that he would be meeting Charles Tupper "one of the greatest — if not the greatest — of Canadians." Ninety-year-old Tupper stepped forward to thankfully greet the gathering. Then, without a single note, he addressed the dinner crowd for over half an hour, never hesitating, barely pausing as he talked. He reminisced about his political life, of the events he'd seen, the people he'd encountered. So much for speaking days being done.

The dinner was also an excuse for the party faithful in London to celebrate not only their former leader but also the return to power in Canada of the Conservatives, this time under Tupper's protégé, Robert Borden. (He had recently defeated Laurier in the September 21 election.)

Frances Tupper had not been well for a number of years and in May of 1911, she passed away at the age of eighty-six. Sir Charles accompanied her body back to Canada and saw to her burial at St. John's Cemetery in Halifax. It was his final visit to his homeland. Returning to England, Tupper settled into a quiet and uneventful final few years at Bexleyheath.

Sir Charles Tupper died in his sleep there on October 30, 1915. Old age had finally caught up with him. His body was returned to Canada aboard the HMS *Blenheim*, the same battleship that had carried Sir John Thompson's body back to Halifax in 1894. A mile-long funeral procession accompanied the old doctor's casket as it travelled streets packed with mourners. Sir Charles was laid to rest beside his wife of sixty-four years.

He had led a long, remarkable life. The sixty-nine days he spent as Canada's prime minister were but one tiny, almost insignificant episode in what was truly a wide-ranging saga. Nearly seventy-five when he reached the peak of the political pyramid, that achievement was anti-climactic when compared to all the other things he'd seen and done. Born the same year that Napoleon died, he lived to see the invention of the telephone, the airplane, and the age of the automobile.

But it was his personality that shone above his achievements. He may have been vain and a self-promoter, but he was truly compassionate as well. He spoke his mind. Although his speeches could ramble on for hours — they quite often did — he took firm positions and expressed his opinions clearly. In politics, that can be a fatal flaw, but Tupper managed to walk a straight line where he stood on principle. Friends and opponents alike knew how he felt about any given issue. Tupper himself saw his goal in life was to not only do good but to show the public what was good. He stated a number of times that he felt that one of the chores for a politician was to educate the voter. He brought a courageous optimism to what he believed. He also had a healthy skepticism and ready critique of laws or legislation that he felt were not in the interests of the country. That held true all through his political life.

Although he often laboured in Macdonald's shadow, Sir Charles justifiably took credit for helping to rebuild the national Conservative Party after the Pacific Scandal. Tupper played a major role in developing the National Policy, especially in soliciting the funding for and directing the construction of the transcontinental railway. He had a say in most of the policy strategy that figured so prominently throughout the 1880s, even as he distanced himself in far-away London.

He was loyal to his native province. Then, in turn, he was loyal to Canada and to the Empire and never saw reason to favour one over the other. That he was such a rabid imperialist made him a man of his times. But those attitudes did not prevent him from pushing for the rights of the religious and linguistic minorities in Canada. Catholics and French-speaking Canadians could look to Tupper for support and tolerance. He expected that same tolerance in others.

On Tupper's passing, Prime Minister Borden commented, "He had a magnificent courage which never quailed before any danger, or in the face of any odds. He had a fine optimism. He was a firm believer in every sense in the resources of this Dominion, and in the greatness of its future."

Although he'd found Dr. Tupper to be arrogant and self-aggrandizing, Wilfrid Laurier, a long-time political foe, also had complimentary things to say about his fellow prime minister upon the latter's death in 1915. Speaking about the last Father of Confederation, Sir Wilfrid first praised some of the other prominent Fathers — Brown, Galt, Cartier, and Macdonald — then focused on the role of Sir Charles. "Tupper brought to the cause more firm conviction and took more chances than did anyone else."

Laurier then went on to comment on the old man's traits. "The chief characteristic of Tupper was courage; courage which no obstacle could down ... but it was not his only characteristic. His mind had been cast in a broad mould.... He seemed to me the very incarnation of the parliamentary athlete, always strong, always ready to accept battle and to give battle."

Tupper would have agreed with Laurier's assessment. And then picked a battle with the Liberal leader.

Chapter Six

———— ◈ ————

After the Deluge: Laurier and Beyond

WHEN CANADA'S NEWEST PRIME MINISTER, the sixth in a span of five years, stood to address the new Parliament in the autumn of 1896, newcomers to the House of Commons gallery were surprised to hear that the Quebec-born francophone spoke fluent English with a hint of a Scottish accent. (He'd learned English at a Scots-dominated private school.) He had a number of things in common physically with the first of Canada's prime ministers, Sir John A. Macdonald. Both men were lean and clean shaven at a time when men were generally short, stout, and sported plentiful facial hair. With his full head of silver, bushy hair, the handsome Wilfrid Laurier bore at least a tonsorial resemblance to John A. Macdonald. (No one ever accused Macdonald of being handsome!) Most importantly, the mantle of power had passed from John A. — after a tumultuous five years — to a man whose reputation among prime ministers would eventually rival that of the Old Chieftain's. Macdonald had held power for almost nineteen years; Laurier would hold office for fifteen years. In the country's first forty-four years, those two men led for thirty-four of them.

Both remain giants on the Canadian political landscape, the dominant figures of their times.

That four other men had briefly held the lofty position of prime minister was seen to be simply a brief, turbulent interregnum. But was it?

The industrious Abbott, the ill-fated Thompson, the ill-suited Bowell, and the old bull Tupper served brief spells that were all much shorter than anticipated, and all marked by controversies, bigotry, grand hopes, and dismal failures. Poor health, a sudden unexpected death, a party revolt, and an electorate ready for change resulted in those four men only briefly filling the gap between two political giants: Macdonald and Laurier.

Laurier came into office with little of the baggage that his immediate predecessors carried. Although it still remained for him to settle the Manitoba Schools Question in 1896, he headed a strong Liberal Party with an outstanding, capable Cabinet. The Grits appeared, in general, to have the potential of achieving nearly anything. All four of Laurier's immediate predecessors on the other hand had been saddled with a dysfunctional Conservative Party that, by comparison to the Liberals, lacked any noteworthy politicians. Laurier, like the "interregnum four," faced the challenges of governing in a time more dominated by religious and racial prejudice than any other era in Canadian history before or since. Being a francophone and a Catholic, Laurier faced a country that was generally suspicious of those two qualities. But Laurier's party was for the most part united under their leader. None of his four predecessors could say that.

The Liberals' strength lay in the number of seats they'd captured in Quebec and the strong men that had been recruited to federal office. The seemingly young prime minister — fifty-five as opposed to Tupper's seventy-five — exuded energy, confidence, and a serene nature. His pronouncement that he would follow "sunny ways" seemed to reassure Canadians at the time that they were in good hands with a Liberal government. By contrast, the Tories were an aging, intransigent group who squabbled and plotted behind their leaders' backs, who had run out of new ideas, and who seemed more concerned with padding their own pockets than nurturing the growing country. Following the election of 1896, the Dominion hoped that it had found a leader who would bring some stability

to the office of prime minister. The previous five years had been anything
but stable.

Laurier had a number of strengths that his predecessors — Sir John A.
excluded — had all lacked. His personal charisma cannot be overstated.
Among Canadian prime ministers, perhaps only Macdonald and both
Trudeaus could boast any kind of similar appeal. Impeccably dressed and
usually soft-spoken, he appealed to the country in that shallow way that
benefits many politicians who are handsome and charming.

But his strengths ran much deeper. He fundamentally believed that the
job of building Canada into a nation was his duty. In that way, he and
Tupper shared a common goal. As a French Canadian, he understood the
nation's dual linguistic nature, but he also had great respect and admiration
for all things British — the institutions, the history, the literature.[1] In that
respect, he was not all that different from the men who'd come before him,
except that all of them were anglophone. Above all, he was a man who
believed in tolerance and moderation, two qualities that would help him
manage the Manitoba Schools Question and Canada's participation in the
upcoming Boer War. Compromise was one of the principles he stood by.
He felt that Quebec and the French culture in Canada could only survive if
there was understanding, cooperation, and the finding of a middle-ground.
It was that kind of thinking that allowed him to eventually find a resolution
to the Manitoba Schools Question where his Conservative predecessors had
stumbled.

Laurier was an intellectual. He preferred to sit and read alone in his
library more than almost anything else. He wrote letters in classical Greek
to Edward Blake. Laurier had eclectic interests well beyond politics. He
was once overheard by a newspaper reporter talking effusively about a rare
cookbook. Although not a robust and energetic man physically, he would
often walk the streets of Ottawa to ponder things that were on his mind.

Sir Wilfrid preferred to be at home with his wife, Zoe. Thompson shared
that kind of preference with Laurier, although he had a house brimming

with young children. The Lauriers, on the other hand, were childless. Until he visited London, for the queen's Diamond Jubilee in 1867, Sir Wilfrid had never sailed across the Atlantic. In contrast, John Abbott had been a gadabout; he could be found on almost a daily basis at one meeting or another pursuing his business connections and personal interests. Tupper made more trips overseas than any Canadian public man of that era. Bowell had travelled to Australia. In that day and age, that was nearly as exotic as going to the moon.

In the political arena, Laurier was a stellar parliamentarian. He could be tough and combative in House of Commons when the discussion touched on issues of particular political or personal importance to him. So could Tupper and Thompson. Even Abbott was an articulate parliamentarian, never cowed by Opposition attacks. Sir Wilfrid's defence of Louis Riel in 1874 (when the Métis leader was expelled from the Commons) helped to establish not only his reputation as a young politician on the rise but as a man who had no fear in parliamentary give-and-take. Again in 1885, he came to the Métis Peoples' defence with a long speech in the House where he pointed a finger at Sir John A. Macdonald, accusing him of being contemptuous of the Métis. Similarly, it was Thompson's defence of the government action in the 1885 North-West Rebellion that had made his great initial impression in Parliament.

But more often, Laurier tended to be reserved, calm, and even congenial, practising what he preached about "sunny ways" in the House. He relied on his skillful logic to skewer adversaries' arguments. Abbott and Thompson both shared that skill, clever lawyers that they were. (Perhaps Sir Wilfrid learned that expertise early on when he had studied under Abbott at McGill law school in the 1860s.) Laurier's famous tolerance for others' opinions was well noted by critics and political opponents. Tupper was a polar opposite in that regard. He was strictly partisan. He openly despised the Liberals and their ideas. To a certain degree, Mackenzie Bowell was that way as well. At times, Laurier was frank and open, but he could also couch his true feelings in flowery rhetoric.

Over his entire political career, he managed to develop a skill for trade-offs and a resistance to taking too rigid a stand on any issue. He was able, like Macdonald before him, to seem to be on both sides of the fence, first taking one position and then qualifying it for a different audience. He often managed to avoid coming down too firmly on one side or the other of an issue. He could just as easily have worn the sobriquet Old Tomorrow as John A. Macdonald did. Procrastination was second nature to him. He was adept in his use of that skill, and it worked a good deal of the time. It was not something easy to master, however. Mackenzie Bowell failed miserably in his attempt.

For a man who faced religious pressure from all sides during his career, Laurier was fearless in taking positions that might offend, on one hand, the Catholic bishops and clergy of his native Quebec or, on the other hand, the Protestant extremists in Ontario. That choice was often risky politically, but it also showed that he had courage to spare. Thompson too had grappled with the vicissitudes of handling both anti-Catholic sentiment and the demands of his chosen denomination throughout his career. John Thompson certainly knew about the systemic bias toward Catholics. He lived it every day, as did Laurier. Both men knew the nature of the country. They could see in their own ranks how the religious prejudices coloured nearly every issue to come before Parliament.

Sir Wilfrid had the skill of focusing on an individual and listening to the person's opinions or ideas. The individual would then come away from the encounter believing that he'd been the only one in the room who was important at the time. That skill played a large part in the way Laurier kept firm control over his party. It also earned him great adoration in the public at large. Macdonald had often shown the same kind of deftness while wooing both supporters and opponents. His personal touch with voters won him many an election. Prime ministers Abbott and Bowell could have learned much from both of them in regard to managing personal relationships.

Laurier was well-liked, acknowledged by contemporaries to be a kind man, polite in manner and courteous, characteristics that were allegedly rare at that time in political life. Not only did Laurier possess great personal charm and remarkable political skills, by the time he had reached the early 1890s, Laurier was the undisputed leader of a party that was far more united, focused, and goal-oriented than the Conservatives at that time.

By the 1890s, his party supported him and stood united behind the policies he advocated. There were no knives in his back from jealous rivals. Furthermore, Sir Wilfrid was almost as diligent in keeping tabs on his party as Macdonald had been with his colleagues.

A Liberal Party convention in 1893 had brought together a massive gathering of Liberals from across the country. They confirmed the policy of reciprocity, the promotion of Canada's resources and new industrial sectors, and attempted to demonstrate to the Canadian people that the Liberal Party was a viable alternative to the ruling Tories. As the Conservatives struggled to cope with changing leaders and stale policies held over from the Macdonald era, the Liberals shone in comparison. Within three years, the Liberals ascended to power, ready to implement those policies they had carefully drafted. Best of all, they had a leader who could sell those ideas to the public.

Not only was Laurier able to showcase Liberal ideas for the future, he was also able to resolve issues that had lingered on the Canadian political landscape for years. He stickhandled the issue that had most plagued the Conservatives during that last decade of the century — the Manitoba Schools Question —far more skillfully than the men who'd come before him. He did it by being careful to never make a public pronouncement about where he stood on the issue. Instead, he expressed his personal sympathy for the minority in the province. He then told the provinces that they had certain rights as independent legislatures. Laurier took on the mantle of protector of the minorities while at the same time putting himself forward as a defender of provincial authority. He adeptly used the controversy to embarrass first Bowell and then Tupper over their handling of the matter. It was a tricky tightrope to walk, but he managed it brilliantly. In the end, he solved the issue with a compromise worked out with Manitoba's Greenway government. Catholic and French education would be permitted in the province on a school-by-school basis, dependent upon there being enough students to warrant those special classes. Laurier had found a middle ground using the sunny way. He succeeded where his predecessors failed. Abbott, Thompson, Bowell, and Tupper had been unable to steer down that road. Had one of them done so, the outcome of the 1896 election might have been very different.

In office, Laurier brought a fresh approach to governing the country. His party had innovative ideas. All the Cabinet members exuded self-assurance in their handling of government affairs. Such was the Dominion's confidence in the Liberals that the Grits remained in office for the next fifteen years, through four successive elections.

Laurier was a master of patronage, using it cleverly to suit his purposes. He became as adept at doling out favours and watching over political appointments as Sir John A. Macdonald and Sir Charles Tupper. He would mete out appointments to friends and associates as a way of saying thank you. He used favours to bring opponents into the Liberal sphere. He even knew how to use it to pay off and get rid of unwanted members of his own party. He oversaw appointments with a watchful eye on even the most trivial of jobs. Like Sir John A., he would know if a lowly paid postal worker deserved a miniscule raise or promotion. He was known to intercede in what were seemingly petty disagreements over government jobs in remote parts of the country. It all paid off, as he developed a strong network across the nation that owed loyalty to the party leader as much as to the local party officials.

Because of Macdonald's long career as Canada's standard-bearer, followed — with a short interregnum — by Laurier's equally impressive term, the four prime ministers who briefly held office in the early 1890s seem to be so much less important. They seem to be lesser men than the nation-builder they followed and the dignified visionary who followed them. Was that true? Abbott, Thompson, Bowell, and Tupper never had the chance to lead for any decent length of time. Nonetheless, they were impressive individuals, who governed through an extremely tumultuous time.

While Macdonald and Laurier shared similar leadership skills, the other prime ministers who sat in that chair in those few short years of the 1890s had their own styles. Thompson was a dynamo and the "smartest man in the room." Abbott led with a quiet, calm, and reassuring manner. Tupper used his blustery personality to, as the modern saying goes, suck all the oxygen out of the room. Bowell had the most meagre social skills of the quartet.

His temper got the best of him too often and his attempts to gloss over his responsibilities and fake knowledge of issues only served to erode respect for his leadership. Yet he had demonstrated over a long career in politics that he knew how to efficiently administer government business.

History, particularly political history, can become a game of "what ifs." Tupper was a great contributor to the founding of the nation, a Father of Confederation who helped to build the country from scratch. Had he assumed office after the Pacific Scandal of 1873, for instance, he may have earned as great a reputation as Sir John A. Macdonald, and he may have led the country for many years. He certainly had the political skills, the confidence, the strategic mind, and the facility to manipulate others — all important talents for handling the job of prime minister. His work as a Cabinet minister, high commissioner, and as an intimate advisor to Macdonald was as admirable as it was influential. That influence was far-reaching. Fiercely loyal to Macdonald and the Tory Party, he had a clear contempt for the Liberal politicians and their ideas, something that inevitably may have hurt his standing with contemporaries. His accomplishments over his long time in politics were impressive. Yet his incredibly brief time in office as premier seems a dramatic anticlimax to such a great career. As with Thompson, we wonder, "If only ..."

Bowell, a man brought down by his own curmudgeonly behaviour, vanity, stubbornness, and false reasoning that he could easily fool others, was destined to fail because of those qualities but even more so by an issue that overwhelmed his entire party. The Manitoba Schools Question hung like an ugly black cloud over his entire time in office. The chaos that existed within his caucus was not entirely of his making. Nor was the upheaval caused by the Manitoba legislation. The religious intolerance of the day peaked just as he took control of the country, and he, unfortunately, lacked the political and personal skills to find a solution. Instead, he was eventually forced to fall on his own sword for the sake of the party. Lacking the innate political intelligence of either Macdonald or Laurier, he had a difficult time adapting to an office that required subterfuge and manipulation. He was too much of a straight shooter and when he attempted to emulate the greatest political manipulator of the day, his efforts fell flat. Furthermore, it seems he rose slightly higher on the political ladder than his skills could handle. He was an example of the Peter Principle decades before that idea was formulated.[2] He was ultimately doomed to fail.

Abbott's personal energy drove him throughout his life to achieve great things in so many diverse areas. His legal accomplishments were impressive enough to merit praise, even if he'd never done anything else. Rising quickly to become dean of a law school and the top barrister in the country were, to say the least, notable. But he did so much more. His knowledge of the railway industry, much of it learned through wise investing and close ties to the industry's entrepreneurs, put him in a special place among businessmen at a time when railways flourished. He was at ease with the major power-brokers of the day. He knew many of their secrets. Regrettably, he shared some of the ethical lapses of Sir John A. His involvement in the Pacific Scandal was an example of that. Yet, he was a competent and efficient man when put in charge of a project, be that a trade mission, a business merger, or a government portfolio. Even in his brief time as premier of the country, a stormy period, he was able to competently steer a huge slate of legislation through Parliament. He was well-liked, a trait he shared with Macdonald, Thompson, and Laurier. His benevolent interests were praiseworthy. Several of his philanthropic endeavours were ahead of their time. Even if he'd never entered the political arena, J.J. Abbott would have been one of the most remarkable Canadians of the nineteenth century.

The prime minister with the greatest untapped potential was John Thompson. Had his term as head of the government not ended so prematurely, it seems he may have been a great rather than merely a good prime minister. He shared many leadership qualities with Macdonald and Laurier. Widely acknowledged as an intellectual giant, he had many other character traits that would have earned him greater fame and respect had he not died so young. His morality as a politician, but more importantly as a man, was unquestioned. He had a great capacity to quickly understand issues and see the solutions to problems. With the fair-minded mien of a judge, he approached politics in a calm and logical manner. He seemed to be above the fray of party squabbles and bickering and seemed to expect the same from his followers. He exuded confidence. Thompson approached much of his work with a diligence that was rarely matched by his peers. Although his wife and family were of utmost importance to him, he never shirked any political duties for the sake of a quiet evening at home. He was a man of many passions — sex (marital that is!), religion, and food being significant ones that we are able to see in examining his intimate personal life. Upholding the law — including the tempering of injustice — was a near obsession that he pursued throughout his professional life.

As prime minister, Thompson held together a feeble Conservative Party. He was the only man in the party who had the personality and skills to do so. That became even more obvious when Bowell succeeded him in office. The racial and religious schisms in the party ran deep, and it took a master's hand to keep the divisive Tories in working order. Both John A. and "Little Sir John" managed to do so by the power of their personalities, especially their wisdom in dealing with people.

Thompson's speeches were well-received and praised for their clarity. His management of government departments showed a mind that could juggle many details at once. He also knew how to supervise the men — and the very few women — who worked under him. He suffered no fools, but he praised good work when he recognized it. His fair, honest, and judicious mind as a judge carried over into his time in elected office, especially when leading his party in government.

He had a personal charm that was especially attractive to women. (Macdonald and Laurier had that same effect.) Lady Aberdeen was quite taken with Thompson, and he made a great first — and final as it turned out — impression on Queen Victoria when he met her at Windsor Castle. The old queen was terribly upset by his sudden death and did all she could to show how much she cared in the days following his fatal heart attack.

Being the leader of a country is by definition a difficult chore. It takes a certain type of person to successfully fill that role. Indeed, only particular sorts of people yearn for the job. For certain men and women, the position of prime minister is a lifelong goal. For some, they strive to accomplish that goal from an early age. For others, the job is thrust upon them. It could be argued that each of the men who rose to power between the Macdonald and Laurier eras — Abbott, Thompson, Bowell, and Tupper — had the job handed to them despite their reluctance to have it. All four viewed their ascension to the premiership as a duty to the Conservative Party.

Abbott took over because of the sudden void left by Macdonald. Sir John A. had not prepared the party for who would follow, so the old backroom deal-maker from Montreal was deemed the least offensive choice. Thompson would probably have preferred to take a seat at the Supreme Court but felt a duty to take on the role of PM out of loyalty to the Conservative Party. Bowell was handed the position at the most inopportune and unexpected time, simply on the basis that he was considered competent enough and was the most senior ranking Cabinet minister. He felt it was his duty to serve his party as best he could. Those were hardly appropriate prerequisites for the job. Once Bowell proved to be not up to the task, Tupper was summoned back to Ottawa from his comfy home in England. He'd likely have preferred to stay on as high commissioner. Yet he was determined to serve the party and ran in the 1896 election despite there being a very good chance he would lose. Then, after that nearly inevitable loss, he stayed on as leader so that he could do what he thought was best for the Tory Party. Out of duty, he carried on until he had groomed Robert Borden to take on the job.

It could also be argued that none of the four truly thirsted for the position the way that some have. All four built outstanding careers and public lives. Becoming the nation's top politician never seemed to be the ultimate goal for any of them (although Tupper may have relished the opportunity in the 1870s, two decades before the job finally fell into his hands). All four believed in public service and even in personal sacrifice for the good of their party and their country. All four took on the job through unusual circumstances in trying times. All four led a divided political party that by its very makeup could not ever be truly united. These men were publicly minded individuals who had other pursuits that could easily have satisfied their personal ambitions.

The six men who were prime ministers of Canada between 1891 and 1896 shared a number of characteristics despite their marked outward differences. Macdonald, Abbott, Thompson, Bowell, Tupper, and Laurier all answered the call to serve their fellow countrymen. All of them knew how to grease the political wheels so that things could be achieved, not the least of which were their own personal elections. All of them knew how to rise to the top of one endeavour or another. Although very different individuals in temperament and personality quirks, each shared the politicians' drive for attention, adulation, and, to a certain degree, power. Every major politician is driven by ego and a need for approval. For those who rise to the very height of power, that drive is usually more ambitious.

The general lack of ambition for the nation's most important political position amongst Macdonald's four successors meant that there was virtually no infighting amongst them. The men knew each other well. Macdonald had been the leader who Abbott and Bowell joined willingly as early as the 1860s. Sir John A. actively recruited Thompson from the Nova Scotia court. He also formed a fast and long-lasting relationship with Tupper as early as their first meeting in Charlottetown in 1864. The men worked together in Cabinet in fashioning the laws and bureaucracy that would service the growing country. All were fundamental components of the political coalition that became the national Conservative Party.

The correspondence among these powerful gentlemen was almost always cordial and complimentary, although they could also be somewhat catty about each other in letters to spouses or friends. For example, during the 1888 fisheries negotiations in Washington, Tupper took credit for something that Thompson thought was more correctly his doing. In a letter to his wife, Annie, Thompson sarcastically commented, "We should be humble in the presence of such gifts." The aspersions Macdonald cast on Abbott's leadership qualities were mitigated when, at the end of his life, he told Thompson that they'd all have to follow J.J.'s lead.

The men spent time together. A snapshot (his own word) from the early 1890s of John Thompson, his family, Senator Sandford, and Mackenzie Bowell shows everyone, especially Thompson, in a happy frame of mind. It is noteworthy to see smiles and laughter at a time when photographs were generally sober. Bowell is grinning from ear to ear, and Thompson seems caught in the midst of a grand laugh. It is difficult to say how close the two men were, but as senior Cabinet ministers, they would have spent considerable time working and, in the setting of that particular photo, playing together.

Abbott and Thompson were both known to invite their Cabinet members to their homes for meetings and sumptuous dinners. Abbott also hosted his fellow politicians at his clubs whenever they visited Montreal. Abbott, Tupper, and Macdonald collaborated for years on the pursuit of railway building. Tupper and Macdonald huddled together when plotting the various Tory strategies from the time of Confederation right up to Macdonald's death. Bowell and Tupper, long-time colleagues on the Conservative benches, knew each other quite well and never seemed to come to any major disagreements. Tupper, upon his return to Ottawa in the winter of 1895, made a point to meet several times with the prime minister. It is highly unlikely that he was nefariously plotting behind Bowell's back. He more or less sat back and waited for the job to finally fall into his lap.

The history of every country's political hierarchy has its triumphs and failures, its glorious highs and tragic lows. Canada is no exception. That four men — six if we count the predecessor and eventual successor — held the position of prime minister in the space of five years is highly unusual, the kind of thing one might expect to find in a nation with an unstable political culture. Frequent changes in leadership have also plagued nations like Italy and Israel, but this is because of their multi-party systems where coalition governments are difficult to keep together. That has generally not been the case in Canada, so it makes the first half of the 1890s such an anomaly.

The four men who held the Dominion's highest office in the 1890s between the end of Macdonald's tenure and the beginning of Laurier's were not the political icons that those two men have become. Most Canadians do not recognize the names of any of them nor are their faces as familiar as those of Sir John and Sir Wilfrid. None of the four accomplished anything along the lines of a transcontinental railway or the settling of the West. Macdonald was the driving force in forging British North America into a nation. He then tied it all together with a ribbon of steel across the continent. Laurier cemented that tenuous amalgamation and saw the country become truly autonomous, one that recognized its French component was an equal partner. He oversaw the early settlement of the western Prairies and the growth of Canada into something more than a cluster of former British colonies on the eastern side of the Great Lakes. He foresaw the potential of Canada, as demonstrated in his often-misquoted line about the nation's future. Speaking at Toronto's Massey Hall on October 14, 1904, he said, "Let me tell you, my fellow countrymen, that all the signs point this way, that the twentieth century shall be the century of Canada and Canadian development.... For the next one hundred years, Canada shall be the star towards which all men who love progress and freedom shall come." He would repeat that message many times. Looking back, it was a prophetic vision that did come to pass in certain ways. He did his best to make it so.

Abbott, Thompson, Bowell, and Tupper could never boast similar accomplishments and therefore have been relegated to the footnotes of Canadian history. Fair or not, that lack of presence in the nation's history books and mythology has consigned these four honourable and distinguished men to rankings much lower than they deserve.

ACKNOWLEDGEMENTS

───────── ◇ ─────────

It may seem a bit odd to acknowledge people from my distant past for a book that was written in 2020. Yet I believe it was my teachers, almost as much as my parents, who sparked a love of history early in my life. I recall my elementary teachers Mrs. Mumford and Mr. March, who taught me about Marco Polo, Pierre Radisson, and even made Lord Durham interesting. In high school, it was Mr. John Palmer who fostered an intellectual approach to history. He could make historical figures like Plato, Metternich, and Garibaldi almost come alive. I then was lucky enough to study history at York University in the early seventies under such wonderful professors as Ramsay Cook, Jack Granatstein, and Paul Stevens. Thank you to all those inspiring teachers.

Thanks again to the staff of Dundurn Press. Their patience, guidance, and support cannot be underestimated. In particular, thanks to associate publisher Kathryn Lane and to my editor, Dominic Farrell, for their acceptance and help in bringing this project into being.

Finally, thanks to my wife, Bonnie, and to my daughters, Erin and Stephanie, for their support and enthusiasm for this book.

NOTES

◈

Chapter One / The Legacy of Sir John A. Macdonald

1 Macdonald's copy of the working document at the London Conference of 1866 is filled with caricatures and doodling, indicating that even when he led the proceedings, his mind was not always fully on the argument at hand. According to some sources, Macdonald himself came up with about fifty of the clauses that made up the final constitutional document. Despite the fact that he had a reason to be excused from some of the meetings (while attending the conference he'd been seriously burned in a fire in his hotel room) he somehow managed not to miss any of the sessions. He also managed to arrange a second marriage for himself.

2 Macdonald had been bestowed with a knighthood (Knight Commander of the Order of the Bath) in 1867, on the recommendation of Lord Monck, the governor general. He was the only Father of Confederation who was entitled to use "Sir" in front of his name. This was a great cause of dissension and resentment. Cartier, Tupper, Tilley, and other prominent men who'd done much to ensure Confederation were not granted similar honours at the time. A.T. Galt was especially angry, going so far

as to refuse the Companion of the Order of the Bath although he got his knighthood two years later. Because of his exclusion from the award, Cartier went so far as to consider a merger of his Parti Bleu and George Brown's Liberals, but Cartier's feeling were assuaged when he was later offered a knighthood.

3   "Manifest Destiny" was a doctrine popular in the United States that maintained that it was both justified and inevitable that the Americans would take over and control the entire North American continent.

4   Lord Selkirk, part owner of the Hudson's Bay Company, had tried to re-settle many displaced Scots in the Red River area in the early nineteenth century, but that colonization effort was controversial and not overly successful. The Métis, with their connection to the rival North West Company, resisted the incursion of Scottish settlers in what was called Assiniboia. Armed conflict, lawsuits, and financial ruin (for Selkirk) were just some of the results.

5   The Orange Order — formally called the Grand Orange Order of British America — was an offshoot of the Orange Order that had been founded in 1795 in Ireland. Established to defend Protestantism, it was made up of members who celebrated the victory of King William of Orange over the predominantly Roman Catholic forces of James II. In Ontario, the organization established itself as the leading political force of the nineteenth century. Sir John Abbott, Mackenzie Bowell, and John A. Macdonald were all Orangemen. In a time when religion figured prominently in all areas of one's life, joining the Orange Order was more often than not akin to joining a men's club for the social and political advantages it might bring. In everyday language, people usually referred to the group as the "Orange Lodge."

6   It was in what we now call Saskatchewan, although that region was at the time called the Northwest Territories. Saskatchewan and Alberta did not join Confederation as provinces until 1905.

7   Donald Creighton, *John A. Macdonald: The Old Chieftain* (Toronto: Macmillan, 1965), 471.

8   Over the years, delegations from Halifax had actually petitioned the Colonial Office in London for the opportunity to secede from

Confederation. The British officials had quickly and consistently told them to cease and desist from such nonsensical talk.

9   By 1854, the Canadian-American Reciprocity Treaty had been enacted. It allowed limited free trade between Canada and the United States. This treaty was abrogated by the United States at the end of the Civil War. Following Confederation, the Liberal Party campaigned for the renegotiation of the treaty. Many years later, Brian Mulroney, a Conservative, would campaign for free trade with the United States. John Turner, his Liberal opponent, opposed it. In the end, of course, the Conservatives won the election and, in 1987, Canada signed a free trade agreement with the United States.

Chapter Two / Sir John Abbott: The Reluctant Prime Minister

1   In the late nineteenth century, the term *pervert* was used to describe a person who had strayed from the accepted method of doing something. At the time, the word had yet to take on the modern meaning of sexual deviance.

2   Chapleau would serve as Abbott's secretary of state, but he refused to become a member of Thompson's Cabinet in 1892. Instead, he accepted the lieutenant governor position in Quebec and spent the years from 1892–98 in the vice-regal post at Quebec City.

3   Reverend Dr. Douglas was the principal of Montreal's Wesleyan Theological College and had made vitriolic attacks on Thompson. At one point, he called Sir John a "Jesuit," a term that was intended to be an insult.

4   John A. Macdonald was said to have been bilingual since he could speak a form of Gaelic. His mother's preferred means of communication was always Gaelic. Alexander Mackenzie, a Scot from central Ontario, likely knew Gaelic as well, but neither of our first prime ministers was truly able to converse in French.

5   Abbott ran for office in the riding of Argenteuil in the 1857–58 election. When his opponent, Sydney Robert Bellingham, a Liberal-Conservative, was declared the victor, Abbott petitioned to have the election overturned

on the grounds that his opponent had enticed men who were not qualified to vote for him. After a hearing that lasted two years, Abbott was
awarded the election. He took office in March of 1860.

6   Dr. Norman Bethune, a hero to Communists in Mao's China, was a des-
cendent of the Montreal Bethune family. Actor Christopher Plummer
was also part of this family.

7   The seigneury was founded in 1672. The seigneur had been a captain
in the Carignan-Salierres Regiment, a French army unit sent to battle and then make peace with the Iroquois. Famed adventurer Charles
LeMoyne purchased the land in 1679. He built a fort there for protection against Iroquois raids. Remains of the fortress still existed in
Abbott's day.

8   Fraser was a businessman in Quebec who, along with Abbott, established the first free public library in Canada and the Fraser-Hickson
institute. It was Fraser's bequest that enabled the institution to operate
for well over a century.

9   At that time, electors could file a petition to remove an elected member
of Parliament if there were sufficient grounds to suspect misdoings or
unscrupulous behaviour.

10   The Canadian Pacific Railway, as established in 1881, was an entirely
different and separate entity from Sir Hugh Allan's Canadian Pacific
Railway company of the 1870s.

11   The practice of retaining a Cabinet one inherits when a leader is suddenly removed from office, dies, or resigns unexpectedly has become a
norm in Western politics. Lyndon Johnson, for example, kept John F.
Kennedy's Cabinet as his own following the November 22, 1963, as-
sassination of the U.S. president. There is a certain wisdom in such an
action since it helps to ensure stability.

12   John Castell Hopkins, *Life and Work of the Rt. Hon. Sir John Thompson:
Prime Minister of Canada* (Toronto: United Publishing Houses, 1895),
205.

13   Courtney had come to Canada in 1869 at the behest of the Conservative
minister of finance John Rose. He became chief clerk and assistant
secretary to the Treasury Board. The Liberals promoted him to deputy

minister. Courtney had a solid reputation as someone opposed to blatant patronage and often spoke out against banks that tried to get business by applying political pressure. Impartial to the core, he was a fine choice as a commissioner.

14 A.H.U Colquhoun, "Civil Service Reform," *Canadian Magazine*, May–Oct. 1896, 569.

15 Pauncefote was officially "Envoy Extraordinary and Minister Plenipotentiary to the United States." That position was changed to less wordy "Ambassador to the U.S." in 1893.

Chapter Three / Sir John Thompson: "The Great Might-Have-Been" Prime Minister

1 He was not all that proficient in French and allegedly would not speak it publicly when he first arrived in Ottawa in 1886. Yet, with characteristic zeal, he learned the language well enough that he was eventually able, when he became prime minister, to speak confidently to francophone audiences.

2 That bit of political manoeuvring came back to haunt Thompson seven years later when Sir Richard Cartwright, a feisty Liberal from Ontario, rose in the House to accuse the then-prime minister Thompson of having "purchased" the Antigonish seat in the Commons.

3 Years later, Thompson, in an interview with a writer for the law review *The Barrister*, said that Blake possessed the greatest legal mind he ever met and went on to say that Blake was very much misunderstood. Blake in turn praised the eloquence and logic of many of Thompson's speeches.

4 Hopkins, 308.

5 The British were not innocents in this dispute. Canadian and British sealers engaged in what is called "pelagic sealing" — the hunting of nursing females in the open sea. This practice nearly exterminated the seals in certain regions. Both the Russians and the Americans objected to the practice outside of their territorial waters.

6 Since he was high commissioner to Britain, many felt that Tupper should not have taken an active role in the election. In the aftermath of

the 1891 contest, the Opposition tried to scandalize his participation, spending an inordinate amount of time on the issue through the 1892 parliamentary session.

7   A short man at only five foot seven, Thompson was becoming increasingly obese. He had put on a great deal of weight during his time in Ottawa. He and Annie had both developed rather substantial jowls. When he first arrived in the capital from Halifax, John weighed 190 pounds, but less than a decade later, he had ballooned to over 225 pounds. His weight was not considered as much of an issue then as it would today; for people in the Victorian age, a stout appearance was indicative of health and vigour. Many of Thompson's fellow MPs were also noticeably overweight and proud of it. While a young lawyer in Halifax, he had been what we'd now call a junk food addict, often living for days on caramel candies. Food (accompanied by a little rum or a fine claret) was an important part of his life.

8   Meredith would eventually be wooed to join the Cabinet of Sir Charles Tupper, but he again refused. Instead, he became the chief justice of Ontario. He is best remembered as the person who initiated the principle of worker's compensation in North America.

9   Emily Stowe has been called Canada's first female physician. In 1879 she was put on trial for administering drugs that would bring about an abortion. The young woman who was Stowe's patient had died after taking what were basically placebo drugs. It was a high-profile case that caught the public's attention. In the end, the presiding judge threw the charges out, citing that Stowe had not done anything wrong.

10   Indigenous people were usually denied the franchise as well, as many of the qualifications to vote were restrictive. For instance, if an Indigenous man gave up his status, he was allowed to vote, but few would agree to such a measure.

11   The term *ultra vires* is used to describe a law that is considered to be beyond the legal power or authority of its authors.

12   Sandford Fleming is best remembered today as the inventor of standard time zones around the world. In the second half of the nineteenth century, he was a pre-eminent railway surveyor and mapmaker, a key figure

in the building of the CPR. He had numerous business interests and ties with the leading politicians of the day. He also designed the very first postage stamp in Canada.

13 Henry Wentworth Monk was a messianic mystic who preached on the streets of Ottawa. Often maligned by traditional thinkers, he advocated for a homeland for European Jews at a time when pogroms in Russia and other parts of Europe resulted in the murder of many Jews and the expulsion of many more.

14 Thompson and Tupper had grown apart over the years. Thompson had confided in Governor General Aberdeen that Tupper was too often promoting "Tupperdom." The prime minister was suspicious of the older man's motives.

Chapter Four / Sir Mackenzie Bowell: The Accidental Prime Minister

1 The prince refused to disembark from his steamship when it docked at Belleville, despite a mass of Orangemen who were gathered there to cheer him.

2 Riel had actually been elected in Provencher in an October 1873 by-election but never took his seat. He was again elected in a September of 1874 by-election, but again, he decided it was not in his interest (or safety) to go to Ottawa.

3 George Bowering, *Stone Country: An Unauthorized History of Canada* (Toronto: Penguin Canada, 2003), 193.

4 P. B. Waite, *The Man from Halifax: Sir John Thompson, Prime Minister* (Toronto: University of Toronto Press, 1985), 379.

5 Mowat articled in Macdonald's law office in Kingston. The two became partners and friends for the early parts of their careers, but that relationship had deteriorated to the point where they became bitter rivals in opposing political parties. Mowat fought for greater powers for the provinces, something that Macdonald vehemently opposed.

6 Lady Macdonald lobbied for Sir Charles to be summoned and given the premier's position.

7   Queen Victoria insisted that the governor general's Ottawa residence
    and place of business be called Government House, as it was in the other
    capitals of the Empire. In fact, she had rebuked Lady Stanley of Preston
    in 1889 for using the name "Rideau Hall."
8   The photograph of the white bearded Smith driving the Last Spike at
    Craigellachie is one of the iconic images of Canadian history.
9   Since 1965, it has been mandatory for senators to retire at age
    seventy-five.

Chapter Five / Sir Charles Tupper: "Finally ... It's About Time You Were Prime Minister!"

1   Sir Charles Tupper was inducted into the Canadian Medical Hall of
    Fame in 2016.
2   Howe, sent to the United States to recruit men to fight against Russia,
    was investigated by a grand jury in New York state for trying to entice
    American citizens to break the neutrality the United States had de-
    clared in the conflict. He was not charged, but some of his subordin-
    ates were.
3   And party they did. The diaries of the participants clearly demonstrate
    that a good time was had by all. The 191-ton steamer was further laden
    down with thirteen thousand dollars' worth of champagne. Some of the
    men brought their wives along on the junket. A mood of optimism and
    cooperation prevailed. Macdonald and his former bitter rival George
    Brown worked collaboratively on their pitch to the Maritime colonies.
    Upon arrival in Charlottetown harbour, no official was there to greet
    the Canadian delegation. W.H. Pope, a legislator from Prince Edward
    Island rowed out — alone — to the ship anchored in the harbour. The
    rest of the town had gone to see a visiting circus. After the first meeting
    of the colonial representatives, Pope invited everyone back to his home
    for a dinner of lobster and oysters.
4   Tupper was the only Father of Confederation to hold a university degree.
5   Archibald was also a Father of Confederation. He attended the
    Charlottetown, Quebec, and London conferences. He faced opposition

within his own party on the issue but persevered until defeated in the 1868 provincial election. He then played a major role in the establishment of Manitoba as a province in the wake of the first Riel rebellion.

6 In the days before the secret ballot, elections would often take weeks to decide. The very first general election in Canada took place between August 7 and September 20, 1867.

7 Joseph Pope, in his first book about John A. Macdonald, imagined a conversation among Tupper, Macdonald, and D'Arcy McGee in which they discussed the formation of the first federal Cabinet. In Pope's imagination, Tupper said, "As leader of the Confederate Party in Nova Scotia, I am entitled to office. In order to remove this difficulty which has arisen, I am willing to forego my claims, and in foregoing them to satisfy the legitimate aspirations of the Irish Catholic body. In my place, appoint an Irish Catholic from Nova Scotia."

8 An anonymous play was written in 1881 called *Sir John and Sir Charles, or The Secrets of the Syndicate*. It imagined a conversation between Macdonald and Tupper. Written in iambic pentameter in the style of Shakespeare, it satirized the scandal and critiqued partisan politics of the age. The conversation was, of course, totally fictional.

9 His law partner in Halifax was none other than future prime minister Robert Borden.

10 Tupper was renowned for his use of patronage appointments in an age rife with such a practice. Many members of his own family received government jobs. The practice inspired critics to label them "public Tuppers."

11 Laurier had promised to negotiate with the Greenway government using "the sunny way." The so-called Laurier-Greenway compromise did not reverse the 1890 legislation, but it allowed for religious instruction at the end of the day and French language usage where the numbers warranted. The Manitoba Schools Question fizzled away.

12 "I highly appreciate the great honour of being presented to Your Holiness."

Chapter Six / After the Deluge: Laurier and Beyond

1   And Britain loved him. When he made his first trip to England in 1897 to attend Queen Victoria's birthday celebration, he made quite an impression on the queen, government leaders, and the public in general. He was granted honorary degrees and medals and was cheered with near–rock star enthusiasm in a parade of the empire's representatives.

2   The "Peter Principle," developed in the 1960s by Laurence Peter, contends that in organizations people will be promoted until they reach a position that will require skills they are unable to master. This situation will result in the person failing at that level. In popular culture, the principle has been simplified, giving rise to the cliché that everyone rises to the level of their incompetence.

SELECTED BIBLIOGRAPHY

Abbott, Elizabeth. *The Reluctant PM: Notes on the Life of Sir John Abbott, Canada's Third Prime Minister.* Montreal: self-published, 1997.

Bliss, Michael. *Right Honourable Men: The Descent of Politics from Macdonald to Mulroney.* Toronto: Harper Collins, 1994.

Bowering, George. *Stone Country: An Unauthorized History of Canada.* Toronto: Penguin Canada, 2003.

Creighton, Donald. *John A. Macdonald: The Old Chieftain.* Toronto: Macmillan, 1955.

———. *John A. Macdonald: The Young Politician.* Toronto: Macmillan, 1952.

———. *The Road to Confederation: The Emergence of the Canadas, 1863–1867.* Toronto: Macmillan, 1964.

Durant, Vincent. *War Horse of Cumberland: The Life and Times of Sir Charles Tupper.* Hantsport, N.S.: Lancelot Press, 1985.

Granatstein, J.L., and Norman Hilmer. *Prime Ministers: Ranking Canada's Leaders.* Toronto: Harper Collins, 1999.

Gwyn, Richard. *John A: The Man Who Made Us.* Toronto: Random House, 2008.

———. *Nation Maker: Sir John A. Macdonald: His Life, Our Times.* Toronto: Random House, 2011.

Hopkins, J.C. *Life and Work of the Rt. Hon. Sir John Thompson: Prime Minister of Canada.* Toronto: United Publishing Houses, 1895.

Longley, J.W. *Sir Charles Tupper.* Makers of Canada, Vol. 1. Toronto: Morang & Company, 1916.

Pennington, Christopher. *The Destiny of Canada: Macdonald, Laurier and the Election of 1891.* The History of Canada. Toronto: Allan Lane, 2011.

Pope, Joseph. *The Day of Sir John Macdonald: A Chronicle of the First Prime Minister of the Dominion.* Toronto: Glasgow, Brook & Company, 1915.

———. *Memoirs of the Right Honourable Sir John Alexander Macdonald.* Volume 1 Ottawa: J. Durie & Son, 1894.

Saunders, E.M., ed. *The Life and Letters of the Rt. Hon. Sir Charles Tupper, BART., K.C.M.G.* Vol. II. Toronto: Cassell and Company, 1916.

Smith, Cynthia M., and Jack McLeod. *Sir John A. An Anecdotal Life of John A. Macdonald.* Toronto: Oxford University Press, 1989.

Waite, P.B. *Macdonald: His Life and World.* Toronto: McGraw-Hill-Ryerson, 1975.

———. *The Man from Halifax: Sir John Thompson, Prime Minister.* Toronto: University of Toronto Press, 1985.

Other Publications

Colquhoun, A.H.U. "Civil Service Reform." *Canadian Magazine,* May–Oct. 1896: 569–71.

Simpson, Jeffrey. "The Perils of Presentism." *Queen's Quarterly* 125, no. 2 (Summer 2018): 252–65.

Waite, P.B. "Love in Code." *Canada's History.* Canada's History Society. Posted February 14, 2017. canadashistory.ca/explore/prime-ministers/love-in-code.

Other Sources

Canada Guide. thecanadaguide.com

Dictionary of Canadian Biography. biographi.ca/en/index.php

Laurentian Heritage WebMagazine. laurentian.quebecheritageweb.com

Library and Archives Canada. bac-lac.gc.ca/eng/Pages/home.aspx

INDEX

◇

ABOUT THE AUTHOR

MICHAEL HILL IS A GRADUATE of York University and the University of Toronto. He is the author of *The Mariposa Folk Festival: A History*. Michael's articles and book reviews have appeared in numerous publications. He wrote a weekly column for the *Toronto Star* for over thirty years and taught elementary school in both Toronto and Orillia. After retiring, he was the artistic director of the Mariposa Folk Festival and is currently the president of Stephen Leacock Associates, which awards the annual Leacock Medal for Humour. His interests — outside of reading, writing, and history — include golf, art, and music. Michael has two daughters and four grandchildren and lives in Orillia with his wife, Bonnie, and his dog, Rocky.